PALM BEACH
CONFIDENTIAL

PALM BEACH CONFIDENTIAL

By Robert Mykle

SLEUTHHOUND BOOKS
ATLANTA, LAKE WORTH

SleuthHound Books

Brumby Holding, Inc.
PO Box 1608
12 S. Dixie Highway, Ste. 203
Lake Worth, FL 33460
USA

www.humanicspub.com

Printed in the United States of American and the United Kingdom

ISBN 978 0 89334 800 7

THIS WORK IS DEDICATED TO THE MEMORY OF
ASENETH VELASQUEZ JACOME

ACKNOWLEDGMENTS

I want to thank my friends at Sleuthhound,
especially Gary Wilson, for all The Island lunches we shared,
as well as my agent, Elizabeth Trupin-Pulli
and my editors, Lynn Vannucci and Peggy Lucke.
I also wish to thank my 'first readers', Clara Cappiello,
Carol Couture, Susan Schlener, and Debbie Quinn.
Their insights and helpful hints were invaluable.
No writer can write without a muse,
thanks to my Morning Muse. Additional thanks to native born,
Ken Goffe for his insights, to my friends and associates
in the Florida Writers Association.
And finally to the people, history, and places
of the fabulous island called Palm Beach.

CHAPTER 1

My Rolex read ten thirty. It was a Monday morning, and I was nursing a nagging uneasiness in the general area of my right frontal lobe, the result of an unwise mixing of good beer and questionable wine. The calendar read the first of December, that nether-time of the year when hurricane season had ended and the full complement of Hampton snowbirds had yet to make their appearance. Bartenders, restaurateurs, and chambermaids examined their checkbooks, praying they could keep bankruptcy at bay for another month. While a living wage was foremost on people's minds, the positive influx of winter people was countered by increased traffic and the inability to get a good table at a favorite restaurant or decent tickets to a top-billed event at the Kravis Center. Still, the Palm Beach winter Season held out many proffered promises, not the least was the anticipated string of parties that served, or at least presumed to serve, quality beverages.

The Season would also bring down the big spenders, those willing to lay down a couple hundred thousand dollars for an old master's painting to hang in their bathroom.

"One can only hope."

Unfortunately, no one, much less yours truly, could have foreseen nor hoped away the string of murders and lost millions that was to soon haunt our island redoubt, testament to the old adage that paradise comes at a price. Perhaps too high of a price.

The stack of this month's unpaid bills weighing heavily in my left hand was about to be tossed into the wastepaper basket when Margot, my five eleven, twenty-five-year-old, Smith-educated, contemporary-art-major assistant knocked softly before opening my office door. She stuck her head in and gave me a big smile, her face surrounded by a halo of luxuriant blond hair. Thank you, Lord, thank you.

"There's a Mr. Ordenoff up front to see you."

Ordenoff. Ordenoff. Oh, yes. Martha Manley's teddy boy. "Alone?" Margot nodded. Curious. Here without the eighty-five-million-dollar bride.

My hand dumped the bills into the basket and I marched through the gallery, past rows of precisely hung paintings and strategically placed sculptures to the starkly decorated reception room; I relish contrast, the keystone of my philosophy. Ordenoff, hands behind his back, was staring out the tinted window facing South County Road, the worst view in the entire gallery. Well, almost. Perhaps the colorless Picasso hanging in my office I had on consignment held that title.

"Good morning, Mr. Ordenoff. What a pleasure."

"Yes. Yes. Mr. Roberts. Thank you," he said, taking my hand with a firm, if slightly moist, palm. I could almost hear his heels click in a perfect display of European manners. He was impeccably dressed in Palm Beach uniform -- navy blue blazer and gray slacks, no tie, shirt opened to second neck-button and a hint of a gold chain crawling on a bed of well-tanned skin and white hair.

"Mrs. Ordenoff?"

"Oh, she's fine. Fine," he said with just a trace of accent.

I directed him to the gallery. We passed through the dark green door between two large Carolyn Sampler custom-made potteries planted in colorful primroses – my primrose path. One can only hope. With slow deliberate steps we walked down the left side of the gallery, the twentieth century side. Two large skylights running the length of the gallery showered the room with a fusion of soft indirect sunlight. I always preferred natural lighting to artificial illumination. Even when making love. Make that, *especially* when. He passed by a small but stunning Braque idiosyncratically placed beside an idyllic country scene by John Constable. Guaranteed eye catchers. Perhaps? Not interested. Obviously, Sergio Ordenoff had more on his mind than buying art. His contact lens blue eyes were glued to the floor as if he were searching for parking meter coins. He stopped in front of a Fernando Botero, and turned his back on a group of round, oversized people cavorting on the banks of a pristine lake, titled "The Bathing Party."

"You have a nice collection here," he said, barely gazing around the room. "You know. I really like the Kandinsky you have on the back wall.

It's his best period," he said, his voice dropping two tones.

It was my turn to thank him.

"I understand you do art appraisals."

"I've done a few appraisals for clients," I said. " Do you have some pieces you'd like me to look at?"

"Oh no, no, not mine. Martha's. Mrs. Ordenoff's paintings."

"By anybody I would know?"

A slight smile lifted his cheeks, revealing a series of evenly placed concentric wrinkles orbiting his drawn and ruddy lips.

"Oh, I think you'd find them interesting." He turned and glanced at the green door then back to me. "Martha would like to have a word with you. She's waiting in the Bentley."

"Martha, I mean Mrs. Ordenoff is outside?" I asked credulously. "Why didn't she just come in?"

The Count stiffened, dropped his hands to his side and pulled at the ends of his coat. "She'd like to see you now, if you 'd be so kind."

"After you," I said. I followed close behind him through the gallery and passed Margot, who gave me a questioning look.

"Martha Manley is outside," I mouthed.

I squinted as we stepped outside into the brilliant morning sun. The traffic on County Road was light. We had just rounded the corner when a driver stepped out of a blue Bentley, its windows so heavily tinted that they reflected the palm trees and the cumulus clouds like a mirror. The driver, dressed in a navy blue uniform, stood ramrod straight. He was tall, with dark wavy hair and an expressionless face. With fluid movements he opened the Bentley's back door. The Count stopped and gestured for me to step inside

"Please have a seat Mister Roberts," a strong voice, a tone below a contralto, sounded. A withered hand with an emerald ring the size of a dove's egg circled by diamonds appeared out of the shadows and patted the back seat by the open door. I stepped inside and sat. As my eyes adjusted to the dark interior, Martha Manley slowly materialized like lottery numbers in a scratch card. Sitting straight up with her legs crossed, she was dressed in a chartreuse linen dress that matched her aquamarine eyes. Her pageboy cropped hair, dyed black, was pulled back behind her ears exposing two diamond-cut emerald earrings. She was smiling, not a humorous smile but a knowing grimace as if she had a private joke understood only by herself.

"Thank you, Raymundo," she said. The door closed behind me with a solid click, leaving Sergio and the driver standing outside.

"It's nice to see you again Mister Roberts," she said.

"It's always my pleasure, I can assure you."

I watched as her eyes gave me the once over. Apparently satisfied, she nodded then leaned towards me, rested her hand on my knee and patted it like she might a pet Chihuahua. I could feel her delicate hand and the hard underside of the ring, as well as and the harder stare of her sea blue eyes. I felt as if she was looking through me searching for another side. Without taking her eyes off mine she said, "A fine strapping young man like yourself should get around more. I hope you're attending this years' Westchester Charities Antique Fair. We all must do everything we can to help those poor children. It's all for a good cause and with your eye you might pickup a bargain."

Martha Manley was board member of the Westchester Charities, an umbrella organization for a dozen nonprofit groups.

"I never miss it. I've always considered it one of the highlights of the Season."

"Bring your checkbook, unless you want to donate a painting."

"You know how to hurt a guy."

She laughed. "Okay, just your checkbook." Another smile. "And please do think of becoming a sponsor. It'd be so appreciated."

"I'd be honored."

She squeezed my knee and paused.

"Two other art galleries are sponsoring booths. And Nigel Jenkins." Her voice trailed off. "You know Nigel Jenkins, don't you?"

"Quite well as a mater of fact. Though I've never had the opportunity to use his facilities."

"Yes," she said almost to herself. "His facilities."

A whiff of Obsession perfume tickled my nostrils. With her hand still locked on my knee, she kept her eyes locked on mine. The whites of her eyes were outlined in a pale red and I wondered if she had partaken in a morning nip.

"You remember the Monet you found for Frederick. It was always one of his favorite paintings. He insisted it hang in the living room a central part of our collection. It's still hanging there."

"Of course. I remember quite well. I hope you're pleased with it."

She looked away, over my shoulder, pressing her lips together. "I'd like you to take a look at it and appraise it along with a couple of other paintings."

"The Monet, I'm very familiar with. Can you tell me a bit more about the others?"

"Let's see, there actually are two Monets, a Gauguin, a Matisse, one small Rembrandt, and a number of others—mostly Dutch and Italian, a few new American artists, you know."

The Manley art collection was one of the better-balanced on The Island. Oddly, she failed to mention the storied Caravaggio rumored to have been bought by her late husband while on the obligatory Grand European Tour immediately after the war.

"It's the Monets that I'm most interested in," she said. "And perhaps the Rembrandt."

"What did you have in mind?"

"It would please me if you could come by tomorrow morning, let's say ten thirty. I'd like you to have a look at the ones that are at the house."

Ten thirty was actually early. During Season, with so many evening events, few of our social island butterflies rise and shine before eleven.

I cleared my throat. "That's rather short notice. But I am intrigued by the quality of the collection. I'd like an inventory beforehand if possible. As you know it takes time to do an appraisal, especially if there are a number of important works involved."

"That won't be necessary. If you could be so kind and just come by the house tomorrow, Mr. Roberts, I would appreciate it," she said, her voice falling a perceptible half pitch. "You don't have to fiddle with silly comparables. I just want your opinion."

"I'll be there at ten thirty sharp, Mrs. Manley."

"Martha. Please, just Martha."

"And I'm plain, Maxie,"

"Yes. Maxie," she said as if savoring the sound over her tongue. "By the way, how is your lovely wife? Her name was Nancy, right?"

"We've been divorced going on three years."

"Oh what a shame. She was such a nice girl. I guess sooner or later we all lose the things we love."

I wasn't sure if she was referring to her late husband Frederick Manley III, her new husband, or her eighty-five-foot Hatteras yacht that sank in hurricane Wilma. She lifted her hand off my knee then tapped the window twice with her knuckles. The door swung opened. "Thank you, Maxie. Tomorrow then."

She gave me her hand. I took it gently and without shaking it said, "Tomorrow at ten thirty."

We stared at each other in silence for a moment. I could hear the soft whir of the Bentley's air conditioning and the smell the polished leather interior. I had the feeling she wanted to tell me more but was hesitant to do so. Finally, she gave a nod of her head and me a smile. "Frederick liked you. And I do too. I hope after you look at the paintings we get to see more of you in the future."

"It'd be my pleasure." I reached into my jacket, retrieved a business card and scribbled my number on the back. "Here's my card with my private direct telephone number on it."

Without reading it, she put the card in her purse,

I stepped into the sunlight as the Count slide into the back seat. Raymundo closed the door, tipped his cap to me, and then climbed into the drivers seat. Before I could blink a third time the Bentley was purring northward up Country Road.

"That was Martha Manley's new husband wasn't it?" Margot said as I closed the gallery entrance door behind me.

"Right. And his bride was waiting outside."

"Is she buying something?"

"One can only hope," we both chimed.

"Does that mean I get paid this month?" she said, and then stopped. "Don't say it."

CHAPTER 2

The Manleys had been part and parcel of the Palm Beach social scene since purchasing an early Addison Mizner mansion just before the war. The Depression was in full swing and I'm sure Papa Manley, as he liked to be called, got himself a good deal. When Papa Manley, a.k.a. Frederick P. Manley III of Pittsburgh fame, died, Martha stopped giving their hallmark Halloween parties, the Season opener. Well, a little early for the real Season but the Manleys liked to arrive early and leave late. They did not have to kowtow to accepted norms. Even in Palm Beach, eighty-five million dollars does give one a degree of freedom.

Unfortunately, the Manleys were not steady customers, those precious few clients who annually bought one or two works from me. Aside from the Monet, six years ago, I did find an interesting Gauguin Tahitian in Canada for Papa Manley. He paid top dollar and had two years to enjoy it before he died – an embolism brought on by a young woman and an oral sex act, if you believe the local gossip. Immediately after the funeral, the grieving widow closed up the house and left for an extended trip to Europe, returning two years later with Count Sergio Ordenoff, a minor noble and former ambassador from Bulgaria, where he was known as Comrade Ordenoff.

Most of the Manley collection was acquired by Papa Manley during the early fifties. Steel was king—the Japanese hadn't gotten the hang of making it yet—and protectionism was public policy. By the sixties Manley had diversified into real estate, shipping, and banking. He bought art early and never sold, even through the alleged bad days of the early eighties when so many people and banks went broke. He was nearly indicted when a bank he owned was taken over by the Resolution Trust Corporation. Something about too many in-house loans to board members. While the Manley fortune was modest by Palm Beach standards, it was comfortable enough for him to acquire a sizeable collection of art, hence my presence at the annual Halloween soirée.

Martha Manley's visit sparked my curiosity. Why had she chosen me for an appraisal? Surely she had her own capable appraisers. Probably one of the big New York auction houses like Sotheby's or Christie's. Someone had to have appraised the artwork for insurance purposes. And why not a simple telephone call, I wondered? Perhaps this might be more than a simple appraisal request.

Don't think badly of paying clients.

I reached in the trash bucket and retrieved the bills. Maybe I'd be able to pay them this month after all.

I thought I'd take a chance and call Kerry Salzhauer who worked at Christie's. We were the same age and not only did we share a love of art, we were beach bums at Fort Pierce for a year.

"Kerry can you call me back on a cell phone?"

"Well dear boy, not even a how are you?"

"Call me."

"Why all the mystery, old boy?"

"I'll explain in a moment." A second after I'd hung up the phone rang. "Still have me on speed dial," I said. "I'm flattered. Did you do an appraisal on the Manley collection?"

There was a pause. "You know that's not information I can give out."

"All I need to know is if you did a recent appraisal."

"Only for you Maxie. Wait a second," I heard the clicking of a keyboard. "The Manley collection. Here it is. The first appraisal we did for Frederick Manley III was in 1954 and the last in 2006. Afraid I can't say anything more but there was a nice painting by one of our more beloved Dutchmen."

"Thanks," I said. "Remember if you get to Palm Beach you've a place to stay and a boat to use. We'll fish Walker's Cay."

"How's the first week in March."

"You're on."

So the Manley collection was recently appraised, belaboring the questions: why me and why now?

I'll take my Dad's often-repeated quip about gift horses and mouths. Just do my job.

First on the agenda was homework. I retrieved three encyclopedic opuses and a painting catalogue on Monet, Renoir, and Rembrandt from the bookcase. I found four paintings owned by Frederick Manley listed.

Taking down a pair of reference books from my shelf, I thumbed through the pages making notes -- painting sizes, price, and periods – then did an Internet search, checking the last time a comparable painting sold, its price and owner, as well as the stolen art directory. If more detail was needed, I'd pay a visit to the Society of the Four Arts library and rummage through their reference stacks.

The last book was an art history tome that I'd used in college—I took art because I knew I'd be the only boy in the class. Those were glory days, eleven open-minded girls and myself. I closed it and laid it with a thud on my desk, then leaned back in my chair and took a deep breath. It was late afternoon and I had to make a decision. I pulled out my last bank statement and rechecked the balance. I had enough to either pay the car, partial payment on the house taxes, or Margot. My father always said, "Keep the help happy."

I wrote out a check and marched to the reception area.

"Payday, my dear," I waved the check victoriously in the air.

Margot grabbed the check and reached for her purse. My head automatically jerked around as she leaned over, giving me a perfect view of the perfectly formed buttocks pressing out softly beneath blue silk. She had the makings of a model. Long legs and a lean figure firmed by morning jogs. Her skin had a radiant quality, almost radioactive, and she had a smile that melted hearts. I admit that her physical appearance was one of the reasons I hired her. You can't have ugly people selling beauty to the rich. Money takes beauty for granted.

Yet even as I admired the view I kept to that other age-old adage—*You don't screw the help*.

Still I felt a tightness in my crotch. She took her time searching her purse, allowing me to eye her. I always admired women who understood the power they held over men. Surrendering, I went to the back office to drown my sorrows and hardness in an early beer. I popped a bottle of Pilsner Urquell and opened the curtains overlooking the enclosed courtyard sculpture garden. The evening sunlight was fading as I saluted the muscular pseudo-Greek bronze Cavanaugh standing vigilant among the flowers. A consignment, he was leaving tomorrow. The alarm light clicked on, another one flashed, signaling that the front door had opened and closed. Margot had left.

Aside from all the hard security on the windows and doors, the gallery had a state-of-the-art alarm system. That was the problem with possessions. You had to protect them, take care of them, to which the alarms and the barred windows attested. They were a responsibility, a burden and you, their beast. Henry VI said it best: "Riches are but snares." At times I wished I was a hippie back in Katmandu smoking opiate hashish without a care or a dollar to my name.

When I get on these self-pitying binges, I know I need a real drink. I marched through the gallery to the reception room, stepped outside, and pulled the door shut. Overhead, a moonless sky hung like a Muslim veil. A wispy chill sent a shudder of goose flesh prancing down my neck. Early evenings and cool nights: winter was here.

I glanced across the street at my madder blue Jaguar XK8 nestled under the protection of a carport in the parking lot behind the bank. Payment was due. *Have got to sell that Picasso.* With brisk steps, I walked south. County Road was lined with blocks of small, drab one-story buildings built, or built to look like they were built, in the 1920s. Anyplace else but Palm Beach and they'd be prime candidates for urban renewal A half hundred steps and a few blocks later at the corner of South County Road and Brazilian Avenue the scenery changed. I pushed through the glass doors of the Café L'Europe and was greeted by the maitre d' with a smile and a warm handshake then directed to the bar in the north room, a mirrored montage of light and sound. It was early and the bar uncrowded.

"Good evening, Mr. Roberts. The Usual," the bartender said. It was a statement not a question. A double shot of vodka and cranberry juice, no lime, was placed in front of the empty stool at the end of the bar. I sat, cupped my hands around the cold glass, took a sip and then turned and glanced over the restaurant's main dining room. It was too early in the evening and the Season for the rich and famous crowd. I did spot one of our city commissioners in the corner chomping on what looked like a wiener schnitzel. Their apple pancakes are to die for. That's what I liked about Café L'Eurpoe, snacks or haute cuisine. Choice. Contrast.

Once I downed half my drink, my choices became more apparent. A leggy brunette in a dress that cautiously accented her fine figure like a Donatello sculpture sat two stools to my left. First impression was that she must be local, though sometimes snowbirds got lost and ended up on the beach at the wrong time of year. It was December, the anything month.

After some silly banter about Palm Beach politics I asked, "What are you doing in Palm Beach? You look like you belong in South Beach." A line that sometimes works.

She had flown down from Connecticut for a stockbrokers' convention and stayed. A wise move. She was living at a friend's Ocean Drive condo until his return sometime after Christmas, at which time she'd move on. A common complaint.

"And what do you do?" she asked.

"Mostly what I like."

She smiled. Making a woman smile is the second greatest feeling a man can have. Probably why I relished my role as the class clown.

"I am a student of beautiful things and things beautiful," I said, pushing my luck.

Another smile. She turned toward the bar, resting her elbows on the counter, staring at the mirrored liquor bottles along the wall, giving me a perfect profile.

"Do I pass muster?" she asked.

A shiver ran up my leg and my bar stool began to shake.

CHAPTER 3

The next morning arrived too fast and too early. Between a shower, the morning paper, and two croissants, I gulped down two hot mugs of my favorite Indian River Coffee, Colombian-Kenyan bean mix, and put on my best "I'm-an-appraiser-pay-me" suit. I gave one last look in the mirror before grabbing my Manley file and the car keys.

As I filed by the kitchen, Margarita Blanco, my seventy-two-year-old Cuban maid, was frying some Caribbean concoction. She looked up and said, "You look so handsome. You'va gotta hot date?"

"An appointment with a client."

"A pretty girl?"

"I wish, Margarita. I wish."

"*Buena suerte*," she said, waving a spatula.

"*Gracias. Ciao, ciao.*"

The Jaguar was parked in the garage beside my trusty rust-ridden Everglades buggy. I put the Jag's top down, revved the engine, and spun out of the driveway. The eight cylinders of the fickle auto hummed like a swarm of killer bees, for how long was anyone's guess. I deliberately let back on the gas. I have been sternly admonished by most of Palm Beach's finest: *County Road is not a drag strip.*

The road led due north. I could smell the sea before I saw her. At the Beach Club I made the turn to the ocean where the road ran along the seawall. With the top down, I was vulnerable. Nothing stood between me, the soothing sea smells and the background noise of waves and gulls. The wind was on shore, blowing from the east. The wind of change.

As I wound past the north curve of Palm Beach Country Club, a fox scurried across the road and disappeared under a hedge. I find it comforting that our little island is lousy with foxes. The Island's resident kitties are another story.

A half-mile later, a few doors down from the old Kennedy compound, I pulled into the drive of the Manley house, discreetly hidden from passing cars by a luxuriant, fifteen-foot-high ficus hedge. The driveway snaked through copious overgrowth to a three-story pseudo-Tuscan sanguine-red manse with ornate stone balconies and four terracotta chimneys. Like many island mansions, the Manley home had an interesting, if jaded, history. That history, I saw, was about to be radically amplified. A half dozen squad cars and unmarked vehicles jammed the circular cobblestone driveway. Instinct said, turn around and leave with as little attention as possible. Official scrutiny, even of the guiltless kind, was to be scrupulously avoided. Then I thought of the clients. Martha Manley was not someone I could afford to slight. After all, it all might simply be an innocent mistake. Right?

A sharp tap on the driver's side door decided for me. I looked up into the dour face of Sergeant Frank Gonzalez. I knew all the Palm Beach cops. Most had ticketed me for a moving violation at one time in their careers. Palm Beach is a small town.

"Hey, Frank, what's going on?" I said, giving him the most chaste look I could muster.

"Mr. Roberts." Sergeant Gonzalez said, and then hesitated. He looked up at the house, then leaned over the car door and in a subdued voice confided, "Martha Manley's been murdered."

Don't think badly of paying clients.

I got out of the car and stood awkwardly, for once at a loss for what to do.

"You'll have to wait here, sir." He stepped between me and the front entrance. "Mr. Roberts is out front," he told his handheld radio, and then to me, "The lieutenant will be right out."

"Thanks, Frank."

A minute later I heard, "Maxie, what brings you to this side of The Island?" I looked up and saw Lieutenant Adam Aldrick waving from the front steps. "It's okay, Frank, let him pass."

Adam was tall and thick, with blue eyes and Celtic-red hair cut short topping a round face that looked years younger than his forty-four years. A slight limp marred his movements as he lumbered down the front steps. He was immaculately dressed in a Brooks Brothers suit bought, I knew, at the Church Mouse thrift shop on the corner of South County and Chilean. Adam and I were friends and occasional drinking buddies. We also shared a love of wine and classic movies. Four years back we had worked together on an art robbery; solving it was the reason he had made lieutenant. Adam Aldrick possessed the rarest of island commodities: gratitude.

Halfway down the steps, he stopped and stretched his leg.

"Damn knee's acting up. I think it's going to rain." Adam shot a glance up at the cloudless sky and blinked a few times. "I assume you were just driving by and wanted to say hello."

"I had an appointment with Miss Martha and her husband," I said.

"Well you're going to have to cancel it. Your client's dead."

"Both of them?"

"No, just Mrs. Manley. The distressed widower is inside. I hate this shit." He swore a rare oath. "You know, I left the big city to get away from this crap. Come on inside but don't touch anything."

We started up the front stoop. As we stepped through the double doors, I smelled the ocean and a bitter, almost cosmetic, smell lingering like centuries-old incense in a Hindu temple.

Spread out before us was a sizable open room stretching forty-feet to a wall of windows and French doors facing the ocean. The Malachite marble floor was covered with oversized hand woven Tarbiz silk rugs. The room, a museum really, was lined with paintings, sculptures and European antiques. Looming over the scene like twin gods in a Roman temple were the two Monets, placed side by side. Absolutely no contrast.

A half dozen uniformed and plainclothes cops moved about the house.

"Have you been here before?"

I looked at him.

"Stupid question."

"I assume you've rounded up the usual suspects?" I asked.

"Yeah. The grieving husband, the butler, and the day help."

"Where was Martha killed?"

"She was murdered upstairs." Adam lowered his voice. "Just between us two, it was a single shot to the temple. Small caliber, probably a .22. A woman's weapon, or someone delicate."

"Or the Mossad."

Adam grunted. "Why did you say you were here?"

I hadn't said but I was not going to state the obvious. "Yesterday morning, Martha and Sergio Ordenoff paid a visit to the gallery and wanted me to appraise some of their paintings."

"These?" He waved his hand across the room.

"Some."

Adam directed me to a corner of the room out of hearing of the other cops.

"So you're telling me that yesterday afternoon Martha Manley and Sergio Ordenoff came to your gallery in person just to ask you to do an appraisal? Why didn't she just call you?"

"I've asked myself the same question. I think Martha wanted to talk to me face to face before hiring me. Other than that, I have no idea."

"So maybe that's why we found your business card lying on top of her desk."

Adam reached into his pocket and pulled out a clear plastic evidence bag. Tucked inside was my card with my private number scribbled on the back.

"I gave Martha my card in case she had to contact me. But feel free to keep it."

"Right." Adam returned the plastic bag to his pocket. "You drove right into the middle of an active crime scene. You'll have to give a statement."

"Good God, Adam, I can't afford to get in the paper. You know how sensitive Palm Beachers are."

"Maxie, just give me the facts."

"Yesterday morning Sergio Ordenoff came into the gallery by himself. We talked for a few minutes. Then he casually told me that Martha wanted to talk to me and that she was waiting outside. I had a brief conversation with her alone in her car. The Count, I mean Mister Ordenoff, waited on the sidewalk. She wanted me to examine some of her collection. Basically told me to come by today at ten thirty and here I am. "

"Was Margot working?"

"Of course. She's very conscientious. Do I need witnesses?"

Again Adam grunted. "Anything else you can tell me?"

"That's it."

"Okay. That didn't hurt, did it?"

I smiled.

"We're almost through with Ordenoff. He's giving a preliminary statement."

"Then Sergio hasn't been arrested?"

Adam shook his head, leaned closer to me and almost whispered; "It looks like Martha was working late at her desk in the back office." He jerked his head slightly towards the French doors. "Sometime near ten o'clock she went upstairs to her bedroom where she was getting ready for bed. She was killed leaning over a makeup table. That's where we found her. A close, clean shot just behind the temple. I'd say she knew her killer. Might have even let him in."

"Or her."

"Ordenoff said after dinner he went out to Ta-boo. Had a couple of cognacs, came home and went straight to bed. Said he didn't hear anything unusual. It is a big house."

"So he's got an alibi."

"The manager and the bartenders at Ta-boo said he was there but he left around eleven and Martha, as far as we know, was killed about that time or before. The autopsy should reveal an exact time of death." Adam glanced out the French doors toward the ocean. "The butler was in his apartment over the garage. Ordenoff drove himself to Ta-boo and back."

"What about the maids?"

"Can you believe with a house this big they had only day help? They come in at nine, clean, and the cook serves Martha breakfast at ten. She's the one who found her. Martha let all of the help and her social secretary go when she left for Europe. Just retained a lawn service. When she returned she kept most of the house closed up. They have nine bedrooms and five baths that they don't even use.   When the children came to town they stayed at the Breakers and the Colony. Talk about a seriously dysfunctional family."

"Show me one in Palm Beach that isn't," I said. "What about motive?"

"Ordenoff told us some of her jewelry was taken. Mostly, as he said, her everyday trinkets, if you can call a five-carat star sapphire a trinket. She left them on the counter at night before going to bed. All her better jewels were locked up in the safe."

Including the emerald ring, I assumed.

"And the paintings. There were million-dollar works of art, and the killer left them where they hung. He just took some jewels and left the paintings."

"Obviously not an art connoisseur. A petty thief taking things he could easily pawn, perhaps? Could have been a drug addict."

"That might be what we're supposed to believe," Adam said. "There's no evidence of forced entry. Either he was good and got past the alarms, or he was let in,"

"Or was already here, waiting."

"We'll see," Adam said. "By the way, how much does an appraiser get?"

"It depends on the quality of the paintings, the types of tests, and the amount of research involved. But, I hate to say it, as of today, I haven't been paid a cent."

Adam shook his head. "Wait here and you can talk to Mr. Ordenoff after we're done. You might get something out of him that we didn't, which I'll expect you'll share with us."

"What about the sanctity of client-confessor privilege?"

"Doubt it. You're an art dealer, not an attorney, and I don't think you've taken holy vows since we last spoke," he said. "Which reminds me, did you see that French movie, *La Vie en Rose,* playing at the Theater?"

"Sure did. Edith Piaff is one of my favorite singers."

"I liked it too. What a voice she had." His hand shot to his chin. "What was that song she did that everyone liked so much?"

"*Non, Je Ne Regrette Rien.*"

"Yeah, right."

"Lieutenant," one of the officers called out. Adam nodded to him. "Wait right here. The second floor is off limits until we're done."

Shaking his head, Adam moved off. He shot over his shoulder, "You should have gotten a retainer."

"I know," I called back with my hands deep in my pockets and under the watchful eyes of two casual but obviously observant officers. There were a lot of quality art objects but no small pieces that have the bad habit of being purloined during well-attended parties.

A painting of Martha hung over a pair of finely carved Chippendale chairs. She had been a young beauty, a first-place trophy wife. Hard to think of a bullet ripping apart that attractive face. Folded on her lap was a pair of delicate manicured hands adorned by the emerald ring, the same hands and ring resting on my knee yesterday.

The painting, according to the date, had been done forty-two years ago when she would have been near thirty. Until yesterday, I hadn't seen her since her marriage to the Count except in photographs of her at charitable events published in the *Palm Beach Daily News* and the *Palm Beach Post* Notables section. They showed an attractive woman who refused to give into the ravages of time. In a community where beauty and power were symbiotic, she had scrupulously kept her part of the unwritten bargain in the marital contract to stay attractive and keep her husband's attention. And the attention of his peers. What exercise and facial creams couldn't cure, the surgeon's knife corrected. In Palm Beach these knives were swung with the abandonment of Attila the Hun's cavalry. Slash, chop, pull, and suck. The amount of blood spilt in the name of beauty would fill the world's blood banks with type O-negative for decades.

There are no ugly women, only poor women.

While most of the body artists resided in New York, a few local surgeons were making the scene including my own surgeon and friend, Doctor Harold Bafitis. I checked my reflection in a mirror. With my index finger I pulled at the crows' feet etched around my eyes. *Maybe next spring.*

The house was as I remembered it from the last Halloween party—the twin Monets, the Steinway grand piano, the ocean view, and the Olympic-sized pool. I glanced to the wall of French doors and the arched walkway towards the back office, where Martha spent her last minutes, before she crossed the great room and ascended the stairs. Did the killer follow her upstairs or was he waiting in her boudoir where he shot her in the head? I thought back to our meeting in her Bentley when she paused, her hand still on my knee, as if she wanted to say something more but hesitated. Now I wondered, what did she want to tell me?

An ornate box resting on an oversized Louis XIV table caught my eye. I thought I had seen it in a catalogue. Since it didn't look like evidence, I turned my back to the officers, picked up the box and cupped my hands around it. I could feel the soothing warmth of centuries extrude from its sides, yet when I gave a subtle sniff, I didn't catch the expected aged smell. Turning it over I checked out the joints, then lifted up the lid and froze. The titillating, tingle disappeared. With my free hand I reached into my pocket and retrieved my reading glasses, actually modified jewelers' magnifying glasses. In one of the corners of the box was a trace of light brown, petroleum-based glue. A glue not used in the 1700s. A sloppy restoration or . . .

I closed the lid, placed the box down and walked across the room to the Monets. The painting to the right was of a languid pond with multicolored water lilies floating in a near haze, confirming Monet's position as the Rafael of water. In its mate, an earlier work, was a young girl standing at the edge of a pond surrounded by spring flowers glowing in the early sunlight. Each feathery petal reflected a beam of August light. Her haunting blue eyes gazed out over the living room in stoic wonder. Yet they did not cry out. Staring at the young girl's eyes, I wanted her to speak to me. Say something. Tell me how the Claude Monet suffered as he slowly, brush stroke by brush stroke, brought her to life. Instead I was met by stone silence. I was deaf and she a mute. A warning shiver etched up my spine.

"Ah, Mr. Roberts. How unfortunate," Sergio Ordenoff said. No handshake. Still, straight and stoic and impeccably dressed.

"You have my sincerest condolences, sir."

"Thank you. Martha was looking forward to seeing you. You know she was a good woman." He paused, searching for words. "This, this is all so terrible. But . . . "

He glanced at the floor then looked up and ran his tongue over his dry lips.

"The police are keeping me quite busy as you can imagine. I'm sorry you had to drive out here," he continued. "If you'd like, I'm sure we can, I mean I'll give you something for your trouble."

Compensated for a seven-minute drive? Was he trying to get rid of me? "I can assure you it was no trouble, but I appreciate the thought."

"No, not at all, Mr. Roberts. If there is anything I can do for you . . ." His hands fell to his sides, reaching for the edges of his jacket.

"Well, actually there is. I hate to bother you at a time like this but I'd still like to examine the Monets and the Rembrandt as Mrs. Ordenoff wished." Then I added, "No charge."

"Why would you want to do that?"

"Do you believe in hunches?"

"No. Frankly, I can't say I ever have," he said, and swallowed hard. "But feel free to make arrangements with our man, Raymundo, to come back in a few days. Let's let things settle. I may be here. I may not."

Was he planning a long trip or figuring he'd be in the county lockup?

"Please excuse me, Mr. Roberts. But do talk to Raymundo here." He nodded toward the chauffeur that yesterday, had driven Martha and Sergio to the gallery. Still in his uniform, the dark and dapper Raymundo was standing in the shadows under the archway separating the living and dining rooms. The Count nodded again; then, pulling at his jacket, he walked aimlessly across the room. I nodded at Raymundo, who stared at me for a couple of seconds before disappearing into the kitchen.

So I was to make arrangements to return and examine the Monets with the other obvious suspect, Raymundo, the butler. Strictly speaking, Raymundo was not a butler but a combination chauffeur-gofor. He had been with the Manleys since before Papa Manley died. Drove Papa to his fatal rendezvous. Obviously Martha hadn't held that against him. Then again, decent help is so hard to find.

So, in my case, is a decent paycheck.

That I hoped to rectify. I checked my watch. It was approaching noon and I had a one thirty appointment with my best client and mentor, Bernie Crown. Adam was nowhere to be seen so I excused myself to the corporal standing guard and left the house.

Outside, Sergeant Frank walked me back to the Jag. "I'd like to get me one of these someday."

"They're not as expensive as they look," I said.

"On a cop's pay? I doubt it. With the big jump in property values few of us cops can even afford to live in Palm Beach County anymore. And the taxes? Forget it."

I agreed.

Trying not to hit any of the police cruisers, I backed out of the driveway before heading south, past Saint Eddy's Catholic Church and the Breakers Hotel.

I was half way to the gallery when the full impact of Martha's murder hit me. I was never a close friend of the Manleys but visions of my few times with Martha played in my head. At their parties, she was a gracious host and made all of her guests feel as if they were the most important of her invitees. It was an inborn talent not shared by many. She was tops in the charitable world, a very generous woman. Who would want to kill her? Money, of course, was likely the prime motive. Murders are rare on our idyllic little island. I was sure Adam would soon find the culprit and make Palm Beach safe once again for us law-abiding citizens.

Then there are the paintings and the haunting suspicion that something was not right.

"Are you all right? You looked a little pallid," Margot said as I entered the gallery.

"Martha Manley has been murdered."

"Oh, my God. How?"

"She was shot last night. Right in her own boudoir. I just drove straight into a hornet's nest."

"What about her husband?"

"I actually talked to him. Grieving of course, but then in these things the spouse is usually the number one suspect."

"This is terrible."

"I know and I have to see Bernie this afternoon." I said. "Nothing is going to happen today. Why don't you take the rest of the day off?"

"Are you sure you don't want me to hang around?" She gave me a concerned, motherly look.

"I'll be all right."

I walked to my back office and closed the door. To keep my thoughts fresh, I jotted down a half dozen notes about the paintings. I hadn't had time to examine them but I wanted to leave my first impressions on paper. As I wrote, most of my thoughts were intuitive and hardly scientific. Below I scribbled a chronology of the last two days including times and places. Like constructing a work of art's provenance, I noted when Ordenoff and Martha Manley came to the gallery, the paintings she mentioned, the time of the murder. I also noted my suspicions about the paintings. I jotted the word 'forgeries' and circled it.

Here again, I was playing the curious cat. I'm no detective, but investigating comes naturally to an art dealer. In fact, curiosity is an occupational necessity. To successfully buy and sell art you must investigate. Positive identification, while not a pure science, is incumbent upon the seller. As a seller, your name becomes part of the painting's provenance—who owned it and what, if any, restorations were made. The best provenance is a work of art that has a continuous documented history. Missing years always bother art dealers, or at least the legitimate ones. Gaps cloud title. You have to be sure what you're selling is authentic. That takes research and investigation. The lazy don't last. *Caveat venditor* or move on.

By the time I finished I had two pages of notes in longhand. I slipped them into the Manley folder and placed it on the desk. Then I locked up the gallery, got into the Jag and headed south.

CHAPTER 4

The eighteen-thousand-square-foot Crown cottage was a khaki-colored, Andalusian villa with large arched windows, black iron balconies, and six chimneys overlooking Route A1A and the Atlantic Ocean. Bernie Crown was, even by Palm Beach standards, well off. During his three tours of duty in Vietnam, he had made his first fortune working the black markets in Hue, Saigon, and Cam Ranh. He was refused a fourth tour of duty because Central Command feared he was about to sell the southern half of the Mekong Delta to the North Vietnamese, or so says hearsay. Back home safely and honorably discharged, he invested his "winnings," as he liked to call them, in real estate. He often spouted: "More money is made in real estate than all the other businesses combined."

Like John D. MacArthur, he was a prodigious purchaser of Palm Beach County farmland—parceled out and sold during boom times, sat on when the economy tanked. In the process he made another fortune, which he, in turn, invested in more real estate, drug stock, and an upstart company called Intel. He divided his time between Palm Beach, his beachfront house in the Hamptons, two wineries—one in Napa and the other in La Rioja, Spain—and a summer estate on the French Rivera. His Gulf Stream G-5 corporate jet was at constant ready at the Palm Beach airport and his fuel bill rivaled Jet Blue's.

Some of the more crass class on The Island called him Bernie Billionaire.

I pulled the Jag into the entrance and waved at video camera. The electric gate silently swung open. The Jag made its way up a palm-lined driveway and parked at the entrance between two Romanesque statues, one of which was soon to be replaced by the Cavanaugh at the gallery. Hilda, Bernie's long-time Germanic housekeeper, opened the twin mahogany doors and without a blink lead me inside to the foyer where I was greeted by a stunning collection of art work tacked up on the walls one over the other, like a seventeenth-century lord's salon. Bernie didn't just like contrast, he like overwhelming anarchy.

High above the array of artwork, covering the entire ceiling, was a copy of Rafael's ornate Heliodorus Room fresco from the Vatican. The muralist had painted Bernie's likeness as Saint Peter being saved by an angel.

Bernie, it seemed, still held out hopes of attaining salvation.

Hilda escorted me to his workroom, stretching along the entire left flank of the house, then left. It was an austere but spacious berth lit by the dull hue of four seventy-two inch computer screens. Not a painting tainted the walls. Bernie called them distractions.

Off to one side against a window, ablaze in light, was an arranged sitting area of comfortable chairs and tables. On one table beside an overstuffed chair was an open copy of Charles Baudelaire's *Les Fleurs du Mal,* in French. I sat down and thumbed through the book. Bernie had highlighted a number of passages in yellow. That's one thing we share, a passion for philosophy, and, I must add, a love of the absurd. Today's events were probably closer to the latter and I was sure Bernie Crown would be impressed at receiving news of the Manley murder from my tittle-tattling lips. Gossip is the grease of societies.

I was on the second poem when Bernie sauntered into the room. He was tall, a good six foot two, and walked straight like a military man. He had long light brown hair swept straight back and eyebrows that needed trimming. He still wore his army dog tags. "For insurance purposes," he'd say.

"Shame about Martha," he said.

How had he heard about the Manley murder? She was still warm. Hell, I was fresh from the crime scene. It hadn't even made the news reports on WJNO talk radio yet. I stared at him, hoping for enlightenment, and was met with a knowing smile. Like a good mentor, Bernie sometimes scared me.

"I liked the old gal. She had the kind of spunk needed to survive in Palm Beach," he said, pouring two glasses of a 1997 Pinot Noir grand reserve from his Eagle's Lair Winery—the California one. "Is it too early for you?"

"Not at all. It's almost lunchtime, isn't it?" I asked.

"For some of us." He planted himself in a large high-backed leather chair.

I dutifully swirled the deep-tinted liquid in the Queen Anne glass, and sniffed the rising bouquet. I sipped and left the wine to linger in my mouth, letting its full-bodied fruit-forward flavor massage my tongue, noting the subtle balance of acidity and tannins followed by a teasing aftertaste of boysenberries, if you believed the back label.

"Not bad," I said.

"You look perplexed, my boy. Anything you want to share with your Uncle Bernie?"

Whether because of the wine or the company, I spurted out my tale: Martha and the Count's visit to the gallery, then bursting onto the crime scene, and finally my suspicions the paintings might be forgeries.

"My dear Maxie. You do have a flare for landing in curious situations," he said, staring at the ceiling. "Don't you think it is a bit too coincidental that the day you show up to examine paintings that you think might be forgeries, Miss Martha is violently dispatched to the next world?"

"I concede that the timing could have been better." I felt the warm, wine-induced inner glow rise to my head.

"I, for one, have found that the 'long arm of coincidence' invariably ends in an armpit."

"A quote from Carlyle?"

"Heavens no, P.R. Chalmers."

"Are you saying you think that the invitation to examine the paintings was a set up to get me to the murder scene?"

"It could have been. You could be. Or worse."

What could be worse?

"You know something you're not telling me?" I asked.

"It's like in the military, son, you're on a need-to-know basis only." He drained the last drops of wine and poured us both another glass. "This is Palm Beach. Like Jake, the Jack Nicholson character in Roman Polanski's *Chinatown* said while lying in bed with Faye Dunaway, 'This case is like working in Chinatown. You never know what's going on,'" Bernie spoke in a perfect Nicholson voice, followed with a perfect Nicholson grin. Scary. "Palm Beach is Chinatown. No one talks to outsiders, at least about anything serious. Frivolity and made up manners are society's shield. Always doubt your instincts, then go with your gut."

"What if the paintings are forgeries and her murder had something to do with them?"

"First, and I trust your instincts, you do not know if the paintings are forgeries. For your own good let the police take care of it. You have an aptitude for research and investigation, but you're not a private detective, you're an art dealer. Keep your inquiries to art. You start talking forgeries in this town and you'll make a barnyard of enemies."

"But it *is* the art."

"What do you mean, the art?" he said. He took another long sip. "I have enough art. And I know you've squirreled away enough paintings to house a museum. Where are the odds? And with your past, Maxie, you can't afford this. Let it go. You have the Gift. Don't abuse it."

"Well, the Gift is not working a well as it should."

"How should it work anyway?" Bernie asked. "I've always been curious."

I thought for a moment. The Gift, as Bernie calls it, is a visceral feeling I get around old art pieces and antiques. "It's nothing scientific or even rational. Nothing I can put into words. It's a feeling, a tingle or a gasp. Sometimes it's physical, other times it's spiritual. It's as if I can feel the artist in the canvas. When these feelings are short-circuited or jumbled, a storm flag rises. Caution."

"Whatever it is, it works. Take good care of it. If you abuse it you could lose it."

"This morning the storm flag was flying hurricane warnings."

"Like all hurricanes, it'll blow over." He slapped his hands on his knees. "Now, what about that Cavanaugh?"

My watch read five when I left with Bernie's check carefully folded in my wallet. I briefly, and I'm afraid to admit how briefly, thought of paying the property taxes, making a car payment, or even sending some extra money to Mrs. Nancy Roberts, my wife. Technically, and legally, my ex.

Before I had turned out of his driveway, I made a call.

"Maximilian Roberts," the voice at the other end said with a yawn. "Don't you know it's midnight here?"

"I always heard that London was a city that never sleeps." I cleared my throat. "Is that Goya etching still for sale?"

"You're in luck. It is available but just this morning a gentleman from Moscow was inquiring about it."

"Are you telling me that the Russian Mafiosi are interested in more than fake Orthodox icons?"

"I'm saying if you want it you'd better say yes now."

"Yes," I said.

I know. I have no resolve. I can't help myself. I did decide to take Bernie's advice. Like he said, there were no odds in following the Manley art trail. And Bernie was always right.

CHAPTER 5

By four o'clock, the Manley murder had hit the national media like a hundred-kiloton thermonuclear bomb. By five, the fallout had circled the globe. Everyone loved Palm Beach scandals. They promised to bring in the three elements that intrigued the rest of the world—big money, big names, big lawyers—and, with twenty-four-hour news shows comes a fourth, big public trials. National media events like the Roxanne Pulitzer divorce, the William Kennedy Smith rape trial, and dear old Bernie Madoff become self-perpetuating feeding frenzies. Blood was in the water and the media sharks were circling. Correspondents from across the globe fought for the last seats on the incoming flights and within three hours all the hotels from Jupiter to Delray Beach were booked. Sure beats Mogadishu.

By the six o'clock news, we were informed, Count Sergio Ordenoff had hired Beebee Alabama, the flamboyant Palm Beach attorney known more for massive litigation cases than capital crimes. Alabama knew everyone and, like every rich alleged felon's best friend, Ray White, Esquire, he rarely lost high-profile cases. By eight, the Manley kids let the world know through their spokespersons that they wanted justice and made little effort to conceal that they thought their stepfather was guilty.

Naturally, I had more than a passing curiosity. I wanted to see justice done. Someone was murdered in my hometown. However, I really did not care who killed Martha Manley as long as the killer was caught. What did bother me were the paintings, the possibility that they were forgeries. I was plagued by a nagging sensation that I could not shake. For twenty years, ever since I lost a priceless Tintoretto that was in my care, I've been haunted by forgeries or stolen art. But I resolved to take Bernie's advice and restrict my interest in the Manley affair to Court TV and The O'Reilly Factor.

As Bernie intimated, parts of my nebulous past would not permit solicitous scrutiny. My conundrum was more financial than felonious, and the magic word was treasure, pronounced slyly by those in the know, almost as a sexual slur. Treasure, especially Spanish treasure, was close to my heart.

I was house-sitting a friend's weather-beaten cottage on the beach near Fort Pierce. It was fall and a tropical storm had just crossed the state. The surf had settled after three agitated days so I decided to take a morning swim before searching for a job. About fifty strokes beyond the surf line I spotted what I thought was a dark log resting on the sandy bottom. I surface-dove to twenty feet and found not a log but a Spanish cannon. Over the next week I followed the scatter trail where in fifty feet of water I found part of the mother load, thirty-two gold bars and hundreds of silver coins that turned out to be from a Spanish galleon sunk in 1638. Nothing corrupts the mind of men more than the word *treasure*.

Alone and mostly at night, I carefully recovered the treasure and in six months went from the poor house to Palm Beach. An everyman's dream but how to justify my sudden wealth, especially to the state of Florida, which claimed all treasure found in state waters? The flip side is that any thing found on land was finders keepers. To avoid the State confiscating most of the treasure, I claimed to have uncovered a few bars in the sand ten miles to the south and they were duly declared. Few professional archeologists believed me, least of all those of the state in the Antiquities Board in Tallahassee And, though over twenty years had passed, the state of Florida had not lost interest me as their regular correspondence from the Antiquities Board attested. Any involvement in the Manley murder, as Bernie pointed out, would bring me unwelcomed attention.

By the time I pulled the Jag into the garage and stepped into the kitchen, my mind had begun the process of placing the Manley paintings into its deepest reaches.

"You'va message from Margot," I heard Margarita say. She handed me a note. It read, "Don't forget the Forester party tonight."

Heat or hurricane, murder or mayhem, Noreen Forester's party was a must-attend affair. Even though the Manley murder that morning would dampen the festive mood, the gossips would be having a field day. The real Palm Beach winter Season, from New Year's to Easter, hadn't arrived but the party calendar was filling fast. Aside from the conga-line of charity galas and balls, every night there are three to four must-attend parties. Palm Beachers like to have fun.

After changing, I headed north and took the back road pass the witch's castle, where it's said that one can hear the forlorn moans of a mourning mother, then north on North Lake Way. The Forester home was on the Intracoastal Waterway, three blocks north of the Sailfish Club. I pulled up to the sweeping driveway entrance to the Forester estate. The Jag, I could tell, felt comfortable rubbing fenders with Bentleys, Mercedes, and Porches. Two racing-red Ferraris were conspicuously parked near the entrance. Beauty is beauty.

There was only valet parking, of course. I reached into my pocket and fingered my last bill, a ten-spot. Well, at least it wasn't a one.

I handed the bill to one of the beach boys and got a, "Thanks." What I really wanted was change. I gave him a, "What's your name? Okay, Shawn, try to leave some rubber on the tires," so he'd hold out the hope of another tenner. Then I ambled up the front marble steps, to the front door, where I passed a cursory inspection by the tuxedoed bouncers.

The charming Noreen Forester's late husband was the U.S. Ambassador to Japan during the trade wars. The party theme was, naturally, Japanese. The waiters and some of the guests were dressed in the obligatory kimonos and some had faces painted as Kabuki players. With a peck-kiss on each cheek and a we-must-see-more-of-you, I gave my regards to Mrs. Forester. She was dressed in a sweeping black Roberto Cavalli dress and a triple strand of large ghost-white Mikies, Mikimoto pearls, hung like apostles down her well-tanned leathery chest. Beside Noreen was the ever-gracious and legendary Barona Goodmann. More cheek kisses. The jewels and the stars were out and shining. A crowd surrounded Ina Trumpet and her new teddy-boy groom. I nodded to yachtsman and America's Cup winner Bobby Notch in deep conversation with our Mayor. I'd had the privilege of viewing Bobby's collection of model and half model American Cub yachts but not his fabled wine cellar. Finally, I made my way to the buffet where I was relieved to see no live gold painted nudes as centerpieces. I snatched a red wine off a tray and was instantly trapped by the delightfully intoxicated Karen Courtney and her companion, Sharon. No last name, only Sharon. Karen grabbed my arm. "Maxie Roberts, you bad boy. You've been avoiding me, haven't you?"

"Can't afford to, Karen," I said.

Suddenly both my arms were in a vice lock as Karen and Sharon led me over to another buffet table. A black kimono-dressed waiter lifted a morsel-covered plate and offered it to us. Karen plucked two still breathing seafood things off the plate and plopped them into her mouth.

"The buffet is superb, but . . ." She paused and looked around for hearing distance. "Remember last year when Melanie Cabot Moore gave a sit down dinner for fifty people? Now, *that* was an affair. People just don't do that anymore," she said. "When her poor hubby died she sold the house, most of her antiques and paintings. Moved into an apartment in the Trump Towers. Imagine? Living in West Palm!"

"Some of my best friends are West Palm Beachers," I said, looking around for a subtle escape route. Over her shoulder I spotted the well-tanned Samuel Hoffman, known as Picasso Man for his extensive collection of the Spanish painter. I gave him a save-me-please glance and he waved me over.

"Maxie, good to see you," he said, holding out his hand. "Thought I'd rescue you from those soon-to-be grand dames. Nothing but ancient widda-women and blue-haired hags in Palm Beach anymore. What this island needs is new blood to replace the blue bloods."

"Be kind Sam. Be kind," I said. "When did you get down?"

"Last week the temperature dropped below freezing at Hyannisport. It was hell on the back nine at Oyster Harbors with that wind blowing off the Sound. Shame about Martha. Anything I'd be interested in?"

"No Picassos."

"None?"

"Manley went more for impressionists and old masters. Still I've one you might want to look at. A crying Dora. But it's pricey."

Now I was going to hear him cry.

"You know things are real tight right now with the economy and all. But do me a favor. Why don't you bring it around, son?"

"I'll call."

He shook my hand. "As you munch into that raw fish stuff, just repeat after me, 'I remember Pearl Harbor,'" he said before moving off.

I gave the party crowd one last glance and saw Henry Tillman, owner of Evernia Art Gallery in Palm Beach, head to head with George Gregory of George Gregory Fine Arts of Worth Avenue. I wanted to pump Tillman for any tidbits of information on the Manley collection, but then I spotted the tall figure of Nigel Jenkins standing on the other side of the pool under a green Chinese lantern. Nigel, a former New York City gallery owner turned fine art guardian, owned a vault-like storage building in Palm Beach Gardens where paintings and sculptures were securely stashed out of season—kind of an Art Depot. His house on Via Linda was a sprawling brown brick ranch with an over-sized tennis racket shaped swimming pool. Martha had said he was on one of her charity boards, so he might have some gossip on the Manley paintings, for curiosity's sake only.

Jenkins was in an animated conversation with a young woman, so I stopped halfway around the pool and waited for them to finish. She had shoulder length auburn hair and a high forehead. Taking a step closer I saw that the light had tricked me. Her hair was not auburn but dark brown, almost black. From this angle, the young lady looked familiar. She was too young and too pretty to be a collector and too innocent-looking to be a fortune hunter. Perhaps she was a gallery girl. With her wide eyes locked like flypaper on Jenkins' every gesture, it was obvious she was enthralled with our man-about-town. Art does that. Two sips later, I was still trying to place her when Nigel leaned over and placed a peck on her cheek. She gave him one last smile then disappeared into the house. My cue to move in.

"Nigel Jenkins, I presume?" I said.

He turned and I was meet with a wide, vivacious smile crammed with large white teeth. He had Cary Grant eyes and a boxer's chin and looked as fit as a man in his fifties could. Nigel Jenkins was always described as tall, so I was surprised that standing together we looked each other directly at eye level. I'm only five eleven. Certain people seem larger than life, like the kid at the center of a group in the school cafeteria, the master sitting at the head of a table, or the winner breaking the tape at the finish line. They attract people, usually of both sexes, with an inner magnetism.

"Maxie Roberts," he said, wrapping his arm around my shoulder in a half *abrazo*. "You never visit anymore. Someone said you were last spotted entering the Uffizzi and never seen again. I was about to believe them."

"Sounds like a plan. Florence does have it's charm but they have something called winter and being a native-born Floridian I've a genetic aversion to the cold."

"Is that an excuse for neglecting old friends?"

"Unfortunately the art market is tough these days. I can't even afford to leave The Island."

"Let's not go overboard. I'm sure you're doing well," he said. "Horrible about Martha. What is the world coming to when you can't be safe on The Island?"

"Tell me about it. I was at the Manley's this morning."

"You're kidding," he said, nearly spilling his drink. "Good God. That must have been awful. In a professional capacity?"

"Confidential, Nigel. Confidential. You know how things are. But actually, Martha did mention you."

"Me?" His eyes widened.

"She told me that you and her were on the board of Westchester Charities."

"Ah, yes. We both believed in good causes. Martha was a ceaseless warrior for the less fortunate." He frowned and cocked his head. "I heard that your friend, lieutenant what's-his-name, is handling the case?"

"Aldrick, Adam Aldrick."

"They tell me he's a good man. At least we won't get an ex-hairdresser investigating this murder. Let's hope they get the killer soon. Don't want people thinking they can't move around The Island unmolested. It'd be bad for business," he said. "She was one of the last of the great ones, I'm afraid. Nothing left but NPs."

New People.

"They buy art too, Nigel."

"Their one saving grace," he said, raising his glass in the air. Probably toasting the god of cash flow.

"Just between the two of us. Have you ever heard of anyone questioning the Manley collection?" I asked.

He paused and gave me a hard look. "Questioning the paintings? That's a pretty nice collection, I hear. Questioning it? No. To tell the truth, I don't even want to think about that." He drained the remains of his drink.

"Nobody likes to think about it, but we all have to be so careful about forgeries." I reached behind Nigel and from a table grabbed a tuna sashimi on toast and popped it into my mouth. "Humm. Not bad." I smacked my lips. "I've been told to leave the paintings alone. It was just a thought."

"Well, don't be a stranger. Why don't you come by the office next week? We've some new facilities I'd like you to see." He gave his glass to a passing white-faced waiter. "You like Japanese?"

"Love it. In Japan."

I polished off three more drinks before the night's entertainment was announced, a must-miss Kabuki Samurai warrior fight. In deference to the Japanese, I quietly made a quick exit.

It was near three in the morning by the time I parked the Jag, gave the bonnet a big kiss for behaving so nicely and made it into the kitchen. The annoying red blinks of the answering machine meant messages. The first two were from Margot and the last two from Nancy. Too late to deal with any distant domestic discommode. I headed to bed, alone as usual.

The ringing in my head, I thought, had to be the genesis of a hangover and I had taken the last of the Percodan. It was four fifteen in the morning for Christ's sake! Finally, my remaining brain cells recognized the offending reverberation as the alarm beeper I carried with me as a backup to the primary alarms at the house and the gallery. It read gallery. My senses came to immediate attention.

Someone was in the gallery.

CHAPTER 6

I dialed the alarm company.

"We haven't had any alarm from the gallery. Do you want us to notify the police?"

"No," I said. "It's probably nothing."

The police hate alarms that cry wolf. Do it enough and they'll charge you a hefty fee or worst ignore it. Also, Adam Aldrick not withstanding, my relationship with the Palm Beach police was touch and go. The less we touch and they go, the better.

I threw on a pair of jeans and a sweater and drove the six blocks to the gallery. As I pulled up to the front door I realized that in my rush I had left my nine-millimeter H-K in my nightstand. Too late to turn back.

I tried the front door, locked and secured. Had I simply not set the alarm when I left? I opened the doors and turned on the reception lights. My gaze darted from the reception desk to the restroom door to the chairs and sofa then along the walls. Everything was in place.

I paused and listened for a half minute before I opened the green doors and lit up the display hall. The lights flashed bright like a police interrogation lamp. I squinted and made a quick visual inventory. Nothing was missing, but a near fear filled the room. The line of portraits along the wall stared at me, eyes replete with dire warning. I took a deep breath and exhaled then, stepping cautiously, I moved down the gallery. An uncanny silence like the first steps into an ancient tomb doused me in beady sweat. My skin tingled. I paused and was overcome again by a sensation of fear that was not my own. Then whose?

As I cocked my head to listen I smelled a trace odor, vague like a beastly warning line pissed in the sand. It was a whiff of something toxic, gas-like. Did I have a gas leak? I sniffed. It wasn't gas; it was too pungent for gas. I turned and moved toward my office, slower now, feeling naked without my pistol. I swung the office door open and was instantly hit by a reeking cloud of gaseous exhaust like a blast of an aerosol fumigant.

I gagged, closed my eyes, and groped for the light switch, then heard hard shoes on tile running behind me. I half turned and saw a bulky figure in night man's clothes plunge through the green doors and disappear into the reception room. Before I could react, I heard a muffled click and a brilliant flare light up my office. From behind the desk, bright angry flames shot to the ceiling. I jerked around and threw myself on the floor, took a deep breath and, without looking back, scampered on all fours down the gallery toward the green doors.

From all sides a deafening siren shrieked and followed by a high-pitched hissing. Streams of high-pressured halcyon gas shot out of hidden ceiling nozzles.

Still on my knees, I scrammed on all fours into the reception area, pushed through the front doors, and rolled out onto the sidewalk to the gutter. I sucked in a breath of night air. Within seconds the entire gallery was filled with cold inert halcyon gas. Deprived of oxygen, the fire was immediately snuffed out. Anyone caught inside would have suffocated.

I was lying face down on County Road when the first police cruiser pulled up to the curb. Officer Tom Tyler rushed over to help me sit up, saving me from the indignation of seeing a photograph of me groveling in a County Road gutter on the front page of the Palm Beach Daily News. I was sitting on the curb nursing my aching elbows when Adam's blue Buick LeSabre pulled in beside the squad car. He stepped out, slipped on his jacket sans tie, and gave the street and the building his trained-observer look before peering down at me.

"I thought I told you this morning. I don't need this crap."

"I guess we're both losing our beauty sleep."

Adam helped me up. "What happened?"

I told him.

Within two minutes the Palm Beach Fire Department had two trucks stationed in front of the gallery. After airing it out, they tromped through in full fireman regalia but, like the professionals they are, they were meticulous in detail, causing little collateral damage. The Palm Beach firemen were some of the world's best; they understood a fire was not an excuse to wage war. No broken-down doors, no hacked-up windows. You never knew when an innocuous wall drawing might be a million-dollar mural in disguise.

Adam and I waited outside, out of the way, for the firemen to finish their job. Police photographers' cameras flashed. Adam's red hair went from auburn to black in the flashing lights of the fire trucks and his blue eyes darkened. He was tired and when he moved he limped a bit more.

"It's definitely arson," the fire chief said, handing Adam an evidence bag with a partially burnt device. It was the size of a cell phone, black with scorched wires protruding from its sides like a mangled spider.

"Is someone mad at you or do you need the insurance?" Adam asked.

"You know I'm the most popular guy on The Island. For Christ's sake, I have an alarm system that cost fifty thousand dollars, I pay a thousand each month for vigilance and a goddamned burglar gets into the gallery?"

Adam examined the device. "Haven't seen one like this before. Not your drugstore variety. I think it's more than a burglary," Adam said. "Come on, let's check out inside. I want you to tell me if anything is missing."

Stepping over fire hoses and puddles of water, I followed Adam through the gallery. Thankfully, none of the paintings were damaged. The fire had been set in my office. A timed ignition device using gasoline as an accelerant ,had been placed on the floor by the file cabinet behind my desk. What the arsonist had overlooked was the halcyon gas system. Most of the damage was from the smoke. The sides of my mahogany filing cabinet were scorched. The curtains would need to be replaced and the office would need a serious cleaning. Again, I thanked my guardian angel. Then I glanced at the Picasso. Perfect. How fortunate for the insurance company.

"Your intruders were professionals," Adam said, stating the obvious. "Lucky for you they missed the gas. I'm sure if they knew it was there they would have disabled it. They were looking for something. To go through all this trouble it must be something valuable."

Adam walked slowly around the office, as interested in the new trinkets I had collected as the crime scene. He stopped in front of the Picasso. "Highly overrated in my opinion. Anything missing? No paintings taken?"

I shook my head.

"I'm to believe that some joker waltzes into your office, disables a state-of-the-art alarm system, sets a fire, takes nothing, and you show up in the nick of time?" Adam paused. "A murder and an arson in twenty-four hours on my quiet island and you're somehow connected to both. Will you tell me what's going on, Maxie?"

"I wish I knew."

Adam scratched the back of his neck. "I'll get the crime scene guys in here to check for prints," he said. "We'll find out who they are."

"They?"

"Arsonists are usually hired hands."

A fireman waved at him from the reception room. "I've got to check with the fire chief," Adam said and headed out of the gallery.

I looked around one last time, shuddering to think of all the damage the fire might have caused. My inner sanctum had been barbarously violated. For what, I wondered? Then I noticed the Manley file was missing off my desk.

CHAPTER 7

I pulled the Jag into my driveway as dawn slashed her red finger across the horizon, flipped off the engine, and sat motionlessly in front of my house, immersed in the silence of early morning. The dim light reflected pink in the glass windowpanes between the soft shadows like a French mood movie. Ghostly arborvitae stood at attention in the front, while along the sides, the faint sparkle of neglected flowers still bloomed even without Nancy's tender guiding hand. Thoughts of Nancy and Eric and Nicole ran me through like a red-hot poker.

Suddenly my entire body began to tremble uncontrollably. Reality erupted through my chest like a shotgun blast at close range. I began to heave. With both hands I grabbed the steering wheel and held on tight and rocked back and forth. I and took deep breaths and slowly exhaled over and over until I recovered control of my body. I was mad. I felt impotent, exposed, and vulnerable. I had no idea what was going on, but knew I was dealing with violent people. If they were capable of setting fire to my gallery, then they were capable of coming after me or my family. Nancy, Nicole and Eric, even Margarita, might be at risk. I had to do something, but what?

No matter what, I was not going to let these cowards bully me

As I calmed down and my senses slowly returned, I tried to piece together the events of the last few days. The arsonist had taken the Manley file. That meant Martha's murder and the fire were related. But how? There was nothing in the file except for some cursory research and my notes from the day of Martha's murder. I had questioned the authenticity of the Monets and had suggested that they be examined closer. Was that motive for arson?

Bernie was right; the easiest route was to let the police handle the murder case. Yet I had been personally attacked. To do nothing was to ask to be attacked again and next time they might succeed in doing serious damage or worse. I had to find out who they were before they could strike again. My only lead was the Manley paintings. Sorry, Bernie, odds or not, I had to know if the Manley paintings were forgeries and if so, what it had to do with me and the gallery fire.

Inside the house, I trudged through the kitchen, to the family room and collapsed on the couch like a rag doll. About an hour later Margarita waddled in.

"What happened?" Margarita asked. "You left so early this morning— Oh Dios. Looka at you pants and you hand."

"I'm okay." I tried to reassure her. "There was a fire at the gallery but it did little damage."

"Ave Maria." She shot a glance at the ceiling, muttering supplications.

I sat up. "I don't want you to worry, but the fire might have been set. Probably kids, but the police said for us to be careful. I want you to keep an eye out for strangers."

"You tink you can upset me? I lived in Cuba. Since Castro that comes naturally to us. I know how to keep eye open. We Cubans have eyes in the back of our heads. The little CDR spies were everywhere ready to de-nounce you. I know what scary people are." Margarita was fingering a ro-sary that she carried in her skirt pocket. "You no have to worry. This house is protected by him." She looked up. "And them." She motioned her head to the cabal of Santeria statues she had place on top of the cupboards.

"That may be. But please let me know if you spot any strange cars or people hanging around outside."

"Nothing happen here as long as they protect us. But I'm gointa light a candle."

I couldn't argue with that.

At eight, I called Margot and gave her the details about the fire.

"Do you want me to come by the house?"

I said it wasn't necessary. "I'm going to keep the gallery closed until Adam assures us it's safe. I'll forward the office phone to your cell so you can take messages. If it's gallery business, just take a message and I'll call them back. Don't tell anyone where you are. "

I waited until nine before I phoned Raymundo. He answered his di-rect line with a grunt, and until he said, "Yes," with a perfect New Jersey accent, I had reckoned he didn't speak English. It took a few more phone calls and a couple of pulled strings but twenty minutes later, I was prom-ised a portable X-ray-like multispectral imaging machine, courtesy of Lee

Lohman, owner and curator of the Fine Arts Restorers.

My final call was to Adam to let him know I was returning to the Manley house.

"Can you tell me why you're getting involved with the Manley case?"

"Martha's last wish to me was to examine her paintings and I have a hunch that they might be forgeries. I'd like to find out if they are or not."

Adam was silent; I knew he was waiting for more.

"It's the art, Adam. It's the art."

I heard a sigh. "I should say no. And I know I'm going to regret this. It's skating close to interfering with an ongoing murder investigation, so be careful."

"Come on, Lieutenant, you know me."

"Please, don't remind me," Adam said sarcastically. Or I hoped sarcastically. "Does this have anything to do with the fire last night?"

"You'll be the first to know," I reassured him.

"That's not good enough." Adam's voice hardened. "I want more than being the first to know. I want to know everything. You got it?"

"Naturally."

"Right. Well, don't touch anything in the upstairs sitting room."

Adam could have, and probably should have, said no. But somewhere deep in his Machiavellian mind the cogs of a shrewd investigator turned. Though we were friends, Adam played by the book. And while he didn't mind giving out tidbits here and there, like all detectives, he always got more information than he gave.

By the time I reached the Manley house, a burgundy van with no markings was waiting in driveway. I recognized Julie Dunlop, the foremost art X-ray technician in the business, as she stepped out of the van.

"Julie, my dear, thanks so much for rushing this." I gave her a peck on the cheek.

"For you, I'd drop everything to help."

"Are you being literal?"

She blushed. "Stop that," she said, and then turned to help move the machine.

Though he was nowhere in sight, I'd been told that Sergio was still living in the house. Obviously, he had not felt the urge to flee nor had he been dragged off to the county clink in cuffs. Did Adam give him the old "don't leave town without my permission" bit?

I found Raymundo brooding in a single bedroom apartment over the five-car garage. Without a word, he escorted Julie and me into the house. It was eerily quiet. Under Raymundo's watchful eye, I took a dozen photographs, sans flash, of Monet's *The Girl in Garden* with my Nikon D2x digital camera. I'd repeat the process for the other Monet and the Rembrandt hanging in the dining room.

I walked over to the twin Monets and pulled a pair of white surgical gloves over my hands. Heaving a sigh, I reached up and took down the first painting. The frame was heavy gilded wood and plaster. Raymundo, dressed in a white housecoat, watched from the kitchen walkway. He made no effort to help.

Carefully I took the first Monet out of its frame and held it firmly. It was a beautiful painting, a happy piece, but it didn't feel right in my hands. The soothing tingling sensation I get when I hold an old art object was absent. I turned it around and looked at the back. The canvas appeared to be at least a century old. But anyone can age a canvas to look old, or simply paint over an old worthless canvas painting from the same period. Lee's tests would tell the age of the canvas and the paint. I examined the edges next. Holding the painting in various positions, first one way then another, I let the light play on the canvas at different angles, looking for subtle changes in paint or color or style. The strokes were Monet's, the color perfect. I took down the second Monet, titled *Water Lilies At Dawn*, and repeated the process.

From the dining room I retrieved the small Rembrandt, examined it like the others while Julie set up the portable machine.

"They're beautiful," she said, then gave me a questioning glance.

I shrugged my shoulders.

I snapped more pictures as Julie took three images of each painting: front, back, and side. In forty-five minutes we were done.

"I'll have these developed by tomorrow," Julie said.

While Julie packed up her machine, I took one of the Monets in my hands, turned it around, and carefully propped it up against a table. I retrieved a pair of surgical scissors from my art kit. My hand hesitated. Mustering up courage, I trimmed a half-inch from the rabbit ear, the corner of the canvas folded back behind the frame. It was painful. Like self-circumcision. Then with a penknife, I chipped off a little paint along the side folded over the wooden frame and placed it into a glassine envelope.

I repeated the process on the second painting. The twin Monets had plenty of excess canvas in the back.

The Rembrandt was trickier. The canvas was painted to the edge, an indication it had been trimmed before. I cut what little exposed back material there was. It couldn't take many more trimmings. Finally, I placed a piece of non-acidic white paper on the table and gently tapped the frame. A sprinkling of paint chips fell like gold dust onto the paper. Satisfied, I carefully replaced the paintings in their frames and handed them to Raymundo, who hadn't said a word.

In all, I had six envelopes of minute paint chips and canvas clippings. I would have preferred to take the paintings directly to the Fine Arts Restorers for examination. I turned the envelopes over in my hand, wondering if they held the answer to a murder or were simply a red kipper.

I heard a throat clear. When I looked up, Sergio Ordenoff was standing directly across the living room in front of me.

"I just got back from the viewing at the funeral home," he said. "Nice crowd of people. Lots of flowers. I'm sure Martha would have appreciated it."

He stepped up to me, grabbed my arm, and without saying a word, escorted me to back of the house. We stopped in an open alcove overlooking the swimming pool area and the ocean. The doors were wide open and we were alone.

"I need your help," he said in a near whisper.

"What you need is a good lawyer."

"I have one. I need someone who can help me objectively."

"You must have plenty of influential friends here on The Island."

"It's odd how so many of your best friends become scarce when the law is involved and scandal looms," he said, gazing out over the back lawn. "I suppose they're afraid I might call them as character witnesses. Truth be told, they were Martha's friends. They've all retreated into their caves and I find myself *persona non grata*, a pariah in my own pond. I'd like to think it's simply because of a drastic reduction in income rather than anything personal. I'm being shunned, Mr. Roberts. I have no illusions. I know my people. You do understand?"

I nodded, not sure where this conversation was going.

"You can help me," he said.

"I can't get involved with a police investigation. It's called obstruction of justice. And let's face it, Mr. Ordenoff, I'm practically a perfect stranger to you."

"A perfect stranger, Mr. Roberts? I hardly think so." He raised his head and squinted at the fair weather clouds scooting across the sky. With his hands buried in his pockets he took a couple of steps and turned to me. "Mr. Manley was a methodical man. Like Martha, he kept detailed records on everyone he did business with. After you sold him a painting, the Monet I believe, he began a file on you. It has everything ever written or printed about you. He trusted your judgment. That's why Martha insisted we visit you. You see, Mr. Roberts, you are no stranger. I actually know you quite well."

We stared, our eyes fixed on each other.

"I need help and I have something you want."

"I'm listening."

"Two more paintings. I'll also tell you what Martha really wanted when we visited your gallery."

"You didn't tell the police this?"

"They didn't ask and I didn't think it prudent to volunteer information. Now my attorney has forbidden me to talk with them. However, I can talk to you."

"Does Beebee Alabama know you're talking to me?"

"No."

"I'd still have to inform the police if they ask me."

"I don't care. Because I trust, Mr. Roberts, that anything you discover will only help me and perhaps find my wife's murderer."

Good Lord, I thought. Can he be that naive? Or is it me? Was I an *en passant* pawn, making a great move forward, followed by a momentary feeling of elation, then doom. Echoes of Adam and Bernie screeching in tandem, "Don't be a fool!" rang in my ears.

But I just couldn't help myself. I rose to the bait.

"You mentioned paintings. Which ones?"

"Actually, it's one painting."

Ordenoff searched me head-on one last time, then he stepped back into the living room and again I followed. We crossed the house to the entrance-hall, walked up the winding staircase and down the long hall-way to Martha's bedroom. The sitting room to the left, where Martha had been killed, was still taped off. I couldn't help but stare at the small dark stain on the carpet. Her blood?

To the right was Martha's boudoir. I followed the Count past a dolmitic marble counter littered with a woman's toiletries and make up. Light perfumes scented the air. He stopped between two walk-in closets. He hesitated then pressed a panel that gave way silently to his gentle nudge. He stood aside and gestured for me to enter.

I paused. "Are you telling me the police missed this?"

"Martha's first husband installed this room," he said. "It was designed by one of the world's top architects."

Still unsure, I took a deep breath and stepped inside.

With that one step I was thrust into another dimension. I was standing in a small light-drenched room. As my eyes adjusted to the light I saw that a mirrored tube in the ceiling brought indirect sunlight into the hidden alcove. The effect was strong and immediate. My senses were assailed from all sides, heightened. I felt disoriented, the way I felt in a recurring dream I had of running naked through the Louvre.

The room was furnished with a single white leather couch facing a large dark object. The couch, I realized quickly, was really a pew, and this a place of worship. Directly before it, lay an altar-like raiment, above which glowed the body of Christ.

I stared at the luminescent corpse, swathed in an angelic light radiating from above, and framed by a dark menacing *chiaroscuro* background. The dead Christ's corpse was misplaced and tortured, yet the stark contrast of light and dark brought me inside the painting, close to him as if I were one of the anguished laborers lowering him from the cross. I could feel their pain and the artist's agony. I recognized a fellow traveler, the "anti-Christ of painting," the bedeviled jailbird, the foremost of Renaissance contrarians. We were, I knew from years of idol worship, one.

It was signed *Caravaggio*.

Then I felt a metal shiver as cold as a Canadian winter clipper ride up my spine. I shuddered and stepped back, horrified.

CHAPTER 8

Driving faster than I should have, I flew across the Royal Palm Way Bridge to West Palm Beach. West Palm was built by railroad magnate, Henry Flagler, in 1893 to house the help. For its first eight decades, it was an obligatory, if slightly distasteful, route to Palm Beach. The Island residents could not be blamed if they held their collective noses driving through the hodgepodge of working class neighborhoods and urban decay. It was the haunt of the faceless minions who kept our island fluid and functioning like a Swiss clock. As in any ghetto, there were demarcations where the townsfolk knew they were not welcomed unasked. The official isolate line was the moat-like Lake Worth Lagoon. Drawbridges were installed on the access roads, ready to be lifted if the rabble became aroused. Of course, the drawbridges were never needed, but the good island citizens could rest assured it was an option.

Once over the Intracoastal Waterway, I took a left on Dixie Highway and two miles later pulled into a driveway just before the Lake Worth city line. The Fine Arts Restorers was located in the most nondescript building imaginable. Nothing advertised that here, each year, passed dozens of priceless pieces of art. Lee Lohman, the owner/curator, was a childhood friend, a high school drinking buddy, and confidant.

The entrance was a metal door at the end of a narrow driveway. I rang and a middle-aged woman in a smock with her hair pinned back let me in. Entering the large, well-lit high-ceilinged room my senses were assailed by smells of turpentine, exotic oil, and a hint of musk. Two women in their thirties were working over dark, grime-covered canvases. A younger girl was hunched over an oversized, gold leaf, baroque frame. Her neck was chalk-white, exposed because her long dark hair was pulled back into a ponytail, a style I've loved since grammar school. From behind, she looked familiar. Okay, I know; they all look familiar from behind. I was about to walk over to the young lady when I heard Lee's soft steps behind me.

"That's Gloria," he whispered into my left ear. "My newest assistant. She joined us about four months ago."

I turned and he winked. Lee had curly, light brown hair and close-set brown eyes staring through gold trimmed granny glasses. He stood about five foot eight and walked with a slight stoop. Dressed in a waist-length white smock, Lee looked more medical than arty.

"Nice," I said then took the glassine envelopes out of my pocket. "Like I said on the phone, I think you'll find these very interesting."

"Well, come on, let's see them," Lee said, rubbing his hands together.

I handed the glassine envelopes to Lee. He eyed the fragments through the paper.

Then I handed him the photographs.

"You're not serious? Two Monets and a Rembrandt?" He let out a whistle.

"As serous as I can get."

"This should be fun. Get back to you in a couple of days." And without a good-bye, he turned toward his office, still eyeing the packets.

I headed out the door and gave one last glance at the appropriately named Gloria. She straightened up, stretched her back, then moved over to the side to examine a corner of the frame giving me a perfect profile. Suddenly, I recognized where I had seen her. She was the mistaken, auburn-haired woman talking to Nigel Jenkins at the party the other night. Good old Nigel gets around. Sure, she was definitely pretty in a Mediterranean way. But an art restorer? I would have thought a nice little wealth-ridden dowager dripping in jewels would be more appropriate for our Mister Jenkins. Then again, as the ancient Romans would say, "*De gustibus non disputandum.*" No telling taste.

Back home after I had a half bottle of wine and a vodka chaser firmly ingested, with the precision timing she was known for, the lovely, flaxen-haired, formerly named Ms. Nancy Roberts, telephoned.

"How are you, Nancy?" I asked in my most sincere voice.

"Doing fine, thank you."

"Is Nicole or Eric there?"

"They just left for a school event and I'm late for a date with Carol Jean Connally. I ran into her at our high school reunion last weekend."

Pause.

"She married a doctor," she said. "And Susan Frye married a lawyer."

Pause.

"And I had to marry an art dealer who's always broke."

"I'm not broke," I said in my defense, then immediately regretted it.

"You sold something?"

"Actually, I did."

"And, of course, you're buying another painting."

Silence.

"You're an incorrigible, obsessive-compulsive. You know that?"

"Isn't that the reason you married me?"

"The reasons I married you could fill an encyclopedia. The reason I divorced you, one line."

I sighed. "I hope you didn't call just to lambast me."

"No, I didn't. The children are out of school early this year, and they're dying to spend the holidays with their father. They'll be flying out of La Guardia, December 19, American Airlines Flight 1125. Eric can't wait to go fishing with his dad and don't forget Nicole needs her asthma medicine close at hand, what with all the rain down there."

"It's winter, the dry season, remember?" I said. And women complain that men don't listen.

"I'm giving you fair warning."

Fair warning? I wondered. What's fair in a divorce? Nothing, absolutely nothing. I was sure she wanted the Long Island house, which I paid for, to be devoid of our progeny; she had a new boyfriend, Eric had told me in all confidence. The boyfriend worked at the Fabric Design Center designing thongs for the masculine set, really good thongs, I was sure. I confess I'm testy and jealous about Nancy. See, she divorced me, not I her. I know, I know; that's obvious.

I wanted to tell her about the Season's concerts, the latest exhibition at the Norton Art Museum, and how I missed her and the kids. I longed to say how I wanted her back but the words never came. In her presence I was a babbling mute. It had always been that way.

"If you want you can come down with them," I said lamely.

"Maxie, you know I could deal with another woman but I can't compete with a damned canvas goddess."

"It is a Rossetti masterpiece."

"For Christ's sake, she can't even give you a decent blow job."

"I still love you."

"I know," she said. And the phone went dead.

I stared at the silent receiver for a moment before hanging up. I had a fleeting vision of Nancy and I walking the beach with fifteen year old Eric and soon-to-be thirteen year old Nicole. The toffee-headed Eric was into engineering, loved to build things, and Nicole had inherited her Dad's love of the sea. She wanted to be a marine biologist.

Kids; I highly recommend them. It's the accompanying obligatory women that are questionable, long-term commodities.

Then it hit me, Eric and Nicole were coming in a couple of weeks and there was an arsonist running loose. They might not be safe here. I can't lock the kids up for three weeks. That would scare the hell out of them. Maybe, I thought, I should call Nancy back but I didn't want to upset her. If I let on that visiting me might put the kids in danger, then I could lose visitation rights. But how long could I not tell her?

Not long.

CHAPTER 9

To the casual kibitzer, the Roberts' homestead looked like a Jersey City architect's idea of a Key West cottage. The boathouse turned guesthouse had suffered a number of injudicious additions that had expanded its original two thousand square feet to four. The house was part of the old Kingsley estate. As the fortunes of the second and third generation of Kingsley offspring fell, parts of their father's company and real estate were sliced off until little was left. Roger Kingsley, the only family member to remain in Palm Beach, sold real estate - other people's real estate.

From the foyer, once the front door is closed, a keen-eyed observer can just make out across the family room and down the hall to the left, a gilded frame and a glimpse of a Mona Lisa-like smile peering out from a Germanic fog-forest. Approaching it gives the sensation of a spectra stepping out of the painting into the hallway.

The figure is the summate amalgamation of all women, a goddess-like portrait of Ophelia, Mary Magdalena, Helen of Troy and Amanda Jones, ten-times-ten. The totality of all feminine sensuality. She has a crown of brilliant red hair, Celtic and pure. Her blue-green eyes shine outward, inviting. A lace shift hangs off her shoulders seductively revealing her right breast to the viewer. At her feet grovels a pair of appreciative vipers, and a goggle-eyed rat terrier yaps silently at her delicate heels. Behind her is a forest filled with large-eyed fauna racked with classic symbolism. A worried wombat stares out between oak leaves. It is a serene scene cocked with subliminal anticipation. The lady, Elizabeth Siddal, was the painter's dead wife. It was Dante Gabriel Rossetti's lost masterpiece, *The Lady and the Lake*—a painting he did for himself and that remained in the family, unseen by the outside world for eighty years until sold by an over-opiated ne'er-do-well great grandnephew for a fix and a drink.

When I come home exhausted and craving comfort, The Lady calms me, and more than once I wanted to climb into the frame and spend eternity with her in ethereal peace, unmolested by the hustle-bustle of a century with which I have so little in common. She is my emotional therapist but lacks something as a marriage counselor. Nancy called my love for the painting obsessive. She insisted I either sell the painting or she'd leave.

The last straw for Nancy was the last time we made love. It was near noon, the kids were in school and Margarita was out shopping. We were on the couch in the loggia, a light rain tickled the windowpanes and a Miles Davis trumpet riff hummed from the family room speakers. Nancy was snuggled up on my chest as I caressed her hair. I could smell the Shalimar she had dabbed on that morning, and a trace of sweet shampoo. I buried my head in her locks; she lifted her head and I kissed her forehead. Nancy opened her mouth and our lips met, hers moist and fleshy. My eyes were closed. Then we were standing and then I was behind her, walking to the bedroom. We never made it. Halfway down the hall I caught a whiff of her and slid my arms around her waist and pressed against her. She turned. Our clothes fell to the floor like leaves in a storm. Miles hit a high trumpet note and we collapsed. We rolled and rollicked down the hall, coming to rest under the painting where she laid back as I parted her legs with kisses and caresses, tasting the sweet and sour juices of her love. We started off in slow motion, my tongue moving with deliberate laps, her stomach rising and falling in shallow steady rhythms. I watched as her body trembled uncontrollably and her legs swayed. I kept pace, increasing the speed and pressure until a steady series of moans and involuntary gasps leaped from her throat.

Catching her breath, she reached up and grabbed me and gave me a kiss, then rolled over onto her stomach and propped herself up on her knees and elbows. Carpet burns be damned, full speed ahead. I was diligently thrusting and straining and she was moaning, her fingers digging deep into the carpet when, feeling a presence, I looked up. The Lady of the Lake was staring down at me, her hand held out in oblique offering. Then she took a step out and I gasped. Nancy glanced back and caught me *in flagrante delicto,* staring up at the painting. Instant *coitus interruptus.*

"You bastard," she yelled and I, still on my knees and erect, watched as she rose, stomped down the hall and slammed the bedroom door.

She moved out that afternoon and filed divorce papers a week later, giving new meaning to Emerson's law, '*Art is a jealous mistress.*'

I don't think I understood what divorce meant.

Thinking back to that fateful afternoon, I don't find blame. That's too easy. It was an act, a bad act, in the unending play between the sexes. I always believed: don't tell me your fantasies and I won't share mine. Women don't get it. We're men, not the bonding, sensitive, communicative creatures they claim to yearn for. Deep down what they really want is another woman with a functioning penis and a half-day's growth of beard.

I suppose I could find some solace in that.

Through trial and error and years of experimenting and experience, I now know what women want—Roberts' Rule # 1: *Women want compliments and cunnilingus*—but can someone tell me what they really *need*?

CHAPTER 10

For a precious moment, the late-rising winter sun blessed South Florida with a roseate-painted sky. It was bright and unusually cool, in the mid sixties. A cold front had moved down the peninsula and, according to the fishing reports, sailfish were striking ballyhoos and streamers in 120 feet. The turmoil and paranoia of the last few days had, thankfully for a few hours, receded into the nebulous abyss of momentary amnesia.

With a steaming cup of black coffee in hand and a Mozart Salzburg piano concert on the radio, I sat down in the breakfast nook overlooking the Intracoastal Waterway. I put the Shiny Sheet, our island information stalwart, aside for later and unfolded the *Palm Beach Post*. The Manley murder still dominated the front page. Titillating tattle of the family's life history, from Papa Manley's untimely demise to a picture of Count Sergio Ordenoff at a diplomatic function in full ambassadorial attire, cocktail in hand, was plastered over the paper. No new news and nothing approaching Pulitzer level investigative reporting. If there were no breaking developments, by the weekend, the story should begin a long and inglorious journey through the back pages.

What did catch my eye was an article on the front page of the Local section.

"Man's Body Found in Canal."

Nothing unusual about bodies in canals. The hodgepodge of drainage canals that crisscross South Florida have always been a favorite dumping ground for unwanted corpses. These unfortunates were usually the result of a rushed killing. Amateurs. No professional dumps a body in a canal where they are usually found within days. A professionally-disposed-of corpse is taken by boat offshore and sliced up before being tossed over the side to become chum for the sharks and barracuda. The advantage of this method is that there is no incriminating body — and you can get a little fishing in at the same time.

Fishing aside, what I found interesting about the corpse was his name. William Jennings Baldwin, known in most circles as Billy Balls. Obviously his parents had a sense of humor as well an appreciation of history.

A single bullet to the head - or as the paper liked to describe it "execution style" - had dispatched Mr. Balls into the next world.

I knew Billy Balls. Everyone in Palm Beach County knew Billy Balls, though I think few knew his real name. He was the local bad boy—a small time car thief, a second-story man, and a con artist, as well as a member of the Pariahs Motorcycle Club. Most Palm Beachers would avoid his type like the bubonic plague. Yet Billy had a bit of quaint charm well hidden under a rough patina. Like most con men, he was entertaining. It wasn't unusual to find Billy at a local party, dressed in his Pariah motorcycle gang colors. Some people thought he added a certain gutter flair to their social affairs. While Billy spiced up the staid island gatherings, he rarely left without some purloined token.

Can't say Billy's untimely demise was unexpected. But the murder of two people I knew in three days was unusual even for me. I half-expected Angela Lansbury to walk out of a scene of *Murder She Wrote* and into the room. And the timing was terrible. Too many murders and publicity will scare the tourists away. Can't have Palm Beach turning into a Miami after the disastrous Mariel boatlift from Cuba.

I felt bad about Billy. No, I'm hardly a bleeding heart looking to excuse every criminal for their crime, crying that they were the actual victims of an inhumane society. But the cards in the game of life had been stacked against Billy. I, on the other hand, recognized that if not actually blessed, I was at least downright lucky. Aside from being cash poor most of the time, which I readily admit is my own fault, for the most part, my life has been a string of great and good fortune.

By nine thirty I began to think my good luck was abruptly ending with a flurry of telephone calls. The first two were from attorneys. Like a police knock on the front door or a telegram from the military, an attorney's call can only be bad news.

The first was from Beebee Alabama. He wanted to meet that morning. "Ten?" he asked. I suggested eleven. Didn't want anyone to think my social or business calendar was so obviously blank. After I'd politely refused to give to the local Democratic political war chests last year, I thought I had been taken off Beebee's let's-meet list.

The second call held out a bit more promise. It was Ms. Kathy Krammer, the Manley children's attorney. I knew Ms. Krammer from a spotlight piece in the *Palm Beach Illustrated* magazine on young up-and-coming female stars. She was smart, well educated, and kept good company. It also helped that, if publicity pictures didn't lie, she was attractive, almost beautiful.

"Mr. Roberts," she said in a voice that sounded like a cross between Madonna and Madeline Albright, "I represent the late Martha Manley's estate. There are a few things I think you could help to clarify. I think we should meet and share information."

"I have an eleven o'clock appointment this morning on The Island," I said. "May I suggest, say, twelve thirty?"

She paused then said, "All right. That's fine. Twelve thirty then. Thank you, Mr. Roberts. See you at twelve thirty." The phone went dead.

Direct, I like that.

While the first two calls were intriguing, the third call caught my undivided attention. It was Lee Lohman from the Fine Arts Restorers.

"You almost got me on these, Maxie. I worked most of the night on them. They're good. The Rembrandt canvas is about three hundred fifty perhaps four hundred years old. The paint looks period, but the ultra-violent light scan showed what looked like new paint. I'll have to get them analyzed to be sure. The two Monets canvases are about a hundred plus years. Again the paints look period. I've sent the three samples out for chemical testing. Should be done in a day or two. At the moment, nothing conclusive there.

"However, Julie did a rush on the multispectral image and there was no under painting on the Rembrandt. Rembrandt, as you know, always drew and redrew before he painted. I know of no Rembrandt that lacks his characteristic under drawings."

"So you think they are fakes?"

"At least the Rembrandt. But where there's one fake there's usually more. With this information, none of the better houses or museums would touch them. Judging from the photographs and the x-rays, if they're reproductions, then they're the best I've ever seen."

"Keep it quiet, Lee. Okay."

"I always do," he said.

"Thanks, Lee."

"By the way—," he cleared his throat, "—where do I send the bill?"

"Get some sleep."

I was relieved that my gut instinct had been correct. I still had what Bernie called The Gift. But I was also perplexed by the old who-done-it. Who forged them, and when and why and how? Most important, where were the originals?

An entire industry revolves around reproductions. From mass-produced prints to meticulously done copies painted by students and enthusiasts, thousands if not hundreds of thousands of copies of paintings are made every year. Copyists have been around since the first Cro-Magnon artist set his brush to the Altamira cave walls in northern Spain. As Plato said in his *Republic*, "*Everything that deceives may be said to enchant.*" Art forgeries are the ultimate deception.

Renaissance artists measured their success by how often their works were duplicated. Most of the great artists were copied repeatedly during their lifetimes. Some of those copies are now three or four hundred years old and valuable in their own right; an unsigned copy of DaVinci's Mona Lisa hangs in Madrid's El Prado Museum.

A number of artists' works have been forged to such an extent that anything by them is subject to extreme scrutiny. An observer noted that of the 2,500 paintings Corot did in his lifetime, 7,800 are to be found in America. Other artists that fall into this category include Van Gogh, Picasso, Dali, Miro, Chagall, and dozens of others.

Some of our most beloved and treasured artists were copyists. The great Michelangelo Buonarroti made drawings of the old masters on paper he had aged with smoke and tint. Often he kept the originals and returned the copy to its owner. Even the incomparable master Peter Paul Rubens resorted to copying and reworking compositions and art created by other artists. He in turn was copiously copied. Despite his own fame, Juan Theodore Delacroix painted hundreds of Rubens and Raphael copies.

That's art.

Copies are reproductions until passed off as originals. Then they become forgeries and my problem.

Again, where were the authentic paintings? Could the entire Manley collection be forgeries? When were the originals switched, or had they been forgeries when Papa Manley bought them? Did the Manleys know they were fakes? Insurance fraud was always a possibility.

Chances are the forger was a local. I didn't think he or she was imported. The Palm Beach art world is so small that the presence of a master copier would not go unnoticed.

First call on my list was Christina Hagan, a gregarious artist who specialized in copying Impressionists and Modern Expressionists. Christina held a master's in fine art from the School of the Museum of Fine Arts in

Boston. She attended most of the local art functions where she picked up painting commissions.

After the obligatory small talk, Christina quickly accepted my offer of early morning cappuccinos and croissants at the Cucina Dell' Arte restaurant on Royal Poinciana Way. She was working nearby on a large Dali for an unnamed client.

I arrived early. Inside, the rustic-red walls were covered with antique mirrors and small chandeliers dangled from the ceiling. The scene was rather sedate. At night, after nine, the restaurant jumps to a younger, energized crowd.

I gave the room a quick once over; all the tables and most of the bar stools were occupied so I returned to the outside lanai and sat at a corner table with my morning paper. Before I had finished reading page two, Christina sauntered down the sidewalk. I waved; she smiled.

Christina was one of those natural beauties who disdained the use of makeup. With a cotton, tartan work shirt and curly brown hair brushing her shoulders like fairy fingers on a country knoll, Christina was a study in contract. Her nails were perfect, as if she had just stepped out of a salon while her blue jeans were dotted with scores of errant paint spots that gave them an odd Jackson Pollock like chic-ness. She was tall, carrying an inch over yours truly. "In school they called me Shorty." she had told me at an art gallery opening last year.

"Beautiful weather we're having," she said after ordering a latte and a cheese croissant. "I heard you had a fire."

"A little electrical problem. We'll be reopening soon."

"You were lucky," she said. "I was surprised by your call."

"When I need information I go to the best."

"So this isn't a social call."

"We could make it one."

She laughed with a deep, full gag then sat up straight in her chair as the waitress brought our food. "What do you need?"

"I'd like to know if you, or anyone you know, has done copies of Monet or Rembrandt?"

"I did a Monet once, a water garden scene, I'd say about fifteen years ago. I've seen lots of students making copies in museums but no one that was any good. Haven't heard of anyone wanting to copy a Rembrandt.

Have you tried Dominic Carranza?"

"No. Is he still around?"

"I'm not sure," she said. "I haven't seen him in over a year. You know Dominic?"

"Actually, I don't. I met him once at a gallery opening in Boca, but never really got to know him."

"That's two of us."

I did know that Dominic Carranza was an Italian-Canadian snowbird and the other star among the local copyists. His *Eve and the Serpent* painted on the wall of a Manalapan living room, was one of the best copies of Michelangelo's fresco I'd ever seen; especially the twisting body of the lady serpent.

"I don't even think he's around anymore," I said.

"I wouldn't know."

Christina took a petite bite out of her croissant then wiped her lips. "There are hundreds of copyists."

"But only a few truly good ones."

Her lips perked a bit at the edges as she took another bite. "Flattery will go a long way."

"Christina, I don't have to flatter you. You're one of the best. It's a fact."

"I keep to what I know best, Modern Expressionism, Surrealism, some Abstract."

"Are you forgetting the fabulous Diego Velazquez portrait you did for Jay Peterson?"

She glanced at me then cocked her head, "I gave it a good try, but not my cup of tea."

"I beg to differ. When I saw the Velazquez, it was hanging in the place of honor in Jay's poolroom. It was a masterpiece."

A bit of color rose in her cheeks. Then she bit her lower lip. "Poolroom, hum."

"And that fine copy of Peter Paul Rubens you did."

Her eyebrows rose and fell.

"What don't you know about me?" Her eyes narrowed.

"You know, the Palm Beach art world is a tight little circle."

"Maybe too tight." She wiped her lips then stood up and grabbed her purse. "I have to get back to work. Thanks for the coffee."

Christina had left her croissant half-eaten.

CHAPTER 11

After leaving the restaurant, I took South County Road south, past the Breakers Hotel and Bethesda by-the-Sea Church to the law offices of Alabama, Cohen, Galindas and Motto. Beebee Alabama's building was a two story modernist Mediterranean structure on the first block of palm-lined Royal Palm Way, better know as Banker's Row. The decor of Beebee Alabama's reception area screamed, "I'm successful! I'll win your case and you will pay me big fees and be thankful!"

The receptionist who looked like Eve Arden in Our Miss Brooks told me, "Mr. Alabama is in a conference meeting and will be with you shortly. Mr. Alabama said for you to wait in his office."

With a perky smile and long strides, she escorted me into Beebee's office.

"Have a seat. Can I offer you something to drink?"

I said I was fine and she left. I strolled over to the room-length window overlooking Royal Palm Way and could just make out the beach and the water. I gazed around at the walls, the awards, the diplomas, the photographs of Beebee Alabama with famous people; Teddy Kennedy, Barbara Streisand, Bill Nelson, Dan Marino, Barack Obama, and Al Gore. I was trying to figure who was in a large picture behind his desk when I notice three files staked neatly on the edge of his desk. The top one immediately caught my eye. It was an eight-by-eleven color copy of the two Manley Monets I had just examined. I peered over and saw a book sized report with the name Atlanta Art Appraisers. It appeared to be full-fledged painting appraisal. What was it doing on Beebee's desk? It took weeks to get a bona fide appraisal done from someone top in the business, like Atlanta Art.

Curiosity won over good manners. I placed myself between Beebee's desk and the door and slid the folders so I could read them. Under the painting report was a legal-sized file titled "Martha Manley Ordenoff" and a two-inch thick one with Sergio Ordenoff's name. Again I checked the door and listened for activity in the hall. Hearing nothing, I opened the report and skimmed through its pages.

It was an analysis of the paintings with the note underlined in red that they were in all likelihood, not painted by Claude Monet.

I glanced around behind me to the door. Beads of sweat dribbled down the insides of my arms. The wall clock ticked down the drawn out seconds, I could hear a printer working down the hall. I swallowed, reached over, and opened to the first page of a sub-report titled: Analysis of Claude Monet's *Water Lilies At Dawn*.

Inside was a cover letter addressed to Sergio Ordenoff. It was an appraisal order, signed by Sergio Ordenoff. I checked the date, three weeks before Martha Manley's visit to my gallery. A receipt stamp on the front was dated last week. My mouth was dry.

The Count knew a week before he visited my gallery that the Monets were forgeries. I checked behind me and turned to the next page and skimmed the analysis when I heard heavy footsteps in the hallway and a male huffing.

I slapped the report shut and dropped it on the other files and took two quick steps away from the desk. I tried not to look too guilty as Beebee Alabama trouped into the room.

"Maxie Roberts, so good for you to come. Thank you."

As we shook hands, I could feel my sweaty palm mesh with his dry, relaxed hand.

"Please. Have a seat." He gestured to one of the leather chairs in front of his desk. He sat down hard, leaned over and straightened out the Manley files into a neat pile before settling back into his high back chair.

I was not sure if it was a calculated tactic or a perverse, personality trait, but Beebee Alabama made you feel as if he was cross-examining you on a witness stand. I took it in good faith, like a practice session. You never know when you'll be a judge's copilot. Born and bred in Palm Beach, Beebee Alabama tried to come off as a good-old-boy, dripping with southern charm and knowing winks. He was smart, at least smart enough not to get indicted in the latest county political-payoff scandal with the rest of the g.o.b.s, many Beebee's life long friends. Politics for profit. Corruption is as Palm Beach as sunshine, sandy beaches and alligators. Still, Beebee was a likeable guy as long as you weren't sitting across from him in court.

"We all mourn Martha's passing. She was one of The Island's great ladies. Always there to support a good cause. We are all going to miss her," Beebee said. He ran his hand through his thick salt and pepper hair. "But you know Maxie, I hate injustice."

Ditto, I thought.

"Especially when it's politically motivated."

Nod.

"To let you know right off the bat, as an attorney I would not have advised my client to allow the paintings to be examined." Lawyers, like bureaucrats, always say no.

"I thought we were all after the truth, Beebee."

"The truth is relative. As you wander farther along the lengthy road of legal process, you understand how relative it can become." He leaned back in his chair, exposing a striking set of lime green suspenders. "In a capital case, we have to be extra cautious. After all, a man's life is at stake."

"Has Sergio Ordenoff been charged?"

"Oh no. Not yet. And based on the scant evidence, Peter Putzer would be foolish to press charges. But you know, in such a high profile case like this one, state attorneys do strange things. Like indict an innocent person. Some just can't help themselves, their one chance at fame and glory and a fifteen second spot on CNN." He glanced at his watch. "Look, Maxie, what I want to ask is if you stumble across something we'd appreciate it if you'd inform us."

"I'm sure you'll get everything at discovery," I said. I watch Court TV.

"What I really mean is, I'd like to see it first, or at least be informed of anything that the police might not be interested in. Sometimes the smallest details can be important. You know we both want what's best for Sergio."

The best for Sergio? You mean the Bulgarian gentleman I just met?

Beebee was someone you did not say 'no' to. And I, the Homeric hero well disguised as an invertebrate nudibranch, was not about to disappoint. He wanted me to share information with him—I think snitch is the word—which I was only too glad to do, though I hesitated at sharing Lee Lohman's information.

"As I've told everyone, I'm interested in the artwork. I don't want to get involved in a murder case. But I'll tell you, *Beebee,* if I hear anything, I'll keep you in the loop."

"I'd appreciate that. By the way," he said, standing up. "Are you attending this year's Children's Home Gala benefit "

"Haven't been invited."

He reached into the top drawer of his desk and pulled out a cream-colored envelope. "Here are two invitations," he said and placed them in my hand.

Without prodding, Beebee Alabama walked over to an oversized walnut cigar humidor and opened the top. The sweet aroma of finely cured tobacco caressed my nostrils. "And a couple of Cohiba Churchills, flown in yesterday."

I left Beebee Alabama's office happily bribed.

Crossing Royal Palm Way I fingered the ticket envelope in my pocket. The Children's Home Gala was a much sought after event on every Palm Beach charitable social calendar. Charity may be the Fifth Pillar of Islam but in Palm Beach it is taken to daring bacchanalian heights. Palm Beachers are generous. They have a lot and they give a lot. They take to heart Francis Bacon's aphorism, "In charity there is no excess." That excess is embodied in opulent galas and extravaganzas that surpass the performances given by Marcus Aurelius at Maximus Circus in ancient Rome. From Alzheimer's to the YMCA, from the Jewish Guild for the Blind to Save-A-Pet, or Martha Manley's Westchester Charities, each charity hosted an annual shindig. If there's a cause, there's a ball. It is an easy way of feeling good about doing good, and Palm Beachers do that quite well. *Panem et circenses.* Bread and circuses. Caligula would be proud.

As I got into the Jag, my thoughts abruptly changed. I wondered, what did the Count know and when did he know it. And why did he want me to appraise paintings that he knew were forged?

CHAPTER 12

Literally changing gears, I turned west, passed the Society of the Four Arts and crossed the Royal Park or middle bridge over the Intracoastal to West Palm Beach. I caught Flagler Drive north and just before the Flagler Memorial Bridge, or the north bridge, I turned left on Sixth Street and into the parking lot of a large black-glassed square edifice, affectionately called the Darth Vader building. A new, but sober, elevator rocketed me up nineteen floors to the law offices of Beck, Goldman, Green, and O'Leary.

From what I'd read, Kathy Krammer, Esquire, who specialized in litigation and estate planning, had everything a lawyer needed in today's legal environment; an Ivy League law school degree, a quick mind, and capability. In court, according to the *Palm Beach Illustrated* article, she had the reputation of a bulldog. One prosecutor was quoted as saying; "Once she got her teeth into you she never let go." Looking at those sensuous lips as she walked through the reception room, I thought that might not be so disagreeable.

"Mr. Roberts, so nice to meet you."

"Ms Krammer." I said, trying not to stutter.

"Call me Kathy. May I call you Maximilian?" she said with a smile that was just this side of a say-cheese pout.

"Maxie, just Maxie."

Ms. Krammer was dressed conservatively, almost severely, even by legal standards. Her shoulder-length raven tresses were pulled back in lady-lawyer style and her perfectly plucked eyebrows, thick and sensuous, rested reassuringly above the bluest of blue eyes this side of County Cork. If the swelling in my scrotum was any indication, I was, once again, in love.

She directed me to her office and sat down behind her desk then picked up a yellow pencil resting on a yellow legal pad. I stepped towards the ceiling-to-floor tinted window. Below me was an expansive view of West Palm Beach, the Intracoastal Waterway, Palm Beach Island, and the Atlantic Ocean. I could make out the Breakers to the south and if I stepped on my tip toes, the Roberts Fine Arts. Well almost.

"Nice view," I said.

"Unfortunately, I hardly have any time to enjoy it," she said.

I took my seat in front of her desk and placed both feet squarely on the floor.

"I want to thank you for coming on such short notice."

"You caught me at a slow time," I said. "Has there been any progress on Martha's murder?"

"Not that I'm aware." She hesitated then said. "She was such a pleasure to work with. A very sharp lady."

"The few times I met her I got the same impression."

"Well, Maxie," Ms Krammer began again. "As you might know, I represented Mrs. Manley after her husband died and now I represent her heirs. Anything that affects the estate is of interest to me." The sharpened pencil in her hand bobbed up and down over a yellow legal pad as she spoke. "May I ask, what is your relationship with the Ordenoffs?"

"I was simply hired by Mr. And Mrs. Ordenoff to appraise three paintings," I said.

"Actually I have a letter on file that I drafted for Mrs. Ordenoff stating that she was hiring you to do an appraisal of her artwork, including the Monet you sold to her first husband. She and I worked closely together." Her eyes narrowed and she leaned forward across the desk, the pencil still bobbing.

"For the record, I didn't sell Mr. Manley the Monet. I found the painting for sale and he bought it directly from the seller. Even so, I was surprised by the Ordenoffs' visit to the gallery." I settled back into my chair. "Let me ask you this, did she think there was a problem with the artwork?"

"If she did she never mentioned it to me," Kathy said, pulling a letter out of a thick folder. "The children are anxious to have the artwork appraised and authenticated. They would like you to finish the appraisal. What more will you need to do a complete appraisal?"

"Do the children, I mean your clients, control the paintings?"

"The Manley art was placed in an irrevocable trust and Mary Martha and Frederick are acting trustees," she said.

"Christie's did the original appraisals in 1954," I said. "And another one in 2006. I'd like to talk with them. Compare notes if you'd like. They'll want a letter from you authorizing them to talk to me. There must be more recent appraisals and I'd like copies of those if possible and any provenance that is available."

"Did Martha tell you about the Christie appraisals?"

"Actually she didn't. But I have my confidential sources," I said and thought, *did Ms. Krammer know about Ordenoff's Atlanta Art appraisals?*

"Humm." The pencil stopped bobbing. "Okay, I'll give you the letter." She called in her secretary, a woman twice her age with a bobbed hairdo, and dictated a letter. In what seemed like thirty seconds, the finished letter was on her desk. Ms. Krammer glanced at it before signing it then folded the letter and slid it into an envelope.

"Here's your letter to Christie's asking them to cooperate with you in any way they can."

She handed me the envelope.

"I don't know why she didn't use Christie's again," she added.

I didn't either, I thought, but said, "I'm cheaper."

"That I find hard to believe." She cocked her head a bit to the right.

"This is Palm Beach, anything is believable," I said.

She closed the file then looked at a small brass desktop clock and asked, "How about lunch?"

I raised my brows for a nanosecond until she smiled.

We took the Jag and drove the long mile across the north bridge to The Island and parked in the angled spaces along the wide palm-lined median on Royal Poinciana Way. Spurning Italian fare we passed Testa's restaurant, a Palm Beach heirloom, to the newest hot place, Nick and Johnnie's Grill, which was the former short-lived Grotto and before, Chuck and Harold's that for awhile was affectionately known as Chuck and Horrible's.

Once seated outside under the canopy-covered veranda facing Royal Poinciana Way, I glanced around the restaurant and shared a couple of discrete nods from acquaintances. At a table for two towards the back, I spotted one of The Island's top real estate brokers with a face so new I almost didn't recognize her. Along with a couple of near billionaires, the eclectic crowd was a study in sophisticated casual, the women in their pseudo-designer dresses and the men in bright almost loud colors.

"Anything to drink?" asked the waitress.

"I usually don't indulge during work hours," Kathy said. "But I think I'll make an exception this time. I'll have a sea breeze."

I ordered a Cape Cod in a tall glass.

"The linguine marinara is fabulous and their crab cakes are to die for," Kathy said.

I knew that, but I liked a take-charge woman and let her order. As she talked to the waiter, I took a hard look at Ms. Krammer. I can appreciate a woman battling in a man's world. Overeducated, strong women don't scare me. In both sexes, I like intelligence, a dangerously dwindling resource.

"I read in the Shiny Sheet you had a fire at you gallery."

"It was nothing. A small electrical problem. No damage."

"That's good to hear," she said. "Tell me about your gallery."

"Not much to tell. It's a small one-man, one-receptionist operation. I have a few well-off clients and manage to keep my head above water." I played with the rim of my drink. "Law must be interesting, but to be honest, I don't get it."

Kathy laughed. "I like litigation. You know, the one-on-one, *mano a mano*. It's like a boxing match."

I nodded.

As she talked, I allowed my eyes to wander. Except for a mole on her lower left cheek, she had perfect skin without a trace of wrinkles, making her look younger than her thirty-six years. Her bright blue eyes contrasted sharply with her dark hair and at this angle she looked Latina. Maybe Cuban.

"My mother's Italian," she said, explaining so much with so few words.

By the time we finished our meals and ordered two cappuccinos, we were gabbing like old lost friends. A strand of dark hair had worked its way loose and dangled over her ear, giving her an asymmetrical look, like a lost gypsy girl. I wanted to reach across the table and gently tuck the errant hair behind her ear. Instead, I fidgeted with my fork. When she reached for a glass of water, I watched her linen jacket open, exposing a silk blouse covering a shapely breast just round enough to make it interesting. She caught my eye and smiled.

"What about you?"

"I'm afraid I live a boring life. A little art and a little fishing."

"Didn't you have something to do with the finding of that stolen

Renoir a couple of years ago?"

"Just doing my civic duty."

"I've always been fascinated by art, but I've never had the time to really get into it."

"You need a good teacher."

"Maybe."

"Do you date clients?" I said, regretting it the moment the words left my mouth.

"Only the ones I like," she said, then looked me in the eyes. "Are you hitting on me, Mr. Roberts?"

"No. . . no, not yet," I said, at a loss for words.

"You're blushing," she said.

That I knew.

She was obviously enjoying the moment, like Perry Mason grilling a witness to confess on the stand. Before I could really make a fool of myself, I was rescued by two frothy cappuccinos accompanied by chocolate squares. She took her chocolate, peeled back the tin foil, and placed it on her tongue like a host. Her lips closed and locked as if forcing the luscious essence deeper into her taste buds. Her mouth moved slowly and the sides curled up slightly in a pleasurable smile of satisfaction. I slid my chocolate across the tablecloth.

She picked it up and skinned it.

"Don't you like chocolate?" she asked.

"I love chocolate, but I like watching a woman enjoy herself more."

I was straightening out a wrinkle in the tablecloth when her hand came down softly on my arm and she gave me a reassuring grasp.

First contact. First hope.

"I'll get the original Christie appraisal for you," she said. "If you'll accept, my clients have authorized two days plus expenses."

Generous of them. Not a big paycheck but at least I wouldn't be footing the bill this time. Maybe I could weasel in Lee's bill for the painting tests.

"Let me think about it. I want to be sure I can give them value for their money."

"Scruples, I see."

"Don't look so surprised. The Island is full of scruples. Like much of its money, it's well hidden."

I paid the bill. When she reached for her purse, I stood up and pulled back her chair. I watched as she rose out of the seat, her body slightly bent as she stood up giving me an ample view of her sensually curved buttocks—it pays to be a gentleman. As she stood up, her shoulders came close to my face and I could smell her hair, ripe and ready, like a breeze through meadow grass.

"Thank you," she said as she turned and looked me in the eye. She held my gaze for an eternally long second.

"My pleasure." And I meant it.

In front of Darth Vader, I was blessed with a warm handshake. Before she disappeared through the doors into the lobby she turned and said, "Don't stop trying."

Amazing how three simple words can alter your thought process. As I drove off, visions of Kathy Krammer drifted before me. We'd look great together at all of the social and cultural functions. What a power couple we'd make, I fantasized, getting a little ahead of myself. Well, according to "Ruby Tuesday," lose your dreams and you'll lose your mind.

My mind and my wet dreams were working quite well, thank you.

CHAPTER 13

The thought of wet dreams and new challenges brought back sweet memories of past passions. Saint Augustine said of his pre-Christian life, "I was in love with loving." Me too. Like a stallion before his mare, I understood it's the pheromones, not the perfume. And I acted accordingly, thrilling and being thrilled by the opposite sex.

Then I met Nancy Ann Wilson, a Boston-born beauty with green eyes, ash-blonde hair, and silky white skin that never tanned. We were two kindred spirits roaming the back alleys in search of the perfect jazz riff and dopamine-numbing sex. One night under a full moon on the Ponte Vecchio in Florence, she whispered a quote from Zelda Fitzgerald in my ear, "*I don't want to live—I want to love and live incidentally.*" Fantastic! Monogamy suddenly became an option.

We married and after a one-year, whirlwind, European honeymoon, bought a house on the Loxahatchee River in Jupiter, moved in, and planned a family. I pictured children and grandchildren rollicking and frolicking in the yard, fishing from the dock, and sails with the clan to the Bahamas. The vicariously living Nancy Roberts dove into the lukewarm embryonic fluids of motherhood as she had with life. Eric and Nicole came within two years of each other. We were on a roll. I, none the worse for wear after two pregnancies, wanted four more children, but sensible Nancy shut down the factory.

We hired Margarita just before Eric was born. Nancy was a bit apprehensive about having a strange woman in her home, a fear not helped by Margarita's penchant for leaving odd, saint-like statues of Santeria Oshians around the baby's room. We compromised. No more Oshian trinkets or sacrificial candles. We did allow the crucifix to remain over the crib.

Nancy hung in there for ten more years. After she took the kids and left for New England, Margarita asked to stay.

"I don't wanna be a burden on my children," she said. "I got nowhere to go."

That made two of us. With the Jupiter house on the market for sale, I wasn't sure of my housing future either.

"As long as I own a house, it's your home too, Margarita."

We hugged and cried and downed a half bottle of white Barcardi rum. Margarita missed the kids as much as I did.

After we sold the house, I insisted that all the proceeds went to purchase a home for Nancy and the kids. My attorney wanted to have me committed.

The converted boathouse I rented after the divorce looked more like a Key West cottage than the normal Palm Beach Tuscan manse. At four thousand square feet, it was small by island standards but more than comfortable. It had four bedrooms, a large family room, a dock on the Intracoastal and enough walls to hang art.

Margarita moved into the in-law loft above the two-car garage.

With Margarita at the helm, the Roberts homestead would never become a confirmed bachelor's pad, which suited me fine. She held down the fort better than any alarm system. Over the last thirteen years, Margarita made the transformation from Cuban nanny to old maid aunt housekeeper to surrogate mother to yours truly. Margarita made the house a home. And, just as important, I thought as I turned into the driveway and parked the Jag in the garage, with Margarita living with me, I had someone to come home to and not a silent and empty house.

Before I had stepped through the front door I knew something was amiss. The radio that usually blared salsa and meringue music was strangely silent. The acrid scent of burnt wax hung heavily in the air, like an elephant passing gas. Either someone was having a candlelight dinner without me or Margarita was burning sacrifices.

Glass candles with pictures of saints and Santeria Orishas were glowing in the living room and kitchen. Each was a supplication to an Orisha, a different god or saint of something. I knew better than to ask and headed to the bedroom. I lay down on my bed with a 1936 art report on Rembrandt forgeries in hand. As I adjusted the pillow, I felt a lumpy object against my left ear. I lifted the pillow and retrieved a grinning, elongated stygian-colored phallus with three beady eyes topped off with a grass cap and a red feather.

I may not know much about Santeria, but I do know a mojo when I saw one.

I took the offending offering to the kitchen and laid it on the counter.

"Margarita, how many times have I asked you not to leave these doohickeys around the house. Especially in my bed."

"Ave Maria, Mr. Roberts. You met a nice girl. You need all the help Oshiam can give you."

"Believe me. I don't need any help. I'm fine, thank you. And who told you that I met someone?"

She winked three times at the eight-inch statue of Elegba perched above the microwave—he was wearing what I thought were miniature designer sungalsses—then she gave me the look of a lost soul, grunted before making a sign of the cross, and swearing a couple of Santeria curses under her breath. Grudgingly, she placed the flaccid phallus into her purse. I was about to ask what the statue said when she turned her back and busied herself at the sink, refusing to waste more breath on someone with little faith.

In Florida, cultures and subcultures exist side by side, sometimes a half block apart, and never know of the others' existence. They are part of the tangled parallelism that makes South Florida the intriguing paradise it is. As I said, I love contrast. Like most Palm Beachers, I tolerate Margarita and her Santeria and all the other curious cults brought in by our legal and illegal visitors from the south. If we didn't, we'd have no help.

It had been a long day. I poured a glass of Muga Reserve, Rioja wine, and walked out to the back deck where the last light of day softly outlined the western horizon. After a few sips, I officially declared it night. I ambled my way back into the den, where I found a five-month-old copy of *Palm Beach Illustrated* halfway down a four-foot-high magazine pile. *Why can't I simply throw things out?* Turning to page forty-five I came face to face with a radiant Kathy Krammer looking up at the camera from the seat of her blue Porsche Boxster. Resting on the side seat was an open briefcase loaded with files in true attorney style. She looked as good in the picture as in real life. I thought of framing the page, but once again I was getting ahead of myself. How quickly this woman had become an obscure object of my desire.

What could I do to show my intentions were pure but real? Now think. Flowers? No, too sentimental. A fresh grouper steak? Get real. The Children's Gala! Yes, an invitation to the Children's Fund Gala. Thank you, Beebee Alabama, thank you.

CHAPTER 14

I awoke early the next morning, as my Guatemalan gardener would say, "like a man." Unfortunately, alone in bed, I had nowhere to place my exuberance except in my left hand, already calloused from overuse. My libidinal alter ego on which, over my life, I have showered an inordinate amount of attention, abuse, and downright love, has returned the favor with untold hours of bliss, consternation, and wonder. As I discovered in my prepubescent period, it has its own personality and a mind of its own, as unfathomable as the mood swings and capriciousness of the alleged fair sex. I have given it a name: Jock.

Living with Jock was like inhabiting a parallel universe with a two-faced Janus, alternately dangling and projecting between my thighs—a veritable Jekyll and Hyde. This, of course, led to some rather erratic behavior. I'm sure men, most of whom have Jocks of their own, confuse the ladies as much as the ladies do us. The sexes equally share Milton's enigmatical *"chaos and old night,"* that I affectionately dubbed MAD—Mutually Assured Discombobulation. I blame it on Jock.

Once downsized, I dressed and gulped two cups of coffee when the doorbell rang. Margarita brought in an overnight package from Kathy Krammer with the Monet provenance and a note: "Do give me a call. Kathy." I resisted calling immediately. Roberts' Rule # 7: *You never show women more interest than they do. It scares them off.*

Inside a tightly sealed folder were a dozen neatly bound letters and documents. I thumbed through them. They were mostly in French—that and Italian are the languages of art and must-knows for any serious art dealer. I spoke French, Italian, and English and, with Margarita's help, I was adding Spanish—hopefully to better understand Velazquez, Goya and El Greco.

The executive summary recapped that Monet finished *Water Lilies At Dawn* in the fall of 1874 at Coulon Gardens during his bold brush period. His technique had matured, which can be seen in the broad strokes and the use of a wide palette of pastel colors. Monet sold the painting to Mers Francois Lambert, a patron of the Montmartre artist cafes where many Impressionists first exhibited their works. In 1875, the painting was purchased by Baron Komaniesky, a renowned Russian art collector, who had discovered a number of Impressionist painters. With more insight than most of his countrymen, he sent the Monet out of Russia just before the Bolshevik Revolution. In 1921 it was purchased by a Dutch collector and remained in his family until 1932 when it was sold to Sr. Lopes of Portugal, where, fortunately, it remained safe from the political and cultural turmoil of the Thirties and Forties when thousands of paintings were looted or burned during World War II. Monet, along with Matisse, Picasso, and most of the Impressionists, Abstract, and Dadaists, were considered decadent by politically correct Nazis. Surviving the war, the Monet was purchased by Papa Manley in 1953.

Tucked in a manila envelope was a letter from The Master's Art Conservers of Philadelphia. They had restored a small rip in the lower left corner. Except for the tear, the painting had no new canvas backing and was in excellent condition. It was last cleaned in 1986.

Not even a vague hint of questionable authenticity.

That was all reassuring in a vague, bureaucratic way.

I was almost finished when my cellular rang. It was the Count.

"Mr. Roberts, if you could so kindly come by the house," he said. "I have a decision to make and I'd rather not discuss it on the phone."

I was about to say I was busy but then I thought, this would be a good time to confront him about the appraisal I saw on Beebee Alabama's desk. "Give me an hour," I said.

Exactly one hour later, I slowly motored up North County Road. Two houses before the Manley place I stopped and cased the area for any active police surveillance. Seeing nothing unusual I motored into the Manley's driveway.

The Count answered his own door. After a handshake he escorted me into the living room.

"Have a seat," he said, waving me to an oversized chair by the piano. He sat on the sofa directly across from me.

"Thank you so much for coming, Mr. Roberts. I can't get anyone to return my phone calls these days. When this is all over, I hope to return to my village in Bulgaria for a few months. You know, let the dust settle."

"You called me."

"Yes. Yes, I did," he said. "I found Martha's appointment book. Oddly, it was in the back seat of the Bentley." He retrieved a comic book-sized brown leather agenda from the mahogany table beside the sofa.

"You telling me the police missed this?"

"At the time the Bentley was in the shop being repaired," he said.

"The same blue Bentley that you and Martha came by the gallery in?"

"Yes. Yes," He nodded. "Raymundo said it was pinging or something and took it in that afternoon."

"I know the Palm Beach cops. There's no way they would have missed one of your vehicles."

"The Bentley is in the name of one of Frederick's, Mr. Manley's, companies' name," he said. He fingered the pages in the leather booklet. "Anyway, Martha had a number of hours marked in red. She'd do that if she had what she called a 'special' appointment."

"Why tell me about it?"

"Oh. One thing. You were here the morning Martha . . . I thought you might have some thoughts on it and . . . and I want someone to believe in my innocence." His arms fell to his sides, on to the sofa, and with a sigh he lowered his head. "Everyone on The Island believes I killed her. I can't even go out to eat without a crowd staring at me." He passed the booklet toward me.

"I can't take that," I said, raising my hands. "I'd have to give it to the police. You had better give it to Beebee Alabama. He has a stable full of the best private eyes. I'm just an art dealer. I'm good at chasing down paintings but this is way over my head."

The Count paused, his hand with the notebook hung in the air.

Was he reluctant to give this evidence to Beebee Alabama? Maybe he didn't trust Beebee. Maybe he had more to hide than he was willing to share with his own attorney.

Carefully, he set the booklet back down on the table.

"You knew the paintings were forgeries didn't you?" I said.

For a second, Sergio looked startled. "No. No I didn't know anything about the paintings except what Martha would tell me. Martha only told me whatever she felt like sharing." He swallowed hard. "You see Mister Roberts, I'm not a curious man. Something I've learned over the years. You might say it's a survival skill. If you know what I mean."

""Then what about the appraisal report that you ordered from Atlanta Art."

"Oh that," he said without blinking an eye. "I never ordered that report. Martha often signed my name. She had power of attorney. It was part of the agreement. I didn't even know about it until Beebee Alabama showed it to me after her death."

"Isn't that rather foolish for a husband or anyone to trust someone with their signature?"

He shrugged his shoulders. "When you have nothing, you have nothing to lose." He swallowed hard then in a near whisper said. "Except in this case it might be my life."

"If she knew they were forgeries then why did she come to me?"

"Martha must have had her reasons. But she did mostly what she pleased. She had some rather strange habits."

"Like what?"

He shrugged his shoulders and said nothing.

I was having a hard time believing what I was hearing. Then I thought, what if Beebee Alabama had left the folders and the report on his desk for me to see? Maybe the files left on Beebee Alabama's desk in plain view weren't a case of a careless attorney. Beebee didn't get where he was by being careless. And if he did deliberately leave the report, why did he want me to see it? Who would it help? Sergio? The Manley estate?

I stared at the Count. "This is getting way too complicated for me. Like I said, give the notebook to Beebee."

"Oh, yes. I suppose you're right." The Count sighed again and placed the booklet on the sofa. Like the last meeting I had with Martha in the Bentley I had a feeling he wanted to tell me more. Instead he lowered his head and went silent.

"You have no idea who the appointments were with?" I asked.

"Could have been any number of her friends. Martha had a lot of friends."

"Did Martha have any new friends? People you were not familiar with?"

"No. Not that I know of."

I glanced around the large room. A house of this size requires help.

"How about any people around the house you didn't know, like new maids or yard men?"

"The police asked the same question. No, all the help came with superb references. Even the handyman who came on his motorcycle. He was big, quite muscular, but discreet. Never, how do you say it, 'gunned' his motorcycle in the neighborhood, though he had a large vulgar tattoo of a shark on his left arm. Quite odd, you know."

"What?" I blurted out.

The room began to spin. I placed my hand on the edge of the table to steady myself. A big biker with a shark tattoo on his arm; the Count had just described the recently deceased Billy Balls. And as far as I know, Billy was no handyman. A good mechanic, perhaps, but no handyman.

"Did you tell the lieutenant this?" I said

"I'm not sure. Should I have?"

"Look, Sergio, give the appointment book to Beebee. He'll know what to do with it. I don't even want to touch it. I could be called as a witness and I don't need that right now."

Nodding , he placed the address book on the coffee table. "Are you all right? You look a bit peaked."

"Just tired."

I repeated my advice to give the booklet to Beebee Alabama then I excused myself and left. Driving back south I wondered, *what was the recently deceased Billy Balls doing working for the Manleys?* That would put Billy solidly at the crime scene. If the police knew that Billy Balls had been employed by the Manleys, then the Count was in more trouble than he realized.

CHAPTER 15

It was a partly cloudy, forty-percent-chance-of-rain sky, which might have explained my pensive mood. I had ruminated all night. The suspicious Elvis-like island sightings of Billy Balls and his oddly timed demise I feared merited closer inspection. The one person I knew who was familiar with Billy on a first name basis was Mike Minsky, my mechanic. Rather, my Jaguar's mechanic. He might know what was the Martha Manley/Billy Balls connection.

An Auburn University graduate, Mike ran a glorified gas station and repair shop in West Palm Beach catering to the Jaguar and Mercedes crowd. Rumor had it that he used to steal the cars. Mike didn't steal them; he had people like Billy Balls boost them and then he fenced them in New York, California, and South America. Through judicious investing of his profits he retired, bought a rundown garage on South Dixie Highway and parked a bright, pink Rolls Royce in the front. The Rolls slowly attracted a somewhat discerning clientele that refused to pay the extortionate rates charged by the 'authorized' Jaguar and Mercedes dealers. He was a good auto-mechanic and hired good people. As I said, I take my car there.

Though claiming to be officially retired, Mike retained his network in the extralegal field and I hoped he might have some information on the Martha Manley/Billy Balls connection.

"It's the carb again," I said, sitting in Mike's office. "Can you get it to run for a month this time?"

"It's a six-year-old Jag, Maxie. You deserve another car," Mike said with a smile. His feet were propped up on his desk. He wore a brown fitted Brooks Brothers suit cut to hide much of his two hundred eighty pound frame. With his round baby-fat face and body bulk he looked like an undersized Sumo wrestler. "I have a new midnight-blue 500 SL that has your name on it."

"I like the Jag. Heard about Billy Balls?"

"Read it in the paper," Mike said. "You know, if you take away his penchant for kleptomania, Billy was not a bad boy. He's a native, born right here at Saint Mary's. Loved his mother. After his father split his mother took in ironing and cleaned houses on The Island. He once told me he wanted money to buy her a house and set her up so that she'd never have to do other people's laundry again. Sadly, she died of cancer first. He hated rich Palm Beachers and loved to boost their cars. But like I've always said, you play Russian roulette for very long and eventually you're going to take a bullet."

Mike had a poignant philosophical side.

"So the police haven't been by asking about Billy?"

"Of course not. Why should they? This is a respectable place of business. They haven't been here and I don't want them here," he said. He leaned further back in his chair. "You know" – he continued with no prodding - "I hadn't seen Billy in months then he shows up a few days ago driving a new Corvette. Fire-red, of course. With the top down."

"You talk to him?"

"No. He drove to the front, honked then waved at me through the office window and drove off. Wanted to show off his new wheels, I guess. He had that goofy stripper girlfriend of his with him." He looked at me. "You know. The one that works at the Landing Strip, tall, dark long hair and a set that could stop a freight train. I think her name is Zora. No, Zelda. Yeah, Zelda. Someone told me she dances at private parties in Palm Beach."

"I might know a few working girls but I hardly know all the strippers in Palm Beach County," I said in a feeble defense of my honor.

"Well, she's a knockout," Mike smiled again. "I think if anyone had information about Billy, it'd be Zelda." He fingered his bottom lip then looked up. "You know you can't live like a wild child all your life. Eventually it catches up to you. It's like the stock market. You have to know when to get out."

I admire savants who heed their own counsel.

"You're telling me you don't know anything about Billy and the Manley murder?"

"Martha Manley's murder? You gotta be kidding." His eyes darted around the room to the ceiling as if scanning for microphones. "I know nothing about any murder. Absolutely nothing."

His denial was too fast and pact. I was positive Mike knew more about Billy than he was telling me but Mike Minsky had survived in his netherworld by keeping a tight lip.

"You know, Mike. There's some serious shit going down about Billy. He might have been involved in the Martha Manley murder and the fire at my gallery. It involves me. So I have to know."

"I don't know anything, I swear. I have no idea what Billy was up to. The last time I talked to Billy was over six months ago. Like I said, the only other time I saw him was when he drove by."

"With Zelda, right?"

"Yeah, Zelda."

CHAPTER 16

I was getting nowhere faster than a speeding bullet and wasting enough time to worry Einstein. Money had to be made and that meant a visit to the gallery. I hadn't been back since the fire and still had a foreboding paranoia. Afraid the gallery might be watched I parked the Jag three blocks up the street in front of the Classic Bookstore owned by an old friend, Jeff Jacobus. Jeff, I was told inside, was in Sarasota at a book fair. So after messing through the stacks, I stepped back out and from the protection of the alcove glanced up and down County Road. Spying nothing suspicious, I hoofed the three blocks to the front door of the gallery, unlocked it and quickly stepped inside. I took a deep breath. I was pleased not to smell any trace of smoke. The high tech air filtration system worked. In the office I pulled down the charred curtains and cleaned up as best I could.

As I stood admiring my handiwork, Margot called on my cellular. "Lee Lohman called, said it was important. Something about his report on the paintings being ready. He wants you to call him immediately."

I dialed Lee. He gave me a quick summary, ending with, "Between the multispectral images, the canvas and paint chip analysis, I believe there is a high probability that they're forgeries. However, until we get the paintings into the lab, I can't certify them as one hundred percent one way or the other."

"You've given me enough information. Fax over the executive summary and send the report over by courier. And Lee, thanks. I owe you big time."

Now I was positive that the deaths of Martha Manley and Billy Balls were related and directly linked to the forged paintings and the fire. Find the forger, find Martha's killer and the arsonists. Or, conversely, find the killer or arsonists, find the forger, right? I knew killers came in all shapes and sizes, but the art world always seemed to have a dearth of assassins. An overabundance of crooks and con artists maybe, but murderers? You know, artist sensitivity, et cetera, et cetera. I tried explaining this to Adam.

"That's a classic case of reverse profiling," he said when I called. "Murderers cover the entire social, racial, and economical spectrum. Believe me, I know. That's why I left New Jersey. And I don't like anyone getting killed on my watch. It's personal, you understand?"

When I suggested we meet, Adam said, "Your visits to the Manley place have created a bit of a negative stir here. It's best we talk somewhere other than the station."

I suggested Renato's.

Renato's was a Piedmontese-fare Italian restaurant locked at the end of the quaint Via Mizner, one of a half dozen cozy alleys that sprouted off Worth Avenue. The vias were Sisyphean vestiges of Island architect Addision Mizner's attempt to imitate the intimacy of a Tuscan village via like Capablio or San Gimignano. One unique if eccentric site on Via Mizner was the gravesite of Johnny Brown, Addison Mizner's pet monkey. Aside from being an in-demand architect, Mizner had a sense of comic hubris. When the political establishment tried to thwart his designs, Mizner put Johnny Brown on the ballot for mayor of Palm Beach. He lost by fifteen votes. Today I'm sure he'd win by a landslide.

I arrived first and asked for a table in the corner of the courtyard, under a market umbrella, with a good view of the adjacent Via Parigi. Like Sicilians, I believe in eating alfresco whenever possible. From my vantage I could see one of the more prestigious galleries, John H. Surovek, whose specialty was American paintings.

Adam casually strolled in and took his seat. Before talking shop we ordered—the yellow snapper for me and lobster salad for Adam. He sipped a diet Sprite and I, a cold, oak-aged California Chardonnay.

Adam's demeanor had a bit more than the usual edge, more strain in his face than normal. Adam and I were here to barter, trade tidbits of information. But I knew he was not going to volunteer much information about an ongoing case.

"This might help." I handed Adam a copy of Lee's painting analyses report.

"How long have you had this?"

"Just got it today." The truth seemed to placate him.

He glanced through the executive summary. "If I read this right, they're definitely forgeries?"

"Legally. Not definite, but highly probable."

"It could be a motive for Martha's murder. Is there more?"

"You're getting everything I know freshly plucked from the tree of knowledge. There are some very serious paintings involved, like a masterpiece by Caravaggio."

"A Caravaggio? Is it a painting worth killing for?"

"Oh, most definitely, yes." I sipped my wine.

Adam stared at me for a moment, searching for either irony or a confession. Finding neither he said, "I'll take your word they're forgeries. Maybe Papa Manley was so hard up for cash he had his paintings copied then sold the originals. None of his high society friends would have known the difference."

"I thought of that. But it's too hard to keep a masterpiece out of the news. Somewhere, at some gallery or auction house, the originals would have surfaced, defeating the purpose of having the forgeries made in the first place."

"If it's not the big switcheroo, then most likely it's an insurance scam."

"That's always a real possibility. However in order to collect the insurance the paintings have to disappear either stolen or destroyed."

"Okay, then what?"

"The way I see it, the original paintings were stolen on assignment," I said. "Someone, perhaps a rogue collector, wanted a certain well known painting. Information on most masterpieces is readily available. Our collector then contracted with an artist who painted a perfect copy. Then a thief or someone with access to the house would make the switch. The collector would have his painting and the owners would be none the wiser for years."

Jack's head was bobbing slightly, either in agreement or he was about to knock on the door to the land of Nod. I continued, "I don't think it was someone who made the forgeries, switched them, then hoped he'd find a buyer. That's too risky for so much work.

"If the paintings were switched first without a rogue collector, then the forger or thief would need proof that the paintings he was selling were the original paintings. He'd need publicity. Something like newspaper headlines that the painting had been stolen so the buyer would know they was authentic. After all, the buyer can't get it appraised, at least not by a legitimate house. Headlines are a thief's best proof that the painting he's offering is an original painting. This guy did the deed without headlines. So, it smacks of a done-to-order job."

"So you have to find a master forger," Jack said. "Who steals paintings from some of our leading island residents before killing them. He then sells the paintings on the black market. Then why go through all the trouble of making a switch when he could just kill the owners and steal the paintings and not go through the hassle of forging them? It doesn't make sense."

"I don't think he intended to kill them. At least not in the beginning. Something happened after the paintings were switched that forced him to kill his victims."

"It sounds like your phantom forger was stealthy, working under the radar. What could force him to kill someone that would trigger a high profile murder investigation? It doesn't make sense."

"I don't know either, but I aim to find out."

"Hold it right there," Adam pointed his finger at me. "I want you to listen to me closely. This county is full of damned bleeding-heart judges looking for any excuse to throw out a case. The state attorney doesn't want any evidence tainted by an amateur. And I concur one hundred percent."

He threw Lee's folder on the table.

"By the way, there was an insurance policy on Martha Manley. Double indemnity and all that. Ordenoff was the beneficiary."

"How much?"

"One million dollars."

"So you think that's motive?"

"You bet," Adam said. "Most crimes are quite simple, you follow the money trail. Here in Palm Beach, only the scale is different."

"Have you forgotten about the gallery fire?"

"No. Of course not. I'll admit the information you've given me is intriguing and we'll look into it. The Chief has quietly told me that the art angle might have merit, but we can't buck Putzer. Did you see the interviews he did for CNN and Fox yesterday?" Adam asked. "He's enjoying the limelight, but all that exposure comes at a cost. If he doesn't make an arrest soon and get a conviction, his chance of a federal judgeship, or of running for the US Senate, is null and void. His career will be flushed down the proverbial tubes and he wouldn't mind taking a few of us with him."

Oops. Where did happy Adam go?

"Oh, and thanks," he said, tapping the folder with a manicured finger. "On second thought, I think I will try a cold limoncello."

With my civic duty done I felt free to put my newfound information to more useful purposes. I watched as Kathy Krammer's eyes romped over the report as if she were reading a page-turning thriller.

"This will change things," she said. "You might not know, but most of the paintings and sculptures were to be donated to the Norton Museum. My clients and I had our suspicions." She looked me in the eye. "They have a proposition that might interest you and would like to meet."

"Are you sure there is no conflict of interest?"

"Absolutely not. Frederick Manley is in town and his sister Mary Martha is flying in tonight for the funeral tomorrow. She was in Hong Kong. Let's give them a few days to mourn. I suggest Wednesday. Say ten a.m.?"

"Works for me."

"Good," she said, writing in her appointment book.

"By the way," I said, clearing my throat. "I just happen to be in possession of two invitations to the January, Children's Home Gala and would appreciate it if you could accompany me." Lame, yes, but it was the best I could do.

"What night is that?"

Not the quick "oh thanks I'd love to" I was hoping for. "Saturday, January the twenty first."

"Let me check." She flipped the pages of her appointment book. Pause. "It's our lucky day. I'm free."

Our lucky day! "Great," I said, trying not to sound too gleeful.

"That reminds me. My secretary informed me that we have more background information on the paintings that might help you. We'll have to retrieve it from the archives, but I'll be on The Island Tuesday around ten. I can drop the info by the gallery."

"My house is only a few blocks away and it just so happens that the plumber is coming over that morning and I'll be home all morning. You know how hard it is to get one to make house calls in a timely fashion. You can bring it by the house."

"The plumber. Right." She smiled and shook her head, "I could almost like you."

"Oh, please do. Please."

"I'll see you Tuesday," she said, trying not to laugh.

Once outside I thought, *that was easy,* and congratulated myself on such a suave delivery. Tuesday. I liked the sound of that. As I drove back to the house, I had images of a lengthy morning tryst in each of the upstairs bedrooms, but I was getting ahead of myself. Taking my head out of my crotch, I began a mental list of galleries and artists I needed to call. I wanted to ask around if anyone had heard of a fake Monet or Rembrandt. Forgeries are a sensitive subject and I had to be especially careful. A false alarm could ruin my reputation.

First, though, I had to pay a visit to Nigel Jenkins and his Palm Beach Art Custodians.

CHAPTER 17

Fifteen minutes north on I-95, I spotted the Palm Beach Art Custodians building, a standout among the lump of modern but humdrum construction in the Palm Beach Gardens Industrial Park. Topped with a Spanish-tiled roof and sweeping gables, it has a warm inviting look, except for its lack of windows. This architectural oddity was compensated for by a series of oversized grand tromp l'oeil arches painted on the outside that give it an appearance of a pseudo-Italian Renaissance *palazzio*.

I parked the Jag in front, next to Nigel Jenkins' white Mercedes Benz S 500 sedan with the vanity plates, ART ONE. On either side of the building entrance, I noticed tall stalks that appeared at first to be bamboo. Upon closer inspection, I saw they were stalks of freshly cut sugarcane stuck like oversized gladiolas in a small fish pool. An odd choice of flora, I thought.

The thick glass double doors opened with a heavy half-tone thud and I was greeted by a blue-eyed Nordic goddess.

"Good afternoon, Mister Roberts," she sang as I walked in. "Mister Jenkins and Mister Oberlin are waiting for you upstairs," she said, pointing to the bronze elevator doors to her left.

The elevator shot me to the second floor and opened directly into Nigel Jenkins' office. It was spacious, clean and minimalist, more Danish than Baroque. Rising from his black Moroccan leather chair, Nigel came around his oversized mahogany desk to greet me with a warm handshake. "Maxie Roberts, this is an honor," Nigel said. " I'm so pleased that you could drop by. This is my partner, Marcus Oberlin."

Marcus stood up. He was a mountain of a man, thick-necked with beefy arms and long brown hair swept back to his collar. He looked familiar and I tried to place the face. Before I could say, "Haven't I seen you somewhere?" he said, "I was a linebacker for three years with the Miami Dolphins before I lost my knee." His smile was wide and white and as we shook hands my palm disappeared into the hard fleshy folds of his massive grip.

"Marcus is a diamond in the rough," Nigel chimed in. "But he does know his art. He won't tell you himself but he graduated from Texas University with honors."

Marcus blushed which made him look more like a cuddly teddy bear than a neckless colossus.

Nigel said, "Let me show you a couple of our unoccupied spaces."

We walked down a wide carpeted hall that had the noble silence of a five star European hotel. Alarm lights lit up the hallways like a department store Christmas display. At a corner vault Nigel punched in a code on the keypad and the four-inch thick door silently opened. It was a small well-lit closet safe, four feet by eight by ten. Nigel continued down the corridor to a second storage area in vault-like room that could accommodate a medium sized dinner party.

"Looks secure," I said.

"All the rooms are humidity and temperature controlled."

The place had the effluvium of a Swiss bank cellar heavy with the unmistakable smell of success. But at heart it was a kennel.

After the tour, we settled in a comfortable den-like conference room off the office area where Marcus served coffee, warm and strong.

I was about to ask Nigel about Lee Lohman's girl, Gloria, when Nigel asked. "Have you heard anything new on Martha's murder?"

"Just the little that I've read in the papers." I shrugged.

"It's a bloody tragedy. You're not safe anywhere today." He crossed his legs and reached over to a humidor and took out a cigar, snipped the end and put it in his mouth. "I only chew. Gave up smoking them ten years ago. And you?"

I took a cigar and slipped it into my pocket. "I'll try it later." I told him.

"Are you still working with the estate?"

"With all due confidentiality."

"Of course. We understand." Nigel looked up at Marcus who had remained standing just to Nigel's right.

I glanced over Nigel's shoulder, past Marcus and spotted, hanging on the wall, a gold framed photograph of Nigel at the White House with President Barack Obama and Margaret Thompson, CEO of the Westchester Charities.

"I'm impressed," I said. "Margaret Thompson."

"I was co-chairperson for Westchester Charities in Florida," Nigel said. "We were at the national meeting in Washington. We're having our fund drive next month."

I pointed to the photograph. "Did you sleep in the Lincoln room?"

"Of course."

"It must seem odd at Westchester with Martha gone."

"It does. Martha supported a number of charities but Westchester Charities was her passion. We funded many causes. Martha was especially interested in supporting the arts and breast cancer. You might not know, but she was a cancer survivor. I worked with Martha and got to know her quite well."

From somewhere behind me I heard a whining and a sharp bark. Nigel clicked his fingers and a gray Great Dane as big as a quarter horse trotted out of the back room. He gave me a one-two sniff and bounded back to his owner, licking him in the face.

"I'm afraid I indulge him too much," Nigel said. He rubbed the dog hard between the ears. "This is Cerberus. Isn't he a real beauty? Won two national championships. Right feller?"

From my angle, the dog could double as the Hound of Baskerville when he wasn't guarding the gates of Hades. Cerberus fell to the floor with a thud, rolled over onto his back, offering his stomach to Nigel who vigorously rubbed his belly. "That a boy. Good boy." Nigel kept rubbing. I began to feel like a third wheel.

Before I left, I said. "If you hear anything about the Manley collection, let me know. Professional curiosity."

"We'll definitely call you," he said and stood. "Here are some brochures," Nigel said. He handed them to Marcus to pass to me. When Marcus leaned over to retrieve the brochures his jacket rode up his back revealing, for a second, a snub-nosed .38 revolver, in a black holster, strapped to his waist.

As we shook hands, Cerberus leaped to his feet and shook himself off. Nigel grabbed his neck, pulled him into his chest, and gave Cerberus a double-armed bear hug.

For a brief moment the two, man and beast, seemed as one.

CHAPTER 18

Outside the air was heavy and foreboding, the sky marred with low black-bottomed clouds. To the west, thunderheads were lining up in order like God's tin soldiers, cannons at ready, usually the harbingers of a hard rain. I looked around for a place to pullover quickly when my cell phone rang. I read the number. It was Dickie Durdle. I hesitated. Did I really need a dose of dalliance? Perhaps. I answered the phone.

"Maxie. I'm so glad I caught you."

"Hello, Dickie."

"Guess who came into my gallery yesterday?" Dickie said.

"I've a funny feeling that you're going to tell me."

"Melanie Cabot Moore." Pause. "Well. She has a magnificent O'Keeffe she wants me to sell. Says she's downsizing her residence. Her driver dropped it off this morning."

"And."

"You know, I'm not real sure about it. If I say anything to her, she'll slay me. Can you come over and look at it for me?"

"I'll check my agenda when I get home and call you this afternoon."

"Oh, Maxie, came you right now," Dickie pleaded. "Aseneth is flying in tomorrow and if I don't have an answer for her, she'll kill me. You know how she is with that Latin temper."

I paused.

"Please."

Before I had time to get bored by talk radio I was moseying the Jag up Worth Avenue past the faux-jewelry shops and the row of haute couture shops from Gucci to Valentino. The west end of Worth Avenue, gallery row, is lousy with galleries, good galleries, but too many from my point of view. Read— competition. But we weren't really competitors. Each gallery specialized in one art school or style or period, from American to Pop Kitsch. Choice.

Spotting a rare parking space, I slid the Jag behind a yellow and black

Rolls Royce two doors down from Dickie Durdle's Wellington Fine Arts Gallery sandwiched in between two establishments, one displaying pop-art and the other neo-expressionism paintings and sculptures.

I liked Dickie. In moderation. While Dickie Durdle was not a member of the overly discreet set, he did get around the South Florida art world—like a city cur and fire hydrants. I would have dismissed him as a charlatan except, as he waddled through the lower depths of the art world, he came across a few artistic gems that he generously shared once I had authenticated them. He also had a good eye. Dickie's one virtue was discovering new talent. He had a knack for knowing which of the thousands of young artists had a chance at making it. Finding virgin virtue is more than a quixotic quest. It is the thrill of catching the freshness of young talent before the once and future artist is transmogrified into a crass commercial concern chasing dollars and endorsements.

I admit I'm an old master snob, lacking a real understanding of modern art. Cubism? Go figure.

Do not misunderstand me. I'm an art dealer. I'll sell anything. While not reaching the levels of harlotry common in real estate, art dealers do make their money buying and selling. I understand that nothing sells itself. But art, by its very nature, has no need for a shill promoting its aesthetic values and worth. *"True art is selfish and perverse—it will not submit to the mold of flattery,"* Beethoven said. True art cannot be promoted. It speaks for itself. The latest hot artist or this year's in-style technique has more to do with publicity than art and will more likely end up, if not on the proverbial trash heap of history, tossed upon the midden of mendacity.

Dickie Durdle was the front man for Aseneth Vasquez, a South American gallerist who had invested in his Wellington Green Gallery. I use the word investor cautiously, as any gallerist knows; an art gallery is not an investment. With few exceptions, Art as an investment is a salesman's pitch. To get a return on your investment you have to love it. Art collecting is not an occupation; it's a disease

As I stepped into the gallery, Dickie marched past me towards the doors. At six foot one Dickie, was tall, made more so by his slim build and immaculate dress. His light brown hair parted high and to the left, was combed in a flip. He wears perfectly pressed European cut silk suits. He walks with long strides with his hand cupped closely to his sides, and he has the habit of gazing around fitfully, especially when nervous.

"I'm on my way to Clermont to throw myself from the top of the Citrus Tower and I'm late," he said.

I grabbed his arm and swung him around. "Calm down. I know for a fact that the Citrus Tower is not going anywhere. Have you been taking your Xanax?"

"You remember I told you Miss Cabot Moore came by?" Pause. "Okay, not personally. Her chauffeur."

"And for this you're contemplating suicide?"

"Well." Another pause for dramatic effect. I waited, "I did expect a little more support from my good friend," he said. Dickie eyed me and raised his eyebrows and asked in a low conspiratorial voice. "Do you have anything I'd be interested in?" One of Dickie's most endearing traits is his short attention span.

To the untrained eye, Dickie Durdle is not of the heterosexual persuasion. He owns the largest collection of Robert Maplethorpe sadomasochist photographs and Luis Caballero prints in the United States, or so he claims. He likes to play his gay New York Jew card, except Dickie was neither gay nor Jewish nor from New York. I'd heard he was born in St Louis. Dickie Durdle thought being a gay New York Jew gave him an advantage in the art world.

I took Dickie by the arm and directed him inside to his office and sat him down in a chair.

"Let me see the O'Keeffe," I said.

He jumped up reached over behind his desk and handed me a two-foot-by-three framed painting. It was an O'Keeffe Lily. I took the painting out of its frame and held it in my hands. I hefted it and ran my fingers lightly across its face, touching the surface like a feather duster, feeling the lines and ridges left by the artist's brush strokes.

I could see the flower set in a vase as a perfect artist's model, prim and pretty, as if suddenly plucked from the garden. The painting looked like an O'Keeffe, in color and emotion. Yet I felt a visceral haze that came and went like I was a sloop sailing in and out of a North Atlantic fog bank. Was it the painting or was it me?

"I don't know, Dickie. Modern art is, you know . . . " I paused, searching for the right word. "Modern."

I turned the painting upside down propped it up against the wall, and stepped back. Georgia O'Keeffe's flowers become more feminine when thus viewed. Sure enough, there were the colorful, anatomically correct vulva and labia. Shaved, of course. Since the first time I saw this image in one of her paintings, I've never been able to view lilies or Jack-in-the-pulpit again in the same light. The power of art.

"Just tell me what should I do," Dickie said.

"Ask for provenance. Then try to sell it until you hear otherwise."

"Oh, thank you so much." He said, grabbed my arm and buried his head on my shoulder, then looked up. "What about that Picasso?"

High with the inner satisfaction that only saving a life from the mortal sin of suicide can give, I headed back home. I'd neglected to tell Dickie that so many O'Keeffes have been forged it's a given you have to prove strict provenance. I wasn't sure about this O'Keeffe but given the current rash of questionable paintings, I had to assume it was possibly forged. The timing and the locale suggested it was done by the same forger who did the two Monets, a Rembrandt, and a Caravaggio. These were not your run of the mill knock-offs. I imagined an evil genius locked in a cave turning out forgeries like an Alsatian wyvern. I hate to say it, but there was a definite European tone in the hues and values that most American copyists lack.

Thinking back to test results on the painting chips and canvases I was dumbfounded and amazed. The sheer mastery of the forgeries was awe inspiring, opening an emotion that dove deep into my libido. The forger was meticulous. The banality of genius was nowhere to be found. The forger loved his copies. It showed in his work. Most forgers specialize in one artist whose style they perfect. These forgeries were all meticulously done with a talent not seen in this century. All forgers make mistakes. But this one didn't. Only a single artist could be consistently that good. I knew I was dealing with one person. And considering the level of violence involved, I preferred to assume it was a man. For this guy to have forged two well-known and disparate painters was an impressive display of artistry. I wanted to meet him, though not in a dark alley.

The sky had cleared; the threatening weather had moved off to the south. Not a drop had fallen, an example of Florida's capricious weather. Just as capriciously, I decided to head west to check out a farmer's market that sold the freshest produce in the county.

As I turned right onto Forest Hill Boulevard, my nostrils were abruptly assailed by the acrid smell of smoke. Fire was in the air. Large ash flakes glided down like black snow out of a blue sky. To the west, I spotted four large plumes of stygian smoke stretching their sinuous fingers toward the troposphere. The Everglades were under siege. The sugar growers were burning cane. A cane burn is a spectacular flash fire that blazes across the sugar fields, then quickly dies out. The dramatic explosion of hundred-foot bright red flames shooting across a green field against a cobalt sky brought out the pyromaniac in me. Burning sugarcane, like the summer thunderstorms, hurricanes, and airplane drug drops, was an essential part of South Florida. Take away one and you lessen the whole. Try explaining that to a transplanted Yankee.

CHAPTER 19

I was never so glad to see a week come to an end. Once home I opened a bottle of Chianti Classico Riserva and plopped into the hammock on the deck.

About an hour later I heard. "Here, eat dis." Margarita handed me a plate of spiced kingfish topped with Mango sauce and a side of baby asparagus. Margarita knew how to get my attention. Near midnight, I popped a couple of Percodans Margarita'd picked up for me at the drugstore, crawled into bed, and slept until ten a.m.

I awoke refreshed and, thankfully, being Saturday, I had nothing planned for the day. After coffee, I took a bottle of Santa Julia Malbec, a glass and my Penn rod and reel spinning set out to the dock, determined not to move until dusk. By noon I managed to hook up a couple of fair-sized snook, which I released. Off in the distance I could make out a row of towering Australian pines swaying dangerously close to power lines. Why no one had cut them down was a wonder. These were bad trees; officially, that is. The state of Florida had banned the planting of Brazilian rubber trees, Australian pines and the malicious Malelueca.

Florida also has banned fish. While the Piranha gets all the press, the list of bad fish is topped by the South American Candiru. A member of the cat fish family, the Candiru is an inch-long, cigar-shaped fish with a ring of sharp, grappling hook-like barbs on its proboscis and an eclectic taste for urine. In pursuit of piss, it swims up urethras where it embeds itself in the walls and can only be removed surgically. Guaranteed to keep skinny dippers out of your pool.

From love bugs to transplanted Yankees, introduced organisms run amuck here. That's what I love about Florida: the rules don't apply.

My rambling thoughts were not restricted to wildlife.

Believe me, I'd have preferred to take Bernie's advice and leave the murder and forgery investigation in the hands of the police if I thought they were going in the right direction. The faster they caught the real killers, the safer I'd feel.

I couldn't understand their reluctance to investigate the forgery angle. Peter Putzer believed that the Count either killed his wife or hired someone like Billy Balls to kill her for her money. End of story. The state attorney wants a quick and clean conviction. Open and shut case. Justice likes clarity. Perhaps stories about forgers and arson were too much information, too many facts that tended to confuse a jury and the state attorney's case. They needed a little nudging in the right direction. If I could get enough evidence to point the investigation to the forgers whom I believe are the real killers, it might convince Adam and Putzer to investigate the forger-as-the-murderer angle. Until then they had their man, the Count, that was that in their eyes. The real killers and the people who tried to burn me out were still at large.

If Billy Balls killed Martha Manley, I had one lead. Unfortunately, it was only a name and a place of business.

The Landing Strip was a single-story, freestanding, box building, one hundred yards west of the main Palm Beach Airport runway off Military Trail. From the parking lot, aircraft enthusiasts could enjoy watching an array of jets and airplanes roar a few hundred feet overhead before feasting their eyes on the delights inside. Through the front doors I was met by a motley mixture of humanity: bikers and hippie wannabes mingling with businessmen and day laborers with only one thing in common. They were men.

As I gazed through the dimly lit room across to the bright stage at the far end, I could see two girls, a blond and a brunette, dancing. My plan, if you could call it a plan, was to have quick interview with Miss Zelda, hopefully to compile a few useful facts about Billy Balls, then leave.

The bar around the stage was full of wide-eyed, half drunk patrons so I took a small cocktail table off to one side with a direct view of the dancers.

"I was looking for Zelda," I said to the topless waitress as I ordered a drink.

"She the one dancing." She pointed to the bar stage. I looked over her bare shoulder to the stage. The dancer was a dark-haired Botticelli Venus with a D-cup slowly coiling like an Anaconda around a chrome pole. And, of course, she was one hundred percent naked. Not nude, naked. As she moved, her hair cascaded over her face and down around her shoulders and suggested a veil if it weren't for its innate sensuality. She had an act that would have made Little Egypt blush. She was good and she was erotic. She gyrated in slow sensual moves and before my drink arrived at my table, I had a you-know-what. Not a hard throbbing drill-bit but enough to feel good and not lose all reason; a thin line, I realize.

After their dance the girls visited each table. I watched as Zelda moved around the room doing lap dances for tips. She finally arrived at my table and I found myself staring not at her ample chest but into a pair of dark kind eyes. My mouth must have dropped because she let out a little laugh, leaned over letting her breasts dangle six inches from my face. My stare shifted and she smiled. "Lap dance will cost you twenty."

Direct. I like that.

"Or would you prefer a private room?"

Such intimate thoughts brought me crashing back to reality. The thin line was blurring. I was not safe. My professionalism—okay, okay, my low disciplinary threshold—was rapidly evaporating. I had to leave. I handed her a twenty, got up and left like a puppy with a bit more than his tail between his legs.

Outside I sprinted to the car, got in and did a series of deep Yoga breaths while thinking of pink-eyed white rats—a surefire boner loser. Talk about stupid. I felt like an idiot leaving the club like that. Now all I could do was wait.

I killed time in the parking lot next door listening to the banal banter on talk radio until the Landing Strip light went out. A little later, just after four a.m., the front door of the club opened and a covey of curvaceous dancers spilled outside. But before I could step out of the Jag, Zelda got into a white Honda and pulled away.

From a safe distance I followed her car down Military Trail, past Haverhill to Greenacres. At Purdy Lane she took a right then a left and pulled into the driveway of a small but neat concrete-block-on-a-slab house with a one-car garage. She parked the car in the driveway then disappeared inside. I wasn't about to knock on her door at four-thirty in the morning but I did want a look around. I waited a half hour after the lights went out before I snuck through the narrow passageway between the side of the garage and a stockade fence. Boxing in the backyard was a four-foot chain link fence. I clambered over the fence and crouched behind a hibiscus bush and listened. It was almost dawn and quiet. Next to the bush were two doors, one I assumed to the kitchen and the other to the garage. By the kitchen door I spotted a doghouse. Not a good sign, but it was a little doghouse. Hopefully not one of those little yipping rat-dogs. I made a quick glance around—no canine outside—then scooted up to the garage back door. The blinds on the window were not drawn tightly. I cupped my hands around my eyes, looked inside. It was dark. I shined my flashlight through the slats. It was a small garage but squarely in the middle was the silhouette of a Corvette—Billy's Corvette. I switched off the light, climbed back over the fence and trotted back to my car. I had found Martha's killer's girlfriend and the Corvette that might have been used in the murder. I should call Adam but what could he do? As he said, "What facts did I have, a biker's girlfriend and a sports car parked in a garage?" I doubt he could get a search warrant on that flimsy evidence. Before I called Adam I wanted to talk with Ms Zelda but I also wanted a look in that Corvette.

CHAPTER 20

The telephone rang. It was nine. I'd had three hours sleep.

"Are you up for a Breaker's brunch?" I heard the Jean Harlow voice of Aseneth Vasquez-Campos croon.

"Before or after Mass?"

"After, silly boy, after. I want you in a purified state of grace. Say eleven?"

In my sleep-deprived fog, I believe I answered affirmatively.

I rolled my feet off the bed and sat up. Before I had my first morning belch, the optimistic aroma of cure-all coffee lured me to the kitchen.

"Margarita, it's Sunday."

"Couldn't sleep. You come in so late. *Muy tarde.*"

"*Mucho Trabajo.*"

"*Claro mucho trabajo,*" she grunted.

The Sunday *Post* was in the breakfast nook where I took my coffee.

"No breakfast, Margarita. *Solo café. Tengo un desayuno con un cliente.*"

"A client?" She glared at me with a *malocchio.* Margarita had her purse at ready on the counter, which she moved around as a sign of disapproval. Even though she lived above the garage she was never without her purse. I was convinced it housed a cocked .44 Magnum revolver, hence, my good behavior.

It was too early in the morning for a double dose of Latina lancination. Maybe I should make the ten o'clock Mass at Saint Eddie's after all.

After a quick shower, I threw on this month's favorite jacket and slacks, took a quick glance in the mirror, and I was out the door. Since the former Mrs. Roberts no longer chose my wardrobe, at first glimpse I screamed, if not bachelor, at least safely unmarried. Men, this is a good time for Roberts' Rule # 5: *When a woman buys you clothes, wear them.* It makes them feel good. But the irony is—and I'm afraid this is lost on them—you are then more attractive to other women. It works every time. Well, almost. Rod Stewart is an exception.

The call was not a request. It was a summons. Aseneth Vasquez was one of South Florida's premier gallerists. She owned galleries in Bogotá, Miami, Paris, and Rome and was a partner in a half dozen others. Ten years ago, she bought into Dickie Durdle's gallery, a business move for which I had yet to discover the whys. "I fly to Palm Beach every month and needed a business write off," she said once.

The stroll through the Breakers' corbel-arched reception area was a walk back into an Italian Renaissance palace. The ornate ceiling painted in Italianate frescos and the stentorian nineteenth-century French tapestries draping the walls spoke splendor with an undertone of the subtle and soothing. I felt at home.

Down the north side hall was the celebrated Circle Room, the setting for the world's most famous brunch. Not shy, the Breakers' chefs prepare fare the Roman emperors would have envied. An ice sculpture of a trumpeter swan dominated the room, around which were spaced tables, each stacked with an array of delectables. One had seafood—quahogs on the half shell, jumbo shrimp and lanky crab legs; another fresh fruit; another roast beef and caramelized vegetables; then there was the indispensable kosher table. No one missed the dessert bar—flavored truffles, garnished fruit, a chocolate fountain, and mountains of mousse, all for breakfast. A musician playing a Paraguayan harp meandered through the room serenading tables and brunchers.

The dog everyone was putting on was present and well accounted for, with liberal doses of Hermés, Versace, Saint Laurent, and a Valentino or two. A few floral hats rounded out the ladies' attire. The less imaginative gents wore blue blazers and gray slacks—the Palm Beach uniform—and, of course with no prejudice, a smidgen of cut-off blue jean shorts and tank tops peppered the tables. The money that had been spent on the clothes alone could have purchased a few oceanfront mansions.

As if on cue, in waltzed Aseneth with the flare of a dark-haired Gloria Swanson. If the caffeine in Margarita's coffee had lacked sufficient stimulation, Aseneth's well-tanned, well-formed breasts bursting solicitously from under a low-cut little-black-dress bordered on cardiac overkill. She had just turned forty and was one of those timeless women who grew more beautiful with age.

"I see you're wearing your Sunday best," I said as she approached,

"You like it?" she said, turning from one side to the other like a ballerina showing off her tutu. "Picked it up in Milan. Giorgio's latest."

Like it? Only my world famous superhuman self-discipline prevented me from ripping it off and ravaging her right then and there on the floor. Thankfully, I had the good sense to wear my loose-fitting silk boxers.

She was tall, nearly six foot two, and carried herself with the studied grace of a Thompson's gazelle. Her long ebony hair was tied back in a bun topped with a black lace headpiece. Not an eye, male or female, was diverted from her. Her thin arms were adorned in throng of gold bracelets and each bejeweled finger carried a precious stone-crowned ring.

We double cheek-kissed and sat down at a quiet table overlooking the Atlantic Ocean.

After a trip to the buffet she asked, "You *are* coming to the Samuel Seahorse opening? He's done a fantastic series of stylized portraits of the local glitterati. Some quite naughty."

"Knowing you'll be there, I wouldn't miss it for all the art in the Vatican."

"Ha! A slight exaggeration but I still love you." She sent me a kiss across the table. "Speaking of love, how is your love life?"

"Nothing to write home about."

"You should have hung on to Nancy."

Words of wisdom from a woman who's been divorced four times.

"Have you seen Bernie?"

"Please. That bore." She sipped from her exotic fruit drink. "Dickie's in a frenzy about his Pissaro. He's practically living on Xanax."

"It's helpful to the emotionally impaired that Xanax is a psychic palindrome."

"Now be kind to Dickie," she said. "I heard you've some misgivings regarding the Manley collection."

I downed half my cappuccino before looking her in the eye. "No longer misgivings. Lee Lohman did a chemical and multispectral imaging analysis and, in his opinion, there's a high probability they're forgeries."

The chatter in the room seemed to dim.

"If I remember correctly, they have a couple of masters. Do you think the entire collection could be fakes?" she asked.

"I saw only four paintings but they were all suspect. I have my suspicions that if I looked at the rest they'd have problems, too. Also, I've been told that paintings from other owners are being put in doubt. It's serious.

They're all by the big boys. There's a Rembrandt, a Monet and a Caravaggio, along with Dickie's questionable Pissarro, among others."

"Good God. That's millions."

"Hundreds of millions, and if there are many more out there it could be a billion or more."

She leaned over the table, much to my delight. In a lower voice she said, "This isn't good. It could cause a panic. If everyone starts to question their artwork then the market will collapse."

"I know. Then we'll have to actually work for a living."

She didn't smile but did stop eating.

"How about just forgetting the whole thing?"

"What do you mean?"

"What I mean is, just leave your suspicions about the Manley paintings as suspicions. No use upsetting the entire art market."

"What, and have a bunch of forgeries out there? And what about Martha? She's being buried today and someone killed her. Maybe because of the forgeries. It's gotten way beyond keeping the market stable."

"You do realize that much more's at stake than a few forgeries and a dead socialite."

"Martha's killers might be the same bastards that tried to burn me out, Aseneth. They failed the first time so they might try again. They're still out there, and I think they also killed this guy Billy Balls who was working for Martha. My file on the Manley art was the only thing stolen the night of the fire. It had the notes I made on the paintings and my suspicions about her murder. They know I know the paintings are forgeries and that I think Martha was killed because of the forgeries. I've no doubt they'll kill me if I don't find them first. It's gotten too personal."

"The word around town is the police think the husband killed her," Aseneth said, toying with a slice of red papaya.

"I think the case against the Count is a contrived subterfuge. I could be wrong, but I think there's a group out there forging paintings and substituting them for the originals and they do not mind killing anyone who gets in their way," I gulped the rest of the cappuccino. It was cold. "Look, I'm not going to broadcast around The Island that there's a possible rash of forgeries. All I want to do is find out if there is a connection between the forgeries, Martha's killing, and the fire and then give it to the police."

"Why you? There's no upside to it."

"What I don't like is being conned." I sat up straight. A knot gripped my throat and I coughed. "I feel like I'm being conned and I've been conned by the best."

"Conned? My dear boy, sounds like you lost money."

"Worse. I lost a painting." My tone rose a quarter octave.

"An important painting?"

"Yes, it was important. Important to me," I stammered and glanced up at Aseneth. She had the glazed look of a father confessor waiting patiently before deciding to give absolution. I fought off vivid pictures of Italian mountains, olive groves and Roman ruins. "It was in Trivoli, within view of Hadrian's palace. I was house sitting for friends who were traveling through Asia. You might know them—Sissy and Garry Murphy."

"I didn't know you knew the Murphys." Her eyes were fixed on mine.

"We met at a museum function in Florence. I the wayward hippie, and he the wealthy patron of the arts. I was like his birddog—no, more like a truffle pig snuffing out those succulent art morsels buried in attics and back alleys. Anyway, the villa was a wonderful place with frescos and sculptures and a classy collection of art. A Canadian I'd befriended needed a place to stay. A week, he said. He called himself 'Jumping Johnny'. Do you believe I trusted a guy named Jumping Johnny!" My gaze hit the floor again. I heard Aseneth munching on a wafer. "Anyway, we shared an interest in wine and marijuana and he was a great conversationalist. A week later he was gone, along with a small, sixteenth century Tintoretto landscape. I've never seen him or the painting since. The insurance covered the loss but I couldn't face the Murphys again."

"Silly boy. It was a simple robbery. Things get stolen all the time."

"No. Something priceless and irreplaceable was left to my stewardship and I failed. For three hundred years that painting had survived fires, brigands, Nazi looters, and Allied bombings, only to be lost by a careless young American. I traced Johnny to England, where the trail went cold. I swore I'd never let that happen again."

"And you think you can compensate for it by finding the original Manley paintings?"

"Well, yes, of course," I said, then, "I don't know."

We both sat silently for a moment.

"Well, do what you have to do but don't let your anger blind you. You'll end up doing something stupid."

"Are we talking in code or are you trying to tell me something?"

"Only that we love you and truly want what's best for your own good."

CHAPTER 21

With a Breaker's brunch grudgingly working its way through my little intestines, I returned home, dressed in my best mourning clothes then stopped by the gallery to retrieve a gilded frame I needed for a client's Chuck Close grid portrait. While I'm widely perceived as an old master snob—Italy will do that to you—I admit I have a longing for surrealists. Proof that surreal art imitates life was only a moment away.

Dickie Durdle pulled up in his red Miata. He had the top down and a branchy potted palm in the passenger seat. He stuck out of the driver's seat like an uptight ramrod with a blond mop.

"Redecorating the hallway," he said, brushing aside an errant frond as he stepped out of the car. "Aseneth is mad at me."

"Anything specific or is it a general, all-encompassing biliousness."

"She said I was gullible."

"And you believed her?"

"Of course."

"She's Latin. It'll pass."

"It's you she's worried about. Seems to think you're going to do something foolish. Aseneth said I'm supposed to watch out for you and if you got hurt she'd circumcise me on the front steps of the Harriet Hillman Theater."

"I appreciate the concern. If it makes you feel any better, I'm not going to do anything that would endanger myself or anyone else."

"Oh. Thank God," Dickie said, instinctively cradling his crotch and letting his shoulders drop. "I'm on my way to the funeral."

"Martha's, I assume."

"Of course, silly boy. Well, who else has died this week?" Dickie picked at a white spot on his lapel.

"More people than I care to mention," I said.

"I'm wondering if there'll be a scene?"

"A scene?"

"You know an altercation between the children and the stepfather? That's the buzz," Dickie said. "But it is Palm Beach and we're all civilized. At least openly, right? Have to show our faces. It's a sign of respect. Plus, you never know whom you'll meet. It'll be a good opportunity to mix with the right people."

"I hate funerals," I said.

"I love them," Dickie said.

Martha Manley was buried at Woodlawn Cemetery next to Papa Manley. Good old Martha was a trouper and Papa's girl to the end. As requested in their wills, a simple stone marker marked both graves.

Dickie was right—half The Island was present. Papa Manley would have appreciated that a third of the mourners were chauffeurs. It was worse than the Red Cross Ball. The black-clad mourners crowded uneasily around the gravesite like a herd of flamenco dancers with hemorrhoids. A mountain of flowers with conspicuously displayed cards crowded the grave site reminded me of Holden Caulfield's quip in *Catcher In The Rye*, "*Who wants flowers when you're dead? Nobody.*"

I spotted Adam Aldrick under the shade of a live oak discreetly casing the crowd from a respectable distance.

"Lovely day for a funeral," he said. "Looks like most of our good citizenry has made their obligatory appearance." He nodded to a plainclothes detective off to his left. "Funeral watches are usually a waste of time but you never know. Murders have been known to do stupid things, like show up at the funerals of their victims."

"To make sure they're dead?"

"Who knows." Adam shrugged his shoulders. "When you fathom the criminal mind, let me know. The grieving husband is here."

"You still think Sergio Ordenoff killed Martha?"

"We can't dismiss the mounting evidence," Adam said. "As circumstantial as it is."

"The Count can hardly tie his own shoes," I said. "I find it hard to believe he could kill his wife and set fire to my gallery."

"Don't underestimate Ordenoff. He's a championship skeet shooter and led a crack commando unit in the Bulgarian army. And as far as the fire, we have no hard evidence linking it to Martha's murder."

"What about the fake paintings?"

"We can't do much. In case you're unaware, no one has filed an official complaint. No complaint, no crime, no investigation." Adam shifted from one leg to the other.

"You saw Lee Lohman's report. I believe Martha's murder, the fire, and the forgeries are all related. "

"I gave the report to the captain and the state attorney's office. They might assign someone to look at it. I can't do anything else."

"But you're fixated on Sergio."

"Captain Lusk goes by the book. We go where the evidence takes us." Again Adam shifted his weight from one foot to the other. "I hate standing around like this, it's bad for my leg." He leaned against the tree trunk. "Officially, I should warn you to stay away from the investigation. I know you too well. But if you bring me something I can use I'll ask Captain Lusk to take it to the state attorney," Adam's eyes darting around the crowd. "Has it occurred to you if these guys, as you think, killed two people they won't mind adding a third?"

"That's exactly why I'm involved," I said. "I'm afraid that they might try something again."

"If you're right, they'd be stupid to do anything. That would bring down a tremendous amount of heat on them. The guys who set your fire are professional. They can't take that risk."

"That might be good in theory but I can't afford to wait and see," I said. "Why is Putzer so reluctant to investigate the forged paintings and their connection with Martha's murder?"

Adam hesitated. I knew he was debating whether to tell me what was happening behind the scenes or what he was really thinking. A cardinal rule in law enforcement is: do not divulge information; it taints testimony.

"I'm telling you this for your own good," he said. "Maybe to show you no matter what you find out, it will change nothing." He took a deep breath. "If there is a formal complaint filed we'll look into the alleged forgeries. But we're cops. I wouldn't know a real Picasso from a fake DaVinci Code. When we investigate the paintings we'll have to spend money to pay experts. Then the FBI will probably get involved. Sure we have good relations with them, after all Captain Lusk is ex F.B.I., but when they get involved we lose control. You get the picture? Putzer doesn't want to share the limelight with the Feds. He believes he has a clean case and doesn't want to muddy the water in the Manley killing with extraneous theories or distracting evidence."

"Like what?"

"With or without your forged paintings, we have motive; opportunity and the insurance policy. We have him at the scene near the time of the murder. No jury is going to believe that anyone could be in the same house for twelve hours and not know his wife was dead a couple of doors away. Rumors are that Ms. Manley wasn't all that happy with her husband."

"As you said it's all circumstantial."

"People have gone to the chair for less."

"Not the rich."

Adam pressed his lips tightly together and nodded.

"This sounds like a classic example of 'don't confuse me with facts'?" I said.

"Unfortunately, you don't have any facts, only hunches. I need facts. Until I get them, I can't buck the state attorney without hard evidence. All I'm getting is a lot of flak about your involvement and I don't need that crap right now. You'd do me a big favor if you'd just go home and let us handle this. I know you won't, but at least I've done my duty and told you."

Adam twisted around and checked out a group of late arriving mourners. "Just be careful," he said. "These guys are killers."

"So you do think there is more than one guy?"

He grunted and waved me off.

Adam sure knew how to liven up a funeral.

I sauntered over behind the mourners to listen to the dirge-like drone of the Episcopal minister. Frederick IV and Mary Martha stood to the left of the minister and the Count on his right, as they listened to the dirge-like drone of the Episcopal minister. Frederick IV was medium height and carried a bit more weight then was healthy while Mary Martha was model slim with a perfectly made up face partially hidden behind designer sunglasses. I spotted Kathy Krammer standing directly behind the children. I caught her eye, she gave a slight smile and I nodded.

The eulogy was the way I like funerals and Sunday services—short, if not sweet. With the liturgy ended, I looked around for Ms. Krammer but she was engaged in a conversation with a Federal judge so I joined the line of people offering condolences. As I passed Frederick IV to shake his hand, he yawned.

CHAPTER 22

Back at the house, I poured an earlier-than-usual grape-based libation and walked out to the back across the yard and onto the dock. The afternoon was steel blue and clear. Hither and thither flocks of crying gulls plunged into the sea and pulled out, again and again, until they flew off, minnows dangling in their dripping beaks. The apparent anarchy was, in reality, a precisely choreographed avian ballet. Not unlike Palm Beach itself.

Nature and the sea have a way of clearing my mind. I inhaled the sea air, drinking deeply of the sea smell. In *Moby Dick*, Elijah said to Ishmael, "There will come a day at sea when you will smell land where there'll be no land." I smell sea where there is no sea. Tourists, seasoned sailors, and sages have pined in poem and prose of a sea that smells of salt, life, exotica, and exuberance. Scientists erroneously reckon it is death, the smell of the decayed and dying. The sea that landlubbers know does smell of dead clams and rotting seaweed. But whiff beyond the shore and it smells of distant lands, of adventure, of anticipation. Yet first and foremost, the sea is the mother womb of all life. The sea smells of sex.

I rested my foot on a piling, feeling it move.

Like Henry Dana, I wanted my two years before the mast. I love the sea. It is the universal equalizer. One's mettle is made or mauled there. The sea is a truth serum. A simple sail can save or slay. Upon the open ocean, faced with adversity, there is choice—to go on or turn back.

Eugene O'Neil said, "*The sea hates a coward.*"

Deep down I am a coward. I hide it with random acts of bravery.

Time for another decision—to go on or turn back.

Time for another wine.

Aseneth had warned me against doing something stupid. I promised her I'd begin tomorrow. However, I had one more task to attend to. I was getting nowhere with my art world contacts. I could not help but think that Billy's girlfriend, Miss Zelda, knew why Billy was killed, what was he doing working for the Manleys and she might know who tried to burn me out. Before I made another venture, and perhaps another embarrassing exit at her place of work, I wanted to examine Billy's Corvette. It was a long shot. But right now I needed anything. Anything.

Billy had just bought the Corvette and I was sure his demise was sudden and unexpected. He might have left something in the Vette related to Martha's murder or his. That something might lead Adam to the forgers or help him convince the Putzer there was a connection between Martha's murder and the gallery fire. If I found anything, I could either ask Zelda about it or give it to Adam. Of course, I should have gone straight to Adam and told him about the Corvette but I wasn't sure he could or would do anything with the information. The Vette might be one big dead-end with nothing inside. I pictured a quick in and a quick out and no one would be the wiser. Like a quick and easy war, I suppose.

At dusk, I slipped on my dark blue sweats and running shoes and drove my trusty Everglades buggy west to I-95 south. I exited at 10th Street North and headed west to Greenacres. It was eight o'clock. Zelda had left for work at seven-thirty. Eight to four, a long time to be on your feet dancing.

I eased the buggy to the curb two blocks down the street from her house. Shoving a flashlight in my pocket, I jogged up to the house and around back, scouting for alarms. Didn't see any so I pulled on a pair of gloves—I watch cop shows—and climbed the fence keeping one eye on the doghouse. At the back door to the garage I played with the lock. It was loose. From my pocket I took out a piece of stiff plastic and shoved it in the jamb by the lock and wiggled. Nothing. It sure looks easy in the movies. After three twists and a little body nudge, it opened. I stood staring inside the dark interior of the garage. How about a reality check here? Was I really breaking and entering a biker's girlfriend's house? I paused. No barks. Hopefully, Fido was asleep. Making one last check around the back yard, I slipped inside and gently closed the door.

The garage was littered with spare motorcycle parts and had the distinct wrong-side-of-an-engine-petroleum-product smell. The Corvette, parked squarely in the middle, had a film of dust on it. I tried the Corvette's driver's door. It was locked but the door to the kitchen was not. When I pushed on it, it opened with a creak. I held it partially opened and listened. No barks. Nothing but my heart pounding in my throat. I flashed the light inside, its beam cutting through the dark like one of those horror films you always wonder how the characters could be so dumb as to go inside a creepy house at night. Slowly I opened the door and passed the light across the room. No beady eyes glowed back, no snarling teeth, so I took a deep breath and stepped inside.

The kitchen looked as if a squad of mini-maids had worked on it all day. The white Formica counter top gleamed and every pot and dish were in place. The stringent smell of lemon cut with lavender tickled my nostrils. The lady was no slouch. It was hard imagining Billy Balls stomping across the squeaky clean linoleum in black engineer boots. I ran the light over the living room. Standard blue-collar furnishings, a three place sofa, two stuffed chairs a metal coffee table and framed landscape prints on the walls. Neat but unimaginative. I stepped back into the kitchen, opened drawers and pantry doors, and found three keys with a Corvette logo key ring in the top drawer next to the door leading out to the garage. I heft the keys in my hands and stepped back into the garage leaving the kitchen door ajar. I unlocked the passenger side of the Corvette and opened the glove compartment. Inside was a registration and insurance papers. The car was in the name of Zelda Sayre Zeitgeist. Using the light from the interior of the Vette, I searched under the seats and between the cushions. My hands were damp in my gloves and a film of sweat beaded on my forehead.

I popped the trunk. The usual trunk trash—a ratchet set, screwdrivers, and a baseball bat that looked more like a weapon than sporting accessory. No burglary tools, nothing that seemed incriminating. I was about to shut the truck but noticed the spare tire was off center. I reached down and grabbed it and, with a huff, lifted it up on its side and set it against the back of the truck. In the bottom tire well, carefully secured with black tape, was a black toiletries bag. Not your typical biker's accessory. I jerked out the bag, pulled off the tape and unzipped it. Inside was a heavy object wrapped in a red cloth. Carefully I unwrapped the cloth, exposing a short barrel twenty-two-caliber Ruger revolver—the same caliber that had killed Martha Manley. It smelled like gun oil, perhaps recently cleaned. Taking a pen from my pocket, I stuck it in the barrel— I watched *Dragnet*—and lifted the pistol to the light. The barrow was smooth with no visible threads for a silencer—*C.S.I.* If it was the murder weapon, then it must have made noise when fired the night of Martha's death. The Count said he had heard nothing.

I laid the gun down inside the trunk and opened the bag again. Tucked at the bottom were five folded newspaper clippings on the Manley murder, a three-page, faded, foldout flyer advertising a Parisian art gallery, and two Polaroid photographs of Billy Balls and an older lady in a compromising position. At first glance, in the dim light, the woman did not appear to be Martha Manley.

Carefully, I wrapped the pistol back in the cloth and was placing it back in the bag when I heard dirt grinding on cement and looked up. All I saw was large figure looming over me like an enraged elephant, then the trunk lid smashed onto my head.

I saw a white flash followed by stinging stars and a white shooting pain. I groaned, fell to my knees, and gasped. A bolt of blue exploded through my head. I was just able to open my eyes to see of a pair of black Florsheim wing-tipped brogues and well-pressed, cuffed pants when the lights and the stars disappeared.

CHAPTER 23

"Can . . . you . . . hear . . . me? Can . . . you hear me?" I heard echoing down a foggy corridor. "Okay. Looks like you're still alive. I suppose that's good."

I thought, yes, and tried to move my head. Nauseating waves of pain, sheer, suffocating hurt swept through my body. I managed a grunt and squeezed my eyes closed. I felt something wet massage my hand.

"Get away, Freddy."

A woman's voice.

"Just relax and don't move. I'll bring you something to drink and some more ice."

I heard footsteps leave and again felt the wetness moving my hand. Blackness swirled across my eyelids and I felt about to pass out again when I sensed a presence. I slowly opened my left eye and saw the vague image of Zelda Zeitgeist leaning over me.

"Get away, Freddy. Sit!" I heard her say. I glanced over and saw a small sniveling half-bred mutt somewhere between a beagle and a malamute. He scampered away a few feet, then sat on his hind legs and watched me. "He won't bite."

Gently Zelda held my head up and gave me a sip of what tasted like stale Diet Doctor Pepper. Then she placed an ice pack on the back of my neck. I was lying on the living room couch. Through the drawn shades I sensed dim light creeping in. That meant I had been out a good three hours.

She handed me three yellow pills and a glass of water.

"Take these."

Without protest I swallowed the pills. She laid my head back down. After fifteen minutes enough of the pain was gone that I could put together a few thoughts.

"Feeling better?" she asked.

"Only if I don't move," I said, trying not to shake my head.

"They were my boyfriend's favorites."

I didn't ask favorite what.

Freddy was sitting at her feet. Without taking her eyes off me she reached down and rubbed his head.

"Now, mister, you're going to tell me what the fuck you were doing bleeding all over my garage floor. If I don't get some answers, I'll get some people here who know . . . Now I remember you. You were the guy who tipped for a lap dance last night, then left without it. Had you down as a fag."

A first.

"Are you stalking me?"

"No." I tried to sit up. Pain. "Oh, Jesus, no." More pain. I lay back down.

"Then what?"

I took a couple of deep breaths and managed to look up at her and say, "I'm interested in why Billy was killed."

Her faced paled then she bit her lower lip and looked away. "You're not a cop. I know cops. So what are you? A friend?"

"I knew him but wasn't a friend," I said, trying not to black out. Every word reverberated pain, pain, pain. I took another deep breath and squinting said, "I was looking inside the Corvette for anything that might explain why Billy was killed. Someone jumped me in the garage and that's all I remember. Did you see anyone when you got home?"

"No. I found the kitchen door wide opened. The back door to the garage was unlocked. Then I saw you behind Billy's car. Figured you were dead. I didn't know if I should have called some friends to dump you in a canal."

"Like they did to Billy?"

She gave me a stare that could have curdled curds, then looked away. Freddy hotfooted over and licked her hands. The cerebral pain pangs began to recede enough so I could move. Straining, I pulled myself up to sit.

"I'm sorry. I really am. Look, my name is Maxie Roberts and I'm just an art dealer. I have a card in my wallet." I reached for my back pocket.

"This?" she said, holding up my wallet in her right hand.

"Yeah." I slid back into the sofa. "I knew Billy and I think his murder might be connected with some paintings."

"Stolen?"

"No, they are forgeries.   A lot of strange things have been happening lately."

"As strange as someone killing your boyfriend?"

"No, no," I said. "Look, I'm really sorry about Billy but lately there have been too many odd coincidences and Billy's name keeps coming up. I think they're related to his murder."

She just stared at me.

"What about the garage?" I asked.

"What about it? It's still there. Left it just like it was when I found you."

"Can you help me up? I found something there I think can help explain a lot."

She thought for a moment, then placed her arm under my arms and pulled me erect, bracing me against her. I stood for a second trying to find my legs. I took two steps then nodded. "I'm okay." Carefully supporting me we crossed the kitchen to the garage. This Zelda might talk tough but she was as gentle as Mother Teresa.

The single overhead light bulb was on and a large amoeba-shaped bloodstain covered the floor behind the Corvette. More blood was splashed against its bumper. My blood, I had to remind myself. If I had seen that much blood, I would have thought someone had been killed.

"This is where you found me?"

She nodded. Freddy was behind the Vette with his tail wagging like a metronome on speed. He was happily lapping at the bloody dark circle on the floor.

The trunk was still open. I looked inside but the black bag was gone. So were the handgun, the picture, the clippings, and the advertisement.

"There was a black bag in the trunk. Do you know where it is?"

"What bag?"

"It was a black, toiletries bag in the trunk under the tire. I don't see it anywhere."

"All I found was the door open and you lying there with all this blood."

I looked under the car. Nothing. I glanced at the trunk, the patch of coagulated blood, then at Zelda.

"You don't seem too upset," I said. "Do you often find strange men bludgeoned in your garage in the middle of the night?"

"Don't fool yourself, mister. I'm pissed. I don't need this crap. I'd rather see your sorry ass out of here." She backed toward the kitchen door.

"I'm sorry. Believe me, I know," I said. "That black bag held important evidence. I don't know what to do."

"This can only be trouble."

"You're right. I'm in a lot of trouble." I thought of Adam's reaction when he found out about the missing revolver.

"I mean for me."

"I'm sorry."

She waved me off.

"It's okay, I'm leaving," I said. "But before I do leave can you tell me something about Billy? We all knew that Billy wasn't your average model citizen. You must have known the Vette didn't fall out of the sky. The money had to have come from somewhere."

"Billy had his secrets," Zelda said. "I knew everything that he did wasn't entirely legit. That goes with the territory. He put the car in my name because he was being hounded by his ex-wife. A real bitch that can't, or won't, hold down a job. I can support myself. I don't need a man for that."

"Ex-wife?"

"She lives in Colorado someplace. I don't think he's seen her in years."

"Can I ask you something? When you found me, why didn't you call the police?"

"Like I said, I don't need the heat. I've nursed many men back from death. Used to ride with the Pariahs."

How did I miss that?

CHAPTER 24

I followed Zelda back into the house. Dawn's early light beamed electric fingers through the front window and my head still ached worse than a vicious hangover. She sat me down on the living room couch.

"Wait here." She disappeared into the back bedroom and emerged with a T-shirt on a wire hanger.

"You can't go out like that," she said. I looked down at my blood stained shirt. "Here, take this."

The shirt she handed me was an, XL. I had forgotten Billy was a big boy. He was tough and knew how to handle himself, and was too street smart to get taken by surprise. Billy's killer had to have been a friend, someone he knew, someone close to him.

Zelda sat down on the edge of the sofa. Freddy jumped up in her lap and she wrapped both of her arms around him. Behind her I noticed three large cardboard boxes taped up and labeled, stacked up in a corner.

"Were you going somewhere?" I asked, pointing to the boxes.

She kept hugging Freddy then lifted him to her face and gave him a kiss.

"Was." She put Freddy gently on the floor and stared straight at the wall in front of her. "You know Billy. He said to pack up, we were moving to California. He had a place all picked out in San Diego. So to please him I put a few things in boxes. I wasn't sure if we were really going, or even if I wanted to go. This is my home. I own the house. But Billy said he was coming into some big money. He was always dreaming."

"Big money? What kind of big money?"

"I don't know why I'm telling you all this." She turned to me.

"It might help in finding his killers."

"You know. He was always talking about big money. Never really made it. Someone would rip him off or the deal fell through. But this time he was so certain, so sure it was going to work out."

"And you believed him?"

"I packed some boxes, didn't I? Maybe I was hoping more than I believed. You know, hoping for a new start or something," she said, eyeing me cautiously. I heard a sigh. "I need some coffee. Want some?"

Magic words.

I followed her into the kitchen and sat down in a white wicker chair with an oversized blue cushion.

"Do you have any idea where this big money Billy was talking about was coming from?"

She poured water into the coffee maker. "He never said exactly. He'd done work for some rich fuckers, as he liked to say, and they owed him his fair share."

"Did he say who or what or where?"

"No. He just went out that afternoon, told me to keep packing and then never came back. Then they found . . ." She dropped her shoulders.

"What about guns? I found a pistol in the trunk."

"He always had guns. They all do."

"They?"

"He and his biker friends. Like Mad Dog and Kiki. Kiki and Billy were like Tom and Jerry for the last year. Kiki loved his guns. Sure made himself scarce right after Billy was found."

"Don't suppose you know where he is."

"No. But you can be sure he hasn't gone far. He's never left Florida in his life. One day he told me that Daytona Beach was as far north as he's ever been."

Hey, why leave paradise? The smell of fresh brew stimulated my nostrils.

"Milk?"

"Black, please."

Zelda handed me a mug painted with jumping blue dolphins. It was warm in my hands. On the wall beside the refrigerator was a photograph of Zelda and Billy on a late model Electra Glide Harley-Davidson, fully chopped.

"How did you meet Billy?" I asked her.

"Why do you want to know?"

"Like I said, the more I know about Billy the better I might be able to help find out who killed him."

For a long two moments she fiddled with her mug then slid it away. She cupped her hands and looked down at them as if in prayer.

"It was six years ago last month, at a biker's rally," she began softly. "I'd like to say it was love at first sight. Maybe it was. He walked up to my old man and told him he was in love with me. Got traded for a half ounce of coke."

Oh. "You know your boyfriend is mixed up in a murder," I said. "Beside his own, I mean."

Again Zelda shook her head but said nothing.

"You don't seem surprised."

"Bikers have short lives. It's better not to ask too many questions." She put her coffee mug down. "Billy was always barking up the wrong tree. Looking for the big one. I guess this one got too big and it came down on him. Since Billy was killed, I really don't care what he did or didn't do. I know it sounds corny, but I loved him. Now that he's gone, I guess I love him even more. That's the way it is with all men, isn't it?"

I said nothing.

"Billy was good to me. He was kind."

"I want to thank you for taking care of me but just so you know, I'll have to inform the police about all this."

"Do what you have to do, but I think you'd better leave now." She handed me my keys, wallet, and cellular telephone.

"You might want to get a lawyer," I said as an afterthought. Hell, I might need one too.

Outside the sun was still low in the east but bright and sharp, silhouetting a row of fair weather cumulus clouds forming off the coast. I squinted through the iron vice gripping my head. By the time I had reached Southern Boulevard, the pain was completely gone and I was feeling a bit giddy. Billy Balls' favorite pills had kicked in. I was floating and knew I shouldn't be driving. I did not need a DUI, but I had to get home, clean up, and face the music with conductor Adam. He wasn't going to be happy. At least he wouldn't throw a punch at an injured man, would he?

CHAPTER 25

The Neo-Spanish style Palm Beach Police Station was a scant five-block, four-minute saunter down County Road from the gallery. Unlike most precincts, where a show of force is *de rigueur*, The Island's finest do not park their squad cars out in the front. The marked cars are discreetly ensconced in the back. For the Islanders, the police, like children, are to be neither seen nor heard. They are part of the help, the army of maids, caterers, and lawn men who make their way over the bridges each morning from West Palm Beach, Lantana, and beyond. Tolerated necessities. They are circumspect and they are some of the nation's best law officers. They do their job well. They stay out of the papers and out of sight. No one wants to be reminded that there is crime in paradise.

At present I didn't need reminding as I sat in a back office with my hands on my lap, like a schoolboy being scolded by his headmaster.

"I should throw your sorry ass into the county lockup for destroying evidence and interfering in an ongoing police investigation."

"Come on. I didn't know I was going to find anything. I was getting ready to call you. You know that."

"No, I don't know that. And I'll tell you, we're pissed. The Captain wants to have you locked up. You're lucky he's not here. Putzer thinks you're dirty and I'm having a hard time keeping the county sheriff from incarcerating you as a material witness."

"You might as well. I can't work looking like this."

"This is great. Just great. Now you've lost what could be the murder weapon. News clippings. Evidence. Important evidence. Why the hell didn't you tell me about the car and the girl?"

"I thought you must have know about Zelda," I said feebly.

"Well we didn't. Those bikers are a closed lipped group. No one shares information," Adam stared out the window and the room went quiet for a long three seconds. Softly he said, "We'll question the girl and see what we can salvage."

"I'd say it looks like your client hired Baldwin to kill his wife."

"Do you really believe that?"

"It makes little difference what I believe. Putzer believes Ordenoff had Martha Manley killed. And I'll begrudgingly say, lost evidence or no, your little escapade last night could go a long way in proving the Balls-Ordenoff connection. We'll know after questioning the girl."

"Then who killed Billy Balls?"

"Perhaps Ordenoff."

"First you thought the Count killed Martha now you think he hired Billy Balls to kill her then killed Billy?"

"We're following the evidence. We'd have more, a lot more, if you hadn't lost that revolver."

"They can't be thinking of indicting the Count."

Adam just stared at me. "I'd worry more about yourself than your client."

"He's not my client."

"What! You still haven't been paid?" He rolled his eyes up into his forehead.

"Not a cent."

"Then what the hell are you doing getting involved?"

"When I get home and look in the mirror, I'll be asking myself that same question."

"Go home. You look in the mirror and if you don't come to some sane conclusion I'll have you locked up for your own protection. Let us take care of it. That's a nasty cut. You'd better get to the hospital. It should leave a nice scar. Maybe it'll remind you not to get involved where you shouldn't."

"Thanks."

As I got up Adam said, "It's a good thing you haven't been paid."

"How so?"

"It helps to keep you out of jail."

CHAPTER 26

Securely ensconced in the Roberts manse, I quietly crept to my bedroom bath. The face staring back out of the mirror was not the Maxie Roberts I knew. The disfiguring swelling and blackness around the eye gave me an asymmetric, Quasimodo look. My hair was plastered punk style with bits of dried blood. I looked like that Picasso hanging in my office but with more color. A lot more color.

I took a long hot shower. Then I carefully combed the tangles out of my hair and dabbed away the last of the dried blood off my face. After a thorough scrubbing and another glance in the mirror, I was almost presentable. But just barely.

It looked as if the Putzer was ready to indict the Count. If Billy Balls is named as the hit man then Zelda would not be far behind. Maybe it was a gut feeling or my weakness for women, but I was sure she had nothing to do with the murder of Martha Manley much less with the forgeries or the fire. I dialed Charles Cromwell, the best defense attorney in the county and gave him Zelda's name, address, and phone number.

"I'll make sure they don't grill her. Unless she gets indicted, it shouldn't take too much time."

"I'll pay for it," I heard myself say against my accountant's wishes. At least Charlie will give her an even playing field.

"I should ask for a retainer but I know better. And I do owe you for that Paul Klee you got me," he said. "But tell me, was she that good?"

"Wait until you see her," I said. Let him think about that for a while.

With my social work out of the way, I thought back to the Manley paintings. Was it possible that the Count hired Billy to kill his wife as Adam suspected? Could it be that simple? Crimes of passion and money are often elementary and straightforward. As Bernie said, Palm Beach was like Chinatown. Nothing is what it seems to be. It was starting to look more like a setup. The question was, who was being set up? And who had given me this head gash and black eye? The intruder at Zelda's house was not there when I broke in. He must have come through the back garage door while I was busy with the trunk. I remembered the shoes and well-pressed pant cuffs. Unless the Pariahs had made a recent and radical change in their official club attire, it wasn't one of Billy's motorcycle friends.

And Zelda? Yes, I'm a sucker for women, especially pretty ones. A woman could tell me anything and, if she smiled, I'd believe her. Zelda hadn't smiled much. If she was telling the truth then the intruder might have gone to search Zelda's house and thanks to yours truly found what he was looking for.

Even I, who so often managed to overlook the obvious, was mired in a quandary: what was the connection between Billy Balls and the forgeries? It's doubtful Billy Balls knew any artists that could have forged such exquisite paintings. Nor did he know the high-end fences needed to sell the originals. And knowing a little about fast-money biker boys, I didn't think Billy Balls possessed the self-control to keep a caper of this magnitude quiet. Maybe there was no connection and we were dealing with two separate crimes. Billy Balls killed Martha Manley and someone forged the original paintings. Two crimes, one victim. Not plausible, but possible.

Suddenly a wave of exhaustion swept through me. I staggered into my bedroom and collapsed onto the bed, fully clothed.

I was awakened by soft sounds around the house. I was under the sheets and my clothes were folded on the chair. A clean scent of freshly washed bedding attacked my nostrils like smelling salts. The window was open. Another aroma, fried dough, drifted in from the kitchen.

Margarita was cooking up a batch of *papoosas*.

The grandfather clock in the entrance hall gonged five times. I had been out for seven hours. I glanced at my reflection. The swelling had receded and the gash on my forehead had scabbed; it was not as bad as I had feared. When I combed my hair to one side I could hardly see it. I trudged into the kitchen.

"You look terrible. You get in a fight or something?" she said.

"Don't worry. It was just a little accident. I'm okay."

Margarita snorted a huff. "You want that I fix you some tea?" Without waiting for an answer she placed the kettle on the stove and poured in water and a mixture of herbs.

"You gotta six messages," Margarita said, pointing to the phone like a stern elementary school matron. "And a certified letter. I signed,"

Margarita said handing me a letter from the Florida State Antiquities Department. I tried smiling. With all that's going on an investigation by the Antiquities Department was all I needed. I dumped the letter on the table and called Margot's cell.

"Where have you been?" Margot asked. "The phone hasn't stopped ringing. Lieutenant Adam Aldrick called. Said you might want to call him, a.s.a.p."

"Hold the rest of the calls. I'll call Adam back". He answered on the first ring.

"We didn't get much from Miss Zeitgeist," Adam said. "She lawyered up. You know what I feel? She must be dirty unless you can tell me how a stripper can afford an attorney like Charles Cromwell."

"I hear a stripper's tips are good."

"Yeah, right. Remember what I said."

"Anything new on the arsonists?"

"Oddly, the trigger device is from Eastern Europe or Russia. Used to set off heavy explosives. No one sells them in the States, so it had to have been brought in or mailed. Unfortunately, that doesn't help us much. Neither did your vague description of the perp."

"Why would they use a Russian device?" I said, and then thought about the Count. He was Russian via Bulgaria.

"Probably because it's untraceable," Adam continued. "The Russians smuggle anything and everything, but mostly in arms. Every terrorist's favorite weapons are AK-47s and RPGs."

"The Russians also smuggle in art, old icons. And good fakes," I said. "Has there been any hint that the Pariahs were involved?"

Adam laughed. "I think the Pariahs have more to worry about than the Manley case or your gallery. The Feds have been in town for months. Racketeering indictments should be handed down any day now. If any of them are involved in either your fire or the Manley killing, we'll get one or two to flip on the others. It happens every time. Putzer's betting one of them will drop a dime on your Mr. Ordenoff. Even if we can't get any of them to flip, there's plenty of circumstantial evidence in the Manley murder, all of it pointing to Ordenoff," Adam said. "By the way, watch the six o'clock news. I think you'll find it interesting."

I moped back into my bedroom and took another glance in the mirror. I couldn't face the world looking like this. I needed help. Cautiously jutting my head into the kitchen, I asked, "Margarita can you make it look better?"

She grunted again, "You wait here," and left. She returned from her apartment hefting an oversized bag of makeup.

"Sit," she said sitting me down in an alcove chair. With deliberate and practiced movements she set out an array of tubes, packages and brushes on the table and began to dab and pat and wipe. After five minutes, a glance in the mirror showed only a faint telltale black or blue.

"You such a handsome man. Why you do this to yourself?"

I wanted to say it was not completely self-inflicted, but I have learned not to interrupt Margarita's chain of thought with logic.

At six I turned on the television, my old reliable Zenith that got little use except for Margarita's Spanish soap operas. Top billing of local news was the Peter Putzer press conference announcing they had a prime suspect in the Martha Manley murder—a recently deceased outlaw motorcycle gang member. He made no mention that yours truly had supplied the tip at a great cost to my personal safety.

Peter Putzer, our beloved crime fighter, was a political hack who never let justice obscure his greater vision--the imprisonment of all his political rivals. He was well known for persecuting small-time offenders for minor infractions. With an unseemly glee he led an aggressive attack on a conservative talk show host that gave him more airtime than Amelia Earhart. Real crime stories bored him. Martha's murder, with its instant national media coverage, however, was a perfect fit and he wore it like a street beggar dressed in a Savile Row suit.

While I contemplated the complexities of unappreciation, Margarita fixed me dinner. She was in the habit of expounding gratuitous maxims as she careened around the house in a state of perpetual motion.

"Men are nothing but heartbreak and heartburn," she said, while cooking up another batch of *papooses*.

"Is that from personal experience?" I asked.

"I tell you, Mr. Roberts, when I was young all the boys in the street stopped when I walked by. They too shocked to even whistle." She paused as if lost in thought. "I was hot stuff." She smiled, waving the spatula.

"Muy buena, si?" I said, practicing my Spanish.

"Buenisima!"

Even now, at seventy-two, she had an ingrained beauty that too many pregnancies and carbohydrates could not hide.

Margarita handed me a mug of steaming something.

"Good for hangover and tough nights," she said with an accusatory glare.

Margarita had an impressive repertoire of Mayan concoctions for every ailment. I gulped it down and in ten minutes was feeling better. Almost as good as Billy's favorite pills.

By nine, merciful sleep once again rescued me.

CHAPTER 27

It was light and the sun was beaming over my left shoulder. I was walking through a Dali landscape: dripping watches as an elongated bull with flared nostrils strutted in the distance. I was naked except for a red cape in my right hand. A crowd of grim-faced spectators sat behind me on folding chairs, whispering in a guttural monotone. They did not clap, but rang little bells as each pass I made with the cape brought the bull closer. I looked for a place to hide. A bloodied nail-studded cross was raised on a distant hill and the bells rang louder. I fell to my knees. Then, just as quickly, I was standing. My right hand was heavy with a sword. I stepped toward the stands and the bells. My hands trembled. I peered down at them. Instead of the sword I was clutching my Heckler Koch 9 millimeter semi-automatic pistol. The crowd faded and I saw the woody grain of my front door. It beckoned me forward and I opened the door and the bells stopped. Outside it was still dark. Long shadows played across the driveway, then a vision of Aphrodite appeared, worried and wanting.

"May I come in?" Zelda asked.

She stood silently clutching an oversized purse to her chest. I buried the pistol in my back pocket.

"May I come in?" she said again.

I moved back and she stepped inside.

"They wrecked my place."

"What? Wrecked your place? Who?"

"How am I supposed to know?"

"Okay. Come on in and sit down." I directed her to the kitchen and sat her at the table. "Let's start from the beginning."

"I got home an hour ago from work and found my place trashed. My clothes were ripped, the furniture was all broken, the food in the kitchen was thrown on the floor."

"Did you see anyone?"

"They killed Freddy," she said.

"Freddy?"

Her eyes watered up. "My dog." She bit her lower lip, fighting back tears. "I'm not like this. I don't cry. I didn't even cry for Billy."

"Believe me. It's all right."

"I'm afraid to go back home."

I put my arms around her and she buried her face in my shoulder and sobbed. With gentle round consoling movements I rubbed her back. Then she sighed deeply.

She dried her eyes with the back of her palm.

"Would you like a drink?"

"Coffee, please. Black."

In less than five minutes I had two steaming mugs of black coffee sitting on the table.

"I got your address from your driver's license." She blew into the steaming mug and sipped. "Nice and hot. Just the way I like it." She blew again. "The cops raked me over the coals. But thanks for the lawyer. He looks expensive."

"Don't worry about it. He owes me some favors." I watched her sip her coffee. Then I force-swallowed an esophageal eruct. I didn't know what was kicking in, Margarita's Mayan remedy, the residue of Billy's favorite pills, or the fried *papoosas* lodged securely in my duodenum.

"I can't go back to the house. I don't know what to do. What are they looking for anyway?"

"You tell me."

"I don't know, but it's been one hell of a long day. First you, then after you left the cops show up. I was sleeping for Christ's sake. I got to work. They take me to the station and the lawyer shows up and they let me go. And tonight there were two guys at the club. They just stood there. I thought they were checking out the girls but they were looking at me. The entire night. Didn't ask for a dance or anything. Even the other girls thought they were creepy. One was a big guy. You know, no neck. Dark hair. He had on a wig."

"A wig?"

"A short one but it was a wig. Girls notice that stuff. He was well dressed. Expensive-looking clothes."

"Well-pressed cuffed pants and nice shoes?"

"That I didn't notice," she said and dropped her eyes. "I just don't know anymore. After Billy was killed, then you, and now this."

"Did you call the police?"

"Are you kidding? After the grilling they gave me?"

"Okay. Listen. We'll go and check out the house later. If you still don't feel safe, you can stay here for a few days. Get some rest first."

I showed her the first floor guest bedroom.

"Make yourself at home. You can take a shower," I said as I opened the guest bathroom door.

"I'd like to wash my things. They smell of gasoline," she said. "Would you have anything to wear?"

"I just happen to have an XL T-shirt someone lent me yesterday."

I brought her Billy's T-shirt. "Shower up and come on out for some breakfast."

It was dawn again and I was wide-awake. My biological clock was in reverse. I retrieved the morning *Post* and The Shiny Sheet and was thinking of what to prepare for breakfast when Zelda came out looking as good as a woman could at six a.m. She had traded her form-fitting blue jeans and white blouse for Billy's oversized tee shirt. As she walked, the hem rose about halfway up her well-proportioned thighs. I'm always amazed at how a woman you've seen naked looks just as sensual dressed. Okay, half dressed.

I sat her down at the breakfast nook with the paper. "At least we didn't make the newspaper," I said.

The second pot of coffee was brewing when I heard the front door lock click and open. Margarita stood in the doorway, her oversized purse secured firmly under her left arm as she fiddled with the keys.

"Good morning, Señor Maxie," she greeted as she came into the kitchen.

"*Buenos dias, Doña Margarita,*" I said.

With surprising agility she crossed the kitchen to the counter. "Up early. *Muy temprano,*" she said. Then her eyes shot over to the breakfast nook and Zelda reading the Accent Section of the morning paper.

Margarita dropped her purse with a deliberate thud on the counter and gave me a fabulous imitation of the evil eye. At least I hoped it was an imitation. Aside from her domestic chores, Margarita had designated herself the gatekeeper of my morality. So far, none of the ladies I had entertained since my divorce had passed muster.

To explain Zelda's plight—and that we had a strictly platonic relationship—would have been futile. For Margarita there was no such thing. If I wanted my crystal glass spotless and my clean underwear to be folded just so, Zelda would have to go.

CHAPTER 28

By nine both Zelda and I were refreshed and ready. From the far reaches of the back of my closet, lost among out-dated suits and polyester bellbottom pants, I fished out a brightly colored floral Hawaiian shirt Eric and Nicole gave me one Christmas as a joke. I slipped it on then took my 9-millimeter H-K from behind my night table, stuck it in my belt and pulled the shirt out over it. A quick check in the mirror. I almost fit the part. What part I had no idea. I hoped for Arnold Schwarzenegger but, in reality, I probably looked more like Mr. Peepers.

Zelda was waiting in the kitchen. I hopped into the Jag, fished my pair of light brown kidskin driving gloves out of the glove compartment before pulling a blue Boston Red Sox baseball cap with no snap, tight on my head. Without a word, Zelda slid into the passenger seat.

"This is the plan," I said to Zelda. "We go and check out your place. Things look a lot different in the daytime. If there's anyone there we leave as fast as possible. Okay?"

Zelda just shook her head.

We had smooth sailing over the middle bridge and up Okeechobee Boulevard, but as soon as I turned south onto I-95 I knew I'd made a mistake. The eight lanes of I-95 snaking past the Palm Beach airport were packed. By the infamous Belvedere curve, the traffic was crawling at thirty-five and by Southern Boulevard it was stopped. I couldn't tell if it was an accident or roadwork ahead that was causing the delay; I-95—the black hole of Florida highway projects—is always under construction. The Jag, a bit too anxious, had moved too far forward. I looked up and saw the oversized brutish behemoth of a cement truck churning ominously a few feet from my freshly polished bumper. I could only read the STAY BACK FIFTY FEET sign if I cocked my head against the windshield and looked straight up. I let him pull forward, grateful when a Toyota Corolla driven by a Marielito-looking Latin immediately cut in and copped the space. Laboriously the left lane moved a car length, then stopped. Then the right lane moved and stopped until this game of tic-tac-toe came to a complete standstill. Fifteen minutes and one mile later we passed a three-car pileup. A pair of paramedics was attending a seasoned citizen with Coke-bottle glasses and a pronounced spinal hump who should have had his license revoked a decade ago. Many of the older generation, their necks stiffened by osteoporosis, can't turn their heads and are forced to change lanes at seventy-five miles an hour without looking, hoping the other drivers will get out of the way. It usually works.

The real problem, however, is not the old folks. It's development. The Palm Beach Commissioners are in an unseemly rush to rezone the remaining South Florida farmland so DiVosta and the other developers can build more subdivisions in the Everglades. The commissioners, along with the developers, the brokers, and state politicians are all lifetime members of the "Pave Florida Now" movement.

True Floridians bemoan the incessant assault on our beloved Everglades. Every year it takes longer to reach them. They are forever drifting farther away, drowning in a sea of cookie-cutter subdivisions of humdrum homes populated by people who hate everything about the Everglades. People are scared of nature. Coming from New York or New Jersey, they're afraid of everything. They detest the heat, the thunderstorms, and the native born. They sequester themselves in fortified air-conditioned abodes, trusting their gated communities to keep out the sunburned, crew cut yobbos. They have a vague notion that a Cracker is not edible. Why are they here? They hate the tropics.

Floridians wish they'd stay home. We fantasize about a Category Five Atlantic hurricane hitting Florida's east coast straight on and blowing all these people back to where they came from.

"One can only hope."

As far as the Everglades, I had to admit, I was an armchair environmentalist. I managed to visit the Everglades only a few times a year, usually by airboat with my Seminole hunting partner Billie Osceola Tommie. We planned to poach a few alligators for new leather boots and feast on their tails, a tribal delicacy. For three days we would swat hummingbird-sized mosquitoes, scrape a crusty bluish mold from our armpits, and pluck black leeches from each other's backs. A rip-roaring time is had by all.

Finally, as suddenly as the traffic jam began, it broke up and in forty seconds I was doing eighty-five due south and thinking positive thoughts.

The positive thoughts ended when we pulled into Zelda's driveway.

"Wait here," I said to Zelda.

"Not on your life buster. I'm going with you."

We stepped out of the Jag and cautiously walk to the front door. It opened with a light shove and we were greeted with the sickening smell of gasoline fumes. I immediately flashed back to the night of the gallery fire.

"Stay back," I said. I took a deep breath, ran into the living room and opened up the windows to air out the house. Zelda stepped inside and let out a cry. All the furniture was turned on its side. The moving boxes had been taken from the bedroom, ripped open, and their contents dumped in the middle of the living room. Gasoline had been poured over them. Clothes, papers and lacy curtains that had been pulled down from the walls were all drenched in gas too.

In the middle of the pile was a stained, partially ripped photograph of Billy Balls. He was saddling his Harley motorcycle in full Pariah colors, his light brown hair swept back over his head to his collar. No denying he was big: big arms, big chest, and a big smile with all his teeth. Like the photo in the kitchen he had a gentle, almost kind face.

The master bedroom was in shambles but the second bedroom had not been touched. It was obviously Billy's room. Along the outside wall, a complete gym and bell bars were set up. I looked at the weights and counted. Four hundred and twenty five pounds. Billy had been a serious lifter.

"Oh, God, Freddy." I heard Zelda cry. I ran into the kitchen. Freddy's broken body was lying in the middle of the floor, his head blown open by a large caliber projectile.

Zelda moved toward him.

"Don't touch him," I said. I grabbed her arm and pulled her back. "Let's let the police handle this."

"We can't just leave him there like that."

"Then let me do it, okay?" From the bathroom I brought back a large towel and placed it over Freddy. We both quietly stared at the lump under the towel.

"We can't stay here much longer. Anything missing?"

"I don't know. I don't think so," Zelda said. Her eyes were red. "I have to get some things."

"Touch as little as you can."

I stepped outside. The gas and the tension were giving me a headache. Zelda came out hefting a black knapsack stuffed with her clothes. She closed the door.

"Leave it unlocked," I told her. Then we left.

No professional ransacked a house like this. Real thieves were masters of human nature and automatically knew where we hide our most precious possessions. Whoever had wrecked Zelda's home lacked that knowledge or imagination. Or loved to destroy things for the sake of destroying. Or it was a warning. The gasoline soaked clothes were a not very subtle threat of fire. Pyromaniacs or arsonists, their MO was the same as the people who'd try to torch my gallery. Zelda was obviously telling the truth and she was not safe. And I had a new houseguest.

On the way back to The Island I dialed Adam's cell phone and explained to him about Zelda and the trashing of her house.

"I thought we already talked about this," Adam said. "You're getting too close, Maxie. "Now, on top of everything, you're involved with the triggerman's girlfriend! Putzer's going to love this. Come on, man, you're not thinking correctly."

Maybe it was Billy's favorite pills.

"I think you'd better find yourself a good psychiatrist," I heard Adam say.

"I already have one."

"And a lawyer."

Silence.

"I'll have the county sheriff send over some people to look at the place."

CHAPTER 29

Back in the Roberts abode, I bathed, changed, and made a mental assessment of the past few days. I wasn't any closer to the paintings or finding Martha's killer or the forger. I had a murder suspect's stripper girlfriend staying at my house, the Florida Antiquities Department was pressuring me, the Palm Beach Police Department and the state attorney were breathing down my goose bumped neck. The arsonist was still out there and the kids were coming for the holidays. Could it possibly get any more complicated?

As if on cue, the doorbell rang.

"Good morning," a smiling Kathy Krammer said. "Like they say, 'I was in the neighborhood.' Are you okay? What happened to your face?"

"I'm now a confirmed member of *Fight Club*," I said in all truthfulness. "Don't I look like Brad Pitt?"

"I'm serious. Are you okay?"

"Thanks, I'm fine," I said. I opened the door wide open.

"Is that your Honda with a Landing Strip bumper sticker outside behind the Jaguar?"

"Come on in," I said, rushing her inside.

She glanced around the foyer. "Nice place you have."

"Thanks," I said and quickly directed her through the kitchen to the loggia.

"I brought over copies of the rest of the information you requested." She raised the folder she was carrying in her left hand.

"Thanks. I'll read it and let you know what I think."

Kathy crossed the loggia and leaned on the railing. "Great view," she said. It was a bright day with a soft breeze blowing off the water. In the distance a couple of sailboats glided past a large Grady White, fishing for snook near the channel. "I think Judge Billlingsworth has a house over there," she said, pointing across the Intracoastal.

"It's the three story one with the blue tile roof and the large white yacht."

Justice pays.

"I can see why you love it here. The water is so peaceful. You're so fortunate."

"When the weather is nice it's peaceful."

"I mean mentally."

"Goes back to our primordial instincts. We all came from the sea and we have an urge to return to it. That's my theory anyway."

"I think you're right," she said. "I have to confess. Last night I actually got out my old undergraduate art history book and thumbed through the pages. I remember more from the course than I believed."

"Art History is where we all start."

"I liked the impressionists. Renoir and Van Gogh."

I nodded my head.

"Not your favorites?"

"Oh, no. If you like them, I like them. How would you like to see an original Renoir?"

"I'd love to."

"We can go by the gallery later, then maybe lunch?"

"I'd like that. I'd like that a lot." She smiled.

I stepped up to the railing beside Kathy. My arm brushed up lightly against hers and I felt a tingle of excitement. She had on a white, lace silk blouse, opened in front and a light blue jacket and skirt. A delicate gold chain necklace with an Etruscan pearl dangled between her breasts. I was about to say how nice she looked when I heard a dishpan clang from inside the house. We both looked back.

"Have a seat. I'll be right back," I said and shot back into the house.

The kitchen was empty. I sprinted to the spare bedroom. Zelda was nowhere in sight. I stepped back into the foyer just as Kathy walked back into the kitchen.

I darted up behind her.

She turned. "Are you okay?"

"Oh. Umm. Ahhh . . . Yes, yes. How about some coffee?"

"I'd love some," Kathy said.

"I drink way too much coffee," I said. "It's my pet addiction."

"Me too," she said.

I dumped four spoons of dark roasted beans into the grinder and hit the on button. An immediate whirling and crunching crackled through the air, followed by the disarming aroma of freshly grounded coffee.

"Umm, that smells so good," Kathy said. She closed her eyes and was inhaling deeply when Zelda emerged from the utility room in Billy's T-shirt.

I straightened up. Kathy opened her eyes.

"Oh, excuse me," Zelda said.

"Oh, ah . . . Zelda, this is Kathy Krammer. Kathy, ah. Zelda."

"How do you do," Kathy said.

"Very nice to meet you," Zelda said. "All my clothes smell like gas so I'm doing a wash. Sorry I'm not decent. Please excuse me."

Kathy and I watched Zelda disappeared into the bedroom.

"The plumber, I assume," Kathy said.

"Actually, Zelda has had some unwanted company at her place and is staying here until it's safe."

"A true gentleman," Kathy said. She handed me the folder, turned and headed for the front door. "I must be going."

"What about your coffee?" I asked behind her.

Before I got to the steps she was in her car. She closed the door with a bit too much force. The window was down and she said, "Safe? I don't think anyone would be safe around you."

"Are we still on for meeting tomorrow?"

"Only under duress," she said, gunning the engine. I always liked the sound of a Porsche motor revving up.

"I'll keep you informed," I shouted.

"You can keep the details to yourself." I heard, just as the Boxster shot out of the driveway, roared down the street, and disappeared behind rows of tall ficus hedges,

Considering, that went off well, I thought.

With Zelda settled in, I made more phone calls to friends and galleries.

"Do you know anyone who has had a Rembrandt quietly examined in the last five years? How about a couple of Monets?" I tried to keep the Manley name out of the inquires, but the art world is a small village of notorious gossips.

By the afternoon, I had exhausted my international contacts in South America and Europe. No one admitted to seeing or authenticating any of the missing paintings. Were the paintings in Asia, where my expertise did not extend?

These forgeries were not done by one of your ordinary art-copying students to hang up over the living room mantel. The canvas was old, perfect for the time period. Contamination aside, the forger used period paints and precise brush strokes and techniques. I could not believe that someone this good could operate anonymously. The forger had to leave a trail.

While trying not to upset the overly sensitive art crowd, like a door-to-door salesman I paid a visit to the leading galleries along Worth Avenue, gently prodding the owners about Monets, Rembrandts, and rogue copyists. The jaunt down Worth Avenue confirmed that the Season was in full swing.

One out of ten people, mostly well-dressed elderly women, walked curly-haired miniature terriers or Chihuahuas. Many of these ladies were coiffured exactly like their poodley pooches, oddly reminiscent of a scene from *Invasion of the Body Snatchers*. Fortunately, strategically placed on the corner of Worth Avenue and Golfview, in the middle of gallery row, was a doggie bar, a blue Spanish-tiled trough with a silver spigot that looked suspiciously like a urinal, where matrons watered their wiggly whelps. The only thing lacking on the avenue was a sign saying, "curb your cur," though most of the cautious canines had too much class and training to do their duty or doodoo on Palm Beach's most fabled street.

A slew of top-of-the-line galleries lined this end of Worth Avenue. The Phillips Galleries, the Irving Galleries, Select Fine Art, DTR Modern Galleries and Arcature Fine Art cluttered the west end along with Dickie Durdle's Wellington Green Gallery. About midway up Worth Avenue, Prince Monyo of Romania's signature yellow Rolls Royce convertible with black top and royal coat of arms on the door was conspicuously parked at the entrance to Via Lela. A former Ft. Lauderdale lifeguard, the good prince is now a much sought after sculptor. The back alleyway in front of the Fourth Dimension Studio is cluttered by his sculptures of children playing ball, eating ice cream and climbing trees. Royalty, in any form, is still in demand in Palm Beach.

Unfortunately all of my inquiries had come up blank. It was nearly noon, and though Ta-boo and Bice were a few steps away, I wanted something light and fast. It was a pleasant day so I footed a block south to Colony Hotel at the corner of Worth and South Country Road. At the first floor corner deli I ordered a ham and cheese croissant and a lemonade, then took my fare up the steps to the lobby and out to the pool area, where I spotted Maria Angelina Bosco and her new husband, Marco something, sunning. She waved me over, lifted her sunglasses and asked, "Are you here for a swim, my dear boy?"

"Only if I can skinny dip," I said.

"You have my permission."

Maria Angelina was a collector-dealer who lived in Grosseto, Tuscany. Twice a year she traveled to Palm Beach to spend a month and a couple hundred thousand dollars on artwork. She studiously shunned the Breakers in favor of the intimacy of the Colony.

I sat down on a lounge chair and unwrapped my sandwich. "Like a bite?" She laughed. "Have you heard anything about Monet or Rembrandt copies?" I asked.

"I did hear that you were asking around about them."

I munched on my sandwich. "It's a tricky subject."

She turned over onto her stomach. At fifty-five with her firm buttocks, lithe legs and hourglass figure, she could model for Vogue. "But I do have a Greco-Roman head that might interest you," she said.

I begged off, downed the rest of my lemonade and left. That was a classic brush-off and I could not afford to alienate people like Maria Angelina.

My last island gallery was the Evernia Art Gallery owned by Henry Tillman located in the battleship grey block a couple of doors down from the old AU Bar made famous by the Kennedy family. The gallery was a study in luminosity. Bright and light, the art works hung in perfect position, along the wall at eye level, the level at which the artist would have painted it - Jackson Pollock being an exception. Henry had taste and bearing, which are the keystones for any art dealer. Hucksters survive but briefly.

Henry's problem was that he believed he was an artist. His critically clobbered work hung around the gallery like Monday's wash on a clothesline—clean, colorful, antiseptic and unwanted in the better communities. Unable to sell his paintings, Henry Tillman was forced to sell other people's art. He had carved out a small but important niche specializing in early twentieth century Abstract Expressionism and Neo-Plasticism. Excuse me! Unfortunately, a client of his had ended up with two meticulously done Mark Rothko forgeries. No one ever accused Henry of selling copies knowingly and he quietly bought them back. But the client, a well-known local gossip, lost no opportunity to play the victim. Henry's business suffered. Most gallerists would have been driven out of town but Henry, a local boy, remained, persevered, and after fifteen years had retrieved a respectable clientele. After the Rothko incident he had grown a beard that now showed the patchy white ravages of age, though it did give him a distinguished air.

"You're looking good except for the black eye," Henry said as we shook hands. He offered me a seat.

"I'm in training for a light-heavyweight fight."

"Doesn't appear to be a healthy pursuit."

"Have to learn to keep my head down," I said, then added, "How about yourself? Getting in any fishing?"

"Too busy, I'm afraid. The market being what it is and all."

"I know. I've been reduced to doing appraisals for a few selective clients.

"Clients. Anybody I'd know?"

"Most definitely, but I'm not at liberty to say who. I was wondering if you had ever come across any unauthorized copies of Monet or Rembrandt."

"Copies? You mean forgeries? I hope we're not going to rehash that old saw?" His eyes flashed red.

"Heaven forbid, Henry. Like you, my clients may be victims. I'm only trying to chase down what may be a disturbing pattern. There might be a master forger turning out copies and passing them off to some of our better collectors. You know, questionable art affects all of us."

"Questionable art? Not all of us, like you, have the luxury of being a dilettante art dealer. I have worked hard to build what I have here and I don't appreciate you coming in here with loaded questions." He started to stand up.

"I'm not implying anything. I've talked with dozens of galleries. It's part of the due diligence," I said. "Look Henry we've know each other for years. I am just looking for names."

"I haven't heard a thing," Henry said. He settled back down in to his chair. "Though a client brought in what she thought was a Hans Holbein portrait done by Christina Hagan." Henry scratched his beard. "It was good. I mean a museum quality copy. Christina had signed it on the back."

"I thought she did only modern stuff."

"That's not what I've been told."

I thanked Henry and left but my curiosity was piqued on two accounts. Why was Henry so sensitive after so many years? And Christina Hagen's name kept surfacing. Why would she not acknowledge the old master copies she'd done?

From the Jag, I called Dickie Durdle. "Have you heard anything about Henry Tillman lately?" I asked.

"Henry Tillman?" Dickie said. "I heard he was in financial trouble again with the real estate boom. The rent went way up then busted. I heard he purchased a load of paintings that he's having difficulty selling. Terrible paintings if you ask me. The man has absolutely no sense of proportion."

"How about Christina Hagan?"

"Is this professional or personal."

"Dickie."

"Okay. Okay. I heard she spends a lot of time on the SunCruise gambling ships plus trips to the Grand Bahama Island casinos."

"Is she a gambler?"

"And a bad one I hear."

"Are there any good ones?"

Exhausted, I called an official end to the workday. Zelda was sitting in the back loggia as I opened a bottle of an Ornellaia, La Volte Super-Tuscan and poured two glasses. The sun was setting and we watched the warm-colored clouds turn and drank in silence.

"What do you want to do?" I finally asked.

"Don't worry. I'll find a place in a couple of days." She tucked the soles of her feet under her thighs.

"You mentioned that Billy had some friends. A Kiki something or other?"

"Kiki Cohen."

"I'd like to talk to him, or anyone else you think might help us discover who ransacked your house and stole the black bag. They might also help us identify Billy's killer."

"If Kiki's still around, I can find him."

A flock of snow egrets, silhouetted against the maroon sky, flew silently across the Intracoastal to their unseen roost.

"I'm curious, why didn't you call Kiki or one of Billy's friends this morning instead of driving all the way over here?"

"For all I know, one of them could have killed Billy. I don't trust any of them," she said. "Motorcycles are great but after a while biker life is tiring. You know. You grow out of it."

"Did Billy?

"No."

Zelda looked out over the water at a school of jumping mullet.

"So what do you want in life? After all this blows over," I asked.

"What all women want—a family, children, security."

"I've been told that women don't want that any more."

"Don't believe it."

Looking at Zelda, want was also much on my mind. But want would wait. Finding the forger and the missing paintings is your first and foremost priority, I keep telling myself and Jock. And tomorrow was the meeting with the Manley children.

CHAPTER 30

Hoping to impress Ms. Kathy Krammer, Esquire with my timeliness, I clocked my appearance at Beck, Goldman, Green and O'Leary to coincided exactly as the bells of Saint Ann's church struck ten. Ms. Krammer greeted me with a smile and a straight and courteous handshake and led me into a conference room. The warmth I longed for was absent, which I wrote off to professionalism. There were, after all, clients in the room. She couldn't still be peeved about the Zelda thing, could she?

Martha's two children, Frederick Manley IV and Mary Martha Manley, were seated at a round mahogany conference table. Had Sophocles searched the ends of the earth twice, he would not have found two more opposite issues from the same womb.

Frederick Manley IV was one of The Island's hundreds of trust fund babies or what is whimsically referred to as "the lucky sperm count." Raised in privilege and wealth, he reckoned the world owed him a living in the style to which he was accustomed. He had never worked a day in his life. His father, wisely, banned him from the family businesses and his mother preferred that he continue his schooling in Europe, even at the age of forty-two. Except for his obvious lack of imagination, he might have been a possible suspect in his mother's murder. Number IV's sister, however, was a different matter. She too had her trust fund but she actually did something with it. She founded, owned, and ran a multimillion-dollar cosmetic company that targeted Latino women. Mary Martha Manley was quiet and shrewd and known in business for always getting her way. She was a youthful replica of the painting of her mother that hung in the Manley living room. Number IV, on the other hand, might have had Papa's bearing but looked suspiciously like the milkman.

I tried to remember that these two adults had just lost their mother and fought to remain sensitive; however, after twenty minutes I fretted about ever being able to explain to them that while I was outraged and saddened by their mothers death, my involvement was not about the Manley family or vengeance, but about the art. The longer I got to know Frederick the IV, the more I longed for Cronos the Titan, whose principal dietary supplement, according to Roman legend, was his children.

How could such good genes go so bad?

"If these are forgeries—," I started to say.

"You know damn well they're fakes," Number IV said.

"If these are forgeries, we have to ask, where are the originals? Contrary to popular belief, there is not a horde of mad millionaires waiting in line to purchase paintings to hang in for-their-eyes-only vaults. The paintings have to go somewhere."

"I don't give a damn about the paintings," Number IV said. "They can burn as far as I'm concerned,"

I believed him.

Tapping his foot against one of the table legs, Frederick the IV cleared his throat, turned to Kathy and said, "I wonder if we could have a word alone with Mr. Roberts?"

Kathy gave him a puzzled looked. She started to object but Mary Martha said, "It's all right we just want a private word with Mr. Roberts. Just five minutes."

"As your attorney I am advising you that I should be present in all the conversations."

"It'll just be a minute," Mary Martha said.

Kathy squinted at me then said, "Okay. I'll be back in five minutes." She picked up her file and legal pad and left.

"We have agreed to pay you one hundred thousand dollars for your help in proving Ordenoff is guilty of mother's death," Number IV said. He reached into his coat pocket and pulled out an envelope, took out a check and handed it to me.

In slow strobe-light-like motions, the check reached my hand and I delicately grasped it in my fingers like a fairy feather. Yes. A one followed by five zeros. I flashed to a beautiful sketch by Sargent for sale in Boston. And I had the perfect place to hang it. Then I heard another voice that sounded strangely like mine: "I appreciate the confidence, but let's wait on any type of payment until I have something concrete."

I laid the check on the table.

"Suit yourself," Frederick the IV said. He snatched up the check and buried it his jacket pocket.

"We do hope you can help us," Mary Martha said. "My mother deserves justice."

"Men like him always make mistakes," Number IV barked. "These damned fortune hunters are all too obvious."

"I know we can count on you to do the right thing," said Mary Martha.

"I'll do everything I can to find the original paintings," I assured them.

Finally, Kathy marched back into the conference room.

"We offered Mr. Roberts a retainer," Mary Martha told her. She didn't say bribe. "He said it wasn't necessary."

Kathy glanced at Mary Martha then Frederick then me. Obviously, she was not pleased at being left out of any conversation. During the meeting she had been strangely quiet for an attorney and I wondered if she was deferring to the children.

Number IV stood and, realizing the meeting was over, I excused myself.

"I'll give you a call if anything comes up," I said to Kathy.

"Feel free to leave any message with my assistant," she said.

Playing hard to get. I liked that. No. Actually I hated it. Coyness was a waste of time. Maybe some flowers would be appropriate after all.

The elevator zoomed me to the basement garage. Before I opened the Jag's door I paused. Had I just refused a hundred thousand dollars? I had an urge to stick my head through the window and push the up button, except the top was down.

The proffered check was blatant bribery. Refrains of Count Von Bulow and onetime princess Sunny Crawford Von Bulow began to ring. Except here there were no planted syringes or bottles of insulin. Instead we had forged paintings and at least one ancillary murder. I could not shake the nagging premonition that I was participating in a public hanging of dear Sergio and I didn't like the sensation. Too often I'd been on the other side. Bernie was right. I couldn't afford the scrutiny. In my life and business, extra-legality was a daily reality. While at the core I abhor injustice, I dislike going to jail more.

CHAPTER 31

Perhaps it was Number IV's check or Kathy's coolness, but I drove home in another pensive mood. Am I chasing phantoms? The paintings could have been switched years ago and have nothing to do with Martha's murder. That made sense, except for the timing between Martha's killing, Billy Balls murder, the gallery fire, and the missing Manley file.

So, who were the forgers? South American or Asian gangs? Maybe Russians. Could it be the long and sticky fingers of the Mafia? The forgeries and the fire seemed too organized not to be organized crime. Also, the fire was not done by your garden-variety slash-and-burn arsonists. Was there a maniacal super criminal, a Doctor Doom or a Joker, with his slimy tentacles in every illegal pie? The stereotyped thugs I'd seen on the History Channel and read about in detective novels were never connoisseurs of fine art, unless, as I'd argued with Adam, the forgeries and the switch were done on consignment. Then we're back to the mad millionaire. And I just didn't buy into that scenario.

All my ruminations had gotten me no closer to the paintings or the forger. Wherever the trail ended, I was faced with a more immediate reality. The money from Bernie's purchase was rapidly disappearing. I should be out selling art and making a living, rubbing shoulders with art buyers, the upper crust of society. Alas, I could hear my bank account whimper that my whimsical toiling should be directed at fattening it, not subjecting it to an economic Atkins diet.

"I don't think your maid approves of me," Zelda said, as I made my way into the kitchen. She was dressed in blue jeans, a T-shirt and was barefooted.

"Margarita? Give her a couple of years. She'll warm up," I said. "Have you eaten anything?"

"She fixed me some Cuban thing."

"See. She likes you. If she didn't, she'd try to starve you out, or make you eat overcooked pasta."

With a glass of orange juice in hand I spread my new Manley file out over the kitchen counter and was rereading the provenance when the doorbell rang. Then rang again. Then again. I opened the door to see the slim but disheveled Dickie Durdle.

"Oh, Maxie, thank God you're home. Someone shot at me this morning; I mean actually shot a bullet at my person. I stared death in the face. It was horrid."

Good old Dickie Durdle had what the illuminati like to refer to as a glib tongue. His language, like his life and art, was a come-again collection of clichés. However, he rarely failed to pique my curiosity and under the circumstances I could hardly refuse him the hospitality of my humble abode. I stepped back. Dickie took a furtive glance at the street, then darted into the foyer.

"You look none the worse for wear," I said, eyeing him for holes. Trying to compose himself, Dickie rubbed at the wrinkles in his suit. "Are you sure it wasn't an automobile backfire?" I was really thinking the alleged perpetrator was a bad shot and wondering if one of the multiple side effects of Xanax was hallucination. Then I thought, *when did the Roberts home become a haven for the endangered?*

"Did you see who shot at you? Where did it happen?"

"I was walking by the Society of the Four Arts sculpture garden when a car with its passenger window down passed by and someone shouted at me and I saw a flash." Dickie shuddered. "I think they were using a silencer or something. But I swear I heard something whizz by my ear."

"It might be nothing but . . ."

From behind me I heard the soft patter of bare feet on marble. We both turned. Zelda passed by the alcove, gave us a demure smile before she disappeared into her bedroom. Dickie raised one eye-lined eyebrow. "What's this? Now we have our own in-house tart?"

"See that door?"

"My, my, my, sensitive, are we? Oh, gracious me, when did we acquire that beautiful Spenser Stenhope?" he said, walking toward the portrait hanging in the study.

I grabbed his arm and swung him around. "Were you not just a few minutes ago fearing for your life?"

"I swear it was gunfire."

"Come on back," I said, directing him to the loggia.

He sat down and looked around at the garden and the Intracoastal and said, "What about mosquitoes? Any alligators in there?"

"Dickie, it's salt water. But if it makes you feel better I do spot an occasional twenty-foot Bull shark. And they relish human flesh."

He shuddered. "What's wrong with your eye?"

"An accident," I said.

"She didn't . . . did she?"

"Are you going to tell me what happened? I have an important appointment at the gallery," I lied.

"I don't know. There was this guy, a big guy, who came in day before yesterday and insisted that I sell him my Pissarro."

"You mean that little portrait of a maid hanging behind your desk?"

"It's an important piece, as you well know. Anyway, he was insistent that I sell it to him, almost threatening. I was so glad when he left. I mean, I didn't think anything of it until today."

"Call the police."

"I can't. There'll be a record. You know how people are in this town."

"Okay." I sighed. "You can stay here as long as you want. You've been here before. Try Eric's bedroom, upstairs third door on the left."

"Thank you. And would you please not mention this to Aseneth? You know, until we know more."

"I won't. You know where the towels are," I said and stood up.

"Don't worry, Maxie, there will not be any commingling of guests, I swear." He raised his right hand and placed his left on his heart.

"Dickie, commingle all you want."

Now I had absolutely no doubt I was being punished by God for missing Mass on Sunday.

CHAPTER 32

While most people claim to want to live life as a function of cognitive consonance, I strive for dissonance, a low-level anarchy. Odd for an art dealer, I know, but, like Mike Minsky, I love adrenalin. It's better and cheaper than crack. At present the thin adrenalin-soaked ice I was skating upon was financial. Art sale prospects were slim and the more time I spent on this quixotic quest, the slimmer they become.

While I am fortunate, fortune, like luck, should not be abused or taken for granted. Maybe it's not fortune, but *a* fortune that was the answer. It was Honoré de Balzac, I think, who said, *"Behind every fortune is a crime."* Perhaps, along with the Caravaggio, there were other skeletons lurking in the Manley closet. Papa Manley had been a keen negotiator, even a ruthless one. What was the Manleys' crime? Did the Count have a past? Billy Balls was more clear-cut, or was he?

I needed professional help. But then why repeat the obvious, right?

The immediate professional help I sought was not psychological but investigative. Michelle James was a local private detective who had found the goods on more cheating husbands and wives than Sergeant Friday had busted felons. Rumor had it that she'd seduce the objects of her investigation herself. I liked that. Dedication.

She answered on the fifth ring.

"How did you know you were next on my must-call list?"

"The story of my life—always number two and I don't mean that scatologically."

"Really, Maxie, I need info on some paintings, and who else to go to but our island's prime fine art expert."

"You're always in need of information, Michelle. But keep the flattery coming."

"I keep you for special assignments."

"Okay, then I'm all ears."

"A certain Palm Beach gentleman, who owns a couple of racetracks, claims he's in hock to his eyebrows and can not spare his poor betrayed spouse her justifiable alimony," she said. "It is rumored that said gentleman has recently purchased a rather high-priced art item that he's naturally hiding so as to deprive his spouse her legal due. Any clues?"

"Interesting. I'm sure the information would send our emotionally abused soon-to-be-divorcee on an all-expense-paid-first-class trip around the world for fifty years."

"Well?"

"Hum. I might have what you need but I'll need something in return."

"The old you-show-me-yours-and-I'll-show-you-mine?"

"Don't you go putting any ideas in my head. It's barter, my dear. The purest form of trade."

"Shoot."

"I know from close associates that said gentleman has purchased a fine and valuable example of a John De Andrea nude from a south county gallery. Very hush-hush, I'm told, and hearsay says it's hanging in his office bathroom, next to the extra-smooth Charmin and the liquid Dial."

"Fantastic, thanks. Now it's your turn."

"You knew Billy Balls, right?"

"Everyone knew Billy."

"Okay. It's been rumored that the late Mr. Balls had been spending an inordinate amount of time on The Island posing as a maintenance man. Have you heard anything about him and what he might be doing?" I asked.

"It's not a rumor. What do you want to know?"

"At the moment anything connecting Billy Balls and Martha Manley will do."

"You mean, besides the fact that both of them have been murdered?" I heard her snicker at her own joke. "Well, some of our higher society ladies like to slum, or rather bring the slums to their bedrooms. I'd say maintenance man described Billy Balls to a T. "

"What are we talking about?"

"Maxie, wake up! Billy Balls was servicing Martha Manley, and a number of our other finer island ladies."

"Are you saying Billy Balls was a gigolo?"

"From what I hear, a good one. In a rough way."

"How did a second rate criminal like Billy Balls get access to Palm Beach royalty?"

"This is for your ears only but you might want to ask Nigel Jenkins."

"You're kidding. Nigel Jenkins? What was he doing? Pimping out Billy Balls to wealthy grand dames?"

"For that information I suggest you ask Melanie Moore . . . "

"What? Now wait a minute. You mean *the* Melanie Moore? Our little island's grandest of grand dames, inheritor of the Cabot and Sillary fortunes, exemplary socialite and philanthropist?"

"The one and only."

""You want me to ask Melanie Moore about Billy Balls and Martha Manley? Do I look insane?" I took a deep breath.

"You asked, Maxie."

"Ah . . .what . . .Listen, Michelle, can I call you back?"

I hung up. My hands were sweating as if dipped in a cauldron of witch's brew. This was one road better left less traveled. I could handle the police, the state and the county. What I couldn't handle was a woman's wrath, especially if she was one of the wealthiest Palm Beach socialites.

Picturing the late Mr. Balls as Martha Manley's and Melanie Cabot Moore's gigolo pushed credulity to the extreme, but then I remembered the photograph in the Corvette. What was it with women? I knew the girls loved the bad boy in high school, but at seventy weren't they supposed to outgrow that?

Was Michelle's information a hot potato or a red herring? Either way it was a lose-lose situation for me. But maybe a little tantalizing information would get Adam more interested in looking for the forger—who I still believed was Martha's killer. This new information could be shared with Adam only under the rules of strict anonymity. If it ever got out that I gave up one of our island's leading ladies in a sex scandal I'd be shamed and shunned. You know, scorned women and hell's fury.

Women are the marrow of The Island's power. Palm Beach is a matriarchal town, run and ruled by the greatest concentration of postmenopausal wealth in the world. The ladies are commonly referred to as SWORDS—single, widowed or divorced. Their diametrical opposites are the *Preemies*, pre-menopausal women. Many Preemies are young and single, trophy-wife wannabes. Trophy wives tend to be younger than their husbands, sometimes decades younger. When Gabriel Dante Rossetti said, "Beauty like hers is genius," he might have had in mind Palm Beach trophy wives. Their presence makes their men look smart, but they, of course, themselves have little power. Until they are widowed. Then they become SWORDs—or should it be scabbards?

"Most of our grand dames were fortune hunters," as Jana Knight told me one evening dining at the Everglades Club. One of the aforementioned ladies who had inherited one hundred and fifty millions form her husband had just passed our table in with her new husband, a young tennis pro.

"I mean that nicely," Judith continued. "Their criteria for a husband is his net worth. And why not?"

Many of our island ladies were studied characters, working on an image or a legacy, others were students of the human condition, and all were horney. The one thing their money couldn't buy was a real man. The Island had plenty of borderline gigolos, teddy boys, and of course, hundreds of the well hung and the not-so well hung waiting in line for the first opportunity to help relieve the ladies of their wealth. A call could procure a walker, those educated, refined gentlemen who are ready to accompany a lady to a function, dinner, or a drive in the country. Most walkers are, unfortunately for our ladies, gay. There were scant few men they would call their equal in status, money, business acumen, or intelligence. Most of the real men had been buried. A few others had quietly slipped away on their yachts and were playing Magellan, circumnavigating the world. Escapists? Most definitely. Palm Beach was synonymous with escapism.

Escapism was not gender specific. Martha Manley had gone to Europe to find her man. The Count had the necessary prerequisites; he was fair looking and well educated, and he had impeccable manners, so wouldn't embarrass her in front of her peers. He had the additional attraction of a title. He lacked only money, and Martha had enough money for both of them.

What was their commonality? Art, perhaps? He did know his art. I remembered the comment about Wassily Kandinsky's best period. That raised the question: was he aware of the quality of the Manley collection before he married Martha? Maybe he saw an opportunity to make a lot more money. He definitely had opportunity to have the paintings copied then make the switch. Did Martha find out and he had Billy Balls kill her? Sergio Ordenoff, the cryptic count from well nigh Transylvania definitely deserved closer scrutiny.

CHAPTER 33

I was still contemplating the complexities of the fair sex as I entered the gallery. Before the front door had closed behind me, Margo said, "You have three messages."

I raised my hand to stop her. "First, will you tell me honestly - what do women see in bad boys? What is the attraction?"

"Is this a rhetorical question?"

"It's part of my unending research into the unfathomable minds of the fair sex."

"From what I hear you don't do too badly."

"Hearsay, my dear, pure hearsay."

"Bad boys. Well, they excite. They're fun, not boring. At least in the beginning. But in the end we always go for the nice guy. It's a security thing," Margot said. "Mr. Durdle came by. Said he found a place to stay and that he'd call you when it was safe."

Good. One less houseguest.

"And Deacon Cleveland Cook called."

"It must be about those Highwaymen paintings," I said. "I'll call him later."

"He said it was important."

"I'll call," I told her.

"By the way," Margot said, dangling a message note between her thumb and forefinger. "Melanie Cabot Moore called. Left a message that she'd like you to come by her apartment."

"Did you tell her I was out of town?"

"No. Should I have?"

"Did she say when?"

"Immediately."

Again, I'd been summoned.

Did Melanie Cabot Moore know she'd been the topic of a rather racy conversation? And if so, how? Money does strange things. It opens doors, and often slams them tight. Money reduces the other sins, venal and mortal, to mere also-rans. It's not the source of all evil, but it attracts banality and greed like Saturn does moons. The rich recognize surfeit urges as exuberance. A person's net worth excuses so many excesses. Even if done correctly, I hear, murder.

Melanie Cabot Moore was born one of the-Lodges-talk-only-to-the-Cabots-and-the-Cabots-talk-only-to-God Cabots from Boston. After her coming out cotillion, the stunning and graceful Melanie Cabot, a much-sought prize in the *haut monde,* was finally reeled in by the most eligible bachelor on the circuit, James Edmonds Sillary, of Sillary Industries fame. James Sillary was perfect: beautiful, Harvard educated, and built like Charles Atlas. The announcement of his marriage to Melanie was front page-fodder for months. Melanie Cabot and James Sillary were a diacritic couple, a holistic matching of Catherine Deneuve and Buckaroo Bonsai. Paired, they would breed perfect children, skipping a thousand years of genetic manipulation. But it was not to be. She found him in bed with two men, twins actually, and she shot her husband and one of the twins. The other twin, escaped only to surface three years later in the Monaco state aquarium, quite blue—and now quite dead.

Melanie Cabot Moore was a survivor, though. She survived the trial, the media blitz, two more husbands—divorced, not dead—and for four decades held court twice a week in her courtyard under the shadow of a bronze Bellini of Poseidon copulating with a bottle-nosed dolphin.

Though Melanie had ten years on Martha Manley, the two women had been best friends. They appeared together at many society gatherings. They summered in the Hamptons and lived near each other in Palm Beach until Melanie gave up the big house and moved across the lake to Trump Towers, where she bought two adjoining apartments and combined them into one large unit.

Unlike Martha, age had not been kind to Melanie. For decades the surgeon's knife had kept Father Time at bay, but then Melanie gave up trying and all hell broke loose. She still had milk-white-skin but her upper arms had developed massive sags that dangled like a Pterodactyl ready to take to the air. Her eyes had droopy lids that gave her a perpetually narcoleptic air, and the folds of her neck almost covered her signature blue-diamond necklace. But her mind was as sharp as a newly stropped straight razor. And she still led with her chin.

The fifteenth-floor double apartment afforded a spectacular view of the Intracoastal, The Island, and the Atlantic Ocean. But as anyone in zip code 33480 would attest, it was not Palm Beach.

Her fourth husband, Juan Guasamani, now known as John, was a former ambassador from Ecuador marooned in the United States after a coup d'état. Penniless and twenty years her junior, his major attribute was that he was strong enough to help lift Melanie out of her furniture. A gracious fellow, he served us tea on Wedgewood china before retiring to the opposite end of the living room where he hovered just in sight, like an at-ready gnat.

After the mandatory two sips of tea, Melanie began. "I understand you are investigating Martha's death?"

"Pardon me, Ms. Moore, I'm not really investigating her death," I said as I put down my teacup. Awful stuff. "I was asked by the Ordenoffs to examine their paintings. After the unfortunate demise of Miss Martha, Sergio Ordenoff allowed me to inspect some of the paintings and I now believe they are forgeries. Miss Moore, to be truthful, I'm only interested in finding the original paintings, though I do hope the police find the killer as soon as possible."

"It seems that everyone on The Island knows who killed Martha, or had her killed."

"And who might that be?"

"Come now, Mr. Roberts," she said, taking another sip. "Martha, you understand, was not completely happy with Sergio. But then what woman is completely happy with her husband?" Sip. "She allowed him his lady friend as long as he was discrete. That was the decent thing to do, you understand."

"Lady friend? Sergio had a girlfriend?" Melanie raised her chin and smiled. "Then why did she marry him? Couldn't she just have him as a male friend?"

"It's a question of arrangements. I know it might be hard for you to understand, but a woman, at any age, needs a man. And Sergio would not embarrass her. Believe it or not, Sergio has a keen sense of humor."

"He hides it well."

"It's his training, my dear boy. It's his training. Breeding will always show, you know. He's a gentle man as well as a gentleman."

"So you don't think Sergio was capable of killing Martha."

"Heavens, no."

"Or perhaps, have her killed?"

"No. No, never. Not dear Sergio." She laughed.

"He had no money of his own. Maybe he was tired of living off Miss Martha's largess, of being Mr. Martha Manley." I paused, she sipped. "Okay, then do you think Sergio could have switched the paintings? Replaced the original with the fakes?"

"Sergio is a dear, but he's not that smart," Melanie said. "What did bother her, and what she didn't want anyone to know, was her preoccupation with her paintings. For years she had a nagging feeling that the paintings might not be what they seemed. Like many of us we let our suspicions and fears linger, afraid of finding out the truth. It wasn't until that silly Wendell Schnelling started the rumor that he was sure that they were fakes. As if he would know. I told her that the same rumor went around about another collection that proved to be untrue. Some people like to spread vicious gossip."

"What did you think about the paintings?"

"Heavens, I know nothing about art. I like what I like and leave the rest for you people."

"I'm curious, Ms. Moore."

"Please, call me Melanie."

"Not to seem indiscreet. But since you mentioned that Martha allowed Sergio his girlfriends . . . "

"Girlfriend. Singular."

"Okay, girlfriend. Do you know who she was?"

"No. Only that she has an apartment on The Island." She motioned to Juan who refilled our cups. "Probably one of those dreadful condos where many of our island philanders stuff their concubines."

"If she allowed him to play around, had Martha lost interest in sex?"

Melanie smiled. "Mr. Roberts, we're here to talk about indiscreet. It always brings out the worst in people, don't you think?"

"Always," I said then thought of Martha and Billy Balls together.

"But believe me, age does not dampen the drive. Her libido was functioning quite well, thank you."

"Where does Nigel Jenkins come in?"

She paused. "He's . . . how would you say it? Nigel is, if I may be blunt, the tall, dark, and handsome man about town. But then you knew that."

"Did he have an affair with Martha?"

"With Nigel Jenkins? Heavens no. She liked the more earthy types."

"Earthy? You mean Billy Balls earthy." I blurted out.

Melanie's hooded eyes locked on to my eyes before she raised her cup to her lips and took a long silent sip of tea. She smiled. She was enjoying this, shocking me. I was not sure if it was age or money or both, but the rules were so different at her altitude.

She set her cup down and motioned for John again. Slipping his arm around her waist and gently lifting her out of her chair. She stood, straightened out her dress and said, "Thank you for coming. I hope to see more of you in the future." Almost the same words Martha Manley voiced to me in the Bentley.

"The pleasure was mine." We shook hands.

"By the way, do you know a Mr. Dickie Durdle?" Melanie Cabot Moore asked.

Touché, checkmate.

"A nice enough fellow," I said. "But I wouldn't necessarily trust him with my daughter."

"I see," she said.

And I hoped she did.

CHAPTER 34

As I left Melanie Moore Cabot's apartment, I was plagued by a nagging foreboding. Like Bernie said, Palm Beach is like Chinatown. And he was right. I had no idea what was going on. The antics of our local grand dames aside, it was the Manley paintings that gnawed at my psyche like a trapped muskrat chewing its leg off to escape. What had I missed? Rudyard Kipling said, "The signs are all there, they're just read wrong." What had I not read right? Was there more to the paintings than I had seen? I had to examine the paintings one more time, if only to give myself a good night's sleep.

Once out of the Trump Towers, I phoned Sergio and asked if I could see the paintings once more.

"Oh, they're gone, Mr. Roberts" Sergio told me. "Freddy and Mary Martha's attorney had a court order and they were taken away yesterday. And all I can say is a good riddance to them."

My heart skipped a beat. "All of them?" I asked.

"Ah. If you'd really like to come over, come anytime. I have no immediate travel plans."

"I'll be right there."

The Count greeted me at the door dressed in blue slacks and a white polo shirt. It was the first time I'd seen him in casual clothes. Sagging dark circles cupped his eyes and he moved with slow and deliberate steps. As we entered the living room, he waved his hand in a wide circle. The walls were bare with discolored squares and rectangles where the paintings once hung. Stripped of its artwork the house sounds rang through the rooms like a dour echo inside an emptied trashcan. The cheerless walls looked as if they'd been assaulted, their clothes ripped brutally from them by uncaring hands.

The Count looked equally dejected.

"I'm being slowly evicted, I fear," he said. "Not that the house or the paintings were mine. This has been my home for the last four years and

I have little to go back to in Europe."

"I know it's not a good time for you and I appreciate you seeing me," I said. "I asked if they had taken all the paintings."

With no hesitation he said, "Come with me." He turned and I followed.

I had no idea what I was looking for or hoping to find as I trailed behind Sergio upstairs directly to the Caravaggio room.

He started to open the panels, then stopped.

"This must look odd to you, Mr. Roberts, but I want you to understand something," the Count said. "I did not keep this painting for myself. Martha wanted it this way. Her husband bought it in good faith after the war, but later he learned it had once belonged to Goering, who had purchased it for a ridiculously low price from a Viennese Jew trying to appease the Reich Marshal. Of course it didn't help him—the poor man and his family died in Auschwitz. His brother's family fled to Argentina in '38, and a few years after the war ended they listed the painting as looted. An international watch was placed on it. For whatever reason, Martha's husband did not want to return it so he built this room. Martha always warned me against letting anyone know about it, even the children. Afraid of *soiling* Papa's image."

"Then why did you show it to me in the first place?"

"I know you find it amusing, but as I said, Mr. Roberts, I trust you. I may be a kept man, but I'm not a thief," Count Sergio Ordenoff said.

He turned on his heels and left. For the first time I realized the title was not merely honorary.

Alone, I took the painting down, removed it from its frame and held it out straight. It was beautiful; it was obviously a masterpiece. What makes a painting a masterpiece is what makes art, art. We are snared by the artist. The paintings draw us in, like sirens draw boats upon the rocks, playing on our senses and our emotions until we tiptoe away exhilarated and exhausted, mere sycophants in the hands of a master puppeteer.

But a painting is not strictly a visual medium. It attacks all the senses. I sniffed the Caravaggio. It smelled genuine as and looked as real as any sixteenth century painting I had ever had the privilege of examining this closely. Yet as I gripped it in my hands, I did not feel the exuberant aura a painter leaves with his paintings. I did not feel the history. I did not feel the past or the pain of that troubled artist, the same intuition I'd felt the first time I examined it.

Not sure what I was looking for, I examined the painting's sides and then laid it against the wall and stepped back. Something was amiss but I couldn't say what. Slowly I took another step back and cocked my head. The dark moody Caravaggio was sucking me in. I paced back and forth in front of the painting like a caged beast trapped in an enigma.

I was about to sit down when I noticed a flicker—no, a flake—of color where no color should be. Then it disappeared.

I stopped and with slow, deliberate motions moved to the left. The painting flickered again. I cocked my head and lifted the painting, turning it slowly to the right. There it was again. On the side in the lower left hand corner, between the grim lines and foreboding hues, almost obscured by the folded canvas rabbit-ear, I could make out an image -- a hologram-like sketch. Lifting the painting up to the light, I slowly shifted my vision to the left and again it flickered.

Then I saw it. Deeply embedded in the background was an unmistakable flaw that could only be seen at an obtuse angle from the left side. It was a black vertical snake less than a half-centimeter long. It was genius. The forger had signed his painting.

I sat down on the couch and let out a sigh. My stomach turned and waves of exhausting exhilaration pounded my senses. The hair on my arms stood at attention and I fought back tears. I wanted to suffer as this lost painting had suffered. I needed pain to understand the painting's agony. First it had survived three hundred years in a troubled Europe. Then it had tolerated the evil eyes of Hermann Wilhelm Goering and his villainous cohorts. Once again, it endured a tedious separation from its proper home and a beautiful, meticulously painted surrogate, with a false claim, lay in its place. It was an injustice that screamed to be righted.

If I had not at first seen the serpent, what else had I missed? What other snakes were laying in plain sight and I couldn't see them? Had my Gift let me down or was I too consumed, too obsessed to listen, to feel, to believe. It would not have been the first time.

I let the copy fall to the floor and ran downstairs.

I found the Count in the library smoking a pipe. He clumsily laid it down in an oversized ashtray and brushed off imagined ashes from his front. "Sorry. Martha hated for me to smoke in the house. Said it damaged the paintings and the furniture."

"You said the handyman came with impeccable references. Do you remember whose?" I asked.

He tapped the ashes out of the pipe and placed it in his pocket. "Martha handled all of that but I'm sure there is an application somewhere. She had a file where she kept all of the work applications."

I followed him towards the back of the house into a study with a view of the manicured lawn sweeping to ocean. He sat down at a large yew desk and rifled through a drawer, finally pulling out a bright green file. He began to leaf through it.

"Funny, his application's gone. I know it was here with the other work applications. Martha was a meticulous record keeper. Wait—," From the back of the drawer, he retrieved a second folder. "Here, I remember he came with a girl who wanted to do cleaning. Here it is," he said, pulling out a formwork application. "Says here both were recommended by Sue Ellen Cornfield."

Of the Cornfield Mining fortune fame.

"And Mr. Nigel Jenkins," he added.

Nigel?

"Do you have the girl's name and her contact information?"

"Dahlia Kapofsky, it says here. Lives in Lake Worth. Is any of this important?"

"I'm not sure," I said

I jotted down the address—7486 Orange Grove Lane—and the telephone number. "I'll give her a call." I watched the Count place the folder back into the drawer. "Sergio, I want to ask you something that's has been bothering me since the first day you came by the gallery. Why did you and Martha want me to appraise your paintings?"

"Martha's paintings. Once they're authenticated, most go to the Norton Museum now, in Martha and her husband's name. It'll be referred to as the Manley Collection, I suppose." He stopped and gave an audible sigh. "You see, Mr. Roberts, Martha insisted on you. She wanted someone discreet."

"You mean someone who wouldn't be forced by law to broadcast to the entire art world that the paintings were forgeries."

Forged paintings, like counterfeit hundred dollar bills, are hard to dispose of once identified, but they often can slip by unnoticed if they're commingled with legitimate paintings.

"You do not give yourself enough credit, Mr. Roberts. You might not know it, but you have a name on The Island as a man who can be trusted. And I concur."

Flattery. I love it.

"You are friends with the lieutenant investigating Martha's death, I understand," the Count said.

"Adam and I've worked together in the past, though this case is straining that relationship."

"Does that make you a private detective or something like that?"

"No, no. Not at all. I deal in art. If you need a PI, I can recommend someone."

"I don't know if I need a PI, as you call them, but I do need some help."

"If you don't mind sharing, I'd like to ask a few questions. Maybe I can help."

"Share? My whole life is plastered over every tabloid newspaper in the country. Ask whatever you want." He turned the chair towards me and crossed his legs, ready for interrogation.

"You two came down in September. Rather early, wasn't it?"

"Martha was hoping to catch a hurricane."

"A hurricane?"

"She wanted to experience one."

"Here?"

"Right here. Said she was going to refuse any evacuation order. She was so disappointed in last year's hurricane season. She was here for Francis and Jeanne and then Wilma. Never evacuated. She stayed right here. Again she was disappointed. None of them were direct hits."

"And what did she expect you to do during a hurricane?"

"A gentleman never abandons a lady. I'd be okay as long as the vodka and Glenfiddich scotch held out. I'm no hero and I don't think she would have really cared if I stayed or not. Please realize Martha had everything. She could go anywhere. She liked the idea of something adventurous coming to her."

"Like men?" I said without thinking. I was afraid I had insulted him, but he shrugged his shoulders.

"How about that drink? I know I need one."

We went into the kitchen. Raymundo was nowhere to be seen. Without asking, the Count poured two Russian Standard Vodkas over ice.

"Martha was an interesting woman," he said, handing me my glass. "Very intelligent and capable. When I first met her, I was nearly broke. Still am. I was living on a Bulgarian government pension and a few family jewels my father was able to hide after the communist takeover. I was still invited to the proper circles—that was where Martha and I met, in Berlin. She wanted a husband and a title and I needed a steady income. Or at least a place to live. So we married. I never saw her fascination with the handyman. Sure he was big and I suppose virile . . . but the tattoos! He was part of their little club."

"Club?"

"Well, not a formal club with presidents and meetings. Martha and her friends would get together and share."

"Share?"

"Yes. Men. Men like the handyman."

"Are you telling me that your wife and her friends were sharing gigolos?"

The Count took a long sip.

Had Melanie Cabot Moore been hinting about this club? A Palm Beach Ladies' Gigolo Club? How intriguing. That information would make the Shiny Sheet shine brighter than a supernova. An entire brave new world of impossibilities had opened up. So many doors, so much danger for someone whose livelihood depended on the goodwill of wealthy patrons -- like yours truly. Billy Balls, Dahlia Kapofsky, and Nigel Jenkins, not to mention Martha Manley and Melanie Moore. Explosive stuff. I could ask Melanie Moore or Nigel about Billy Balls and Dahlia Kapofsky, but I'd lose two potential customers and I was not about to burn any bridges on a vague hunch. Still I had to ask myself, was Sue Ellen Cornfield another one of Billy's clients?

Before I tried to jump that grand canyon, I made some simple inquires. First I called Ms. Kapofsky's number. A woman who only spoke Spanish answered. "No live here. *Numero nuevo.*" Information informed me that they had no listing for a Ms. Kapofsky. I knew the area and MapQuest showed the address a block from the Intracoastal in Lake Worth.

CHAPTER 35

Following the map I'd printed out on MapQuest, I took Route 1 along the coast, past Ibis Island though south Palm Beach, where stately homes begrudgingly gave way to a tropical New York City on a small short strip of land that the more parochial referred to as the Gaza Strip.

At Lake Worth Casino, a former gambling den now bath house, I crossed the Intracoastal to the town of Lake Worth. Four blocks later I spotted the four-story apartment building, a nineteen eighties idea of neo-modern Florida architecture. Painted rosette and teal, its one redeeming quality was the lack of pink plastic flamingos standing in the entrance. Inside, a uniformed doorman looked up from a Frank Miller comic book. He was short and dark with a scowl that had prematurely creased his forehead. A five o'clock shadow discolored his recessed jaw and a pair of granny glasses rode low on his pug but off-centered nose.

"Good day," I said with my biggest disarming smile. "I'm looking for Dahlia Kapofsky." I said.

"Not here. Never hear of her," he answered with a thick non-Hispanic accent.

"She worked for a client of mine and left this address as her place of residence."

"No. I tell you no Dahlia here. Never here."

He pressed his lips together and hunched his shoulders in close like a cobra ready to strike. Before I could ask another question, he waved me away. I thanked him and turned to leave. Before I made it to the door, I heard him dialing a telephone and talking loudly in a foreign language.

As I hopped into the Jag a pair of seasoned citizens pedal down the sidewalk on oversized tricycles loaded with plastic Publix grocery bags. Another dead end, I thought.

I dialed Margot.

"Carmine Colletti just hung up. Said please call him a.s.a.p. Didn't say why," she said. "Are you coming in?"

"Okay, I'll see what Carmine wants first then I'll be in. Didn't know he was back from Italy."

Carmine Colletti was owner of Colletti Galleries on Worth Avenue's gallery row. Carmine specialized in early twentieth century Italian landscapes and prints. Over the years he had traded me quality Italianate paintings.

"I'm glad you called," Carmine chimed. "I have something that might interest you."

"Another print?"

"Maria told me you stopped by while I was in Italy asking about old master copies," he said. "I might have something that'd interest you."

"I'll be right over," I said and started the engine. As I was about to pull away from the curb, a dark green Lincoln Navigator came around the corner and stopped in front of the apartment building. Two men dressed like undertakers got out. One turned and stared at me. I was used to people checking out the Jag so I gave a friendly wave, put on my driving hat and drove off.

Worth Avenue was crowded; every parking space was preempted by a Mercedes, a BMW, or a Lexus. Not wanting to pay for valet parking I took a left onto Golfview Road, ignoring the private way sign, and made another left in front of the tennis courts next to the Everglades Club down the tight alley that sliced between Worth Avenue and Golfview Road. On the left was the working end of the commercial establishments along Worth Avenue and on the right the garages and parking area of the houses overlooking the Everglades golf course. The intentionally un-maintained way looked more like a Lantana back alley than Palm Beach but it kept out the drive-throughs. About half way down I pulled into a cramped parking area in the back of a house that fronted Golfview. A Belgian client owned the home and I knew he wouldn't be down until after the New Year. During Season it was my secret parking area.

The alley way was, as usual, empty so I hoofed back out to Golfview then across Worth Avenue. The Colletti Gallery was on the north side of the street near the entrance of Via de Mario and caddie corner from the Philips Galleries and Arcature Fine Art galleries and just up the street from Dickie Durdle's Wellington Green. Location, location, location.

"Nice of you to stop by," Carmine greeted me with a toothy smile as I walked through the double-doors. He was round, with a round face, brown hair, bright brown eyes, and thick eyebrows that gave him a Botero look except for perfect cut of his hand-tailored Brioni silk suit. Maria, his attractive dark-haired Moderna-born wife, waved from the back desk. She was his hands-on, receptionist, archivist and vender, and the reason Colletti Galleries did well.

"The place looks good," I said. "Nice set of early manniseristic prints on the side wall."

"Thank you. Just got them in. Would you have anyone who'd be interested in them?"

"Not right, I'm afraid. But . . . "

"I understand. If you hear of anyone you'll call."

We both laughed. Carmine had a hearty laugh that sounded like a love-struck bufo toad.

"How was Italy?"

"The Euro is still killing us. I was in Reggio Calabria. It's the only place you can find bargains in Italy anymore." Carmine stood up straight cleared his throat and glanced at the front door. "The reason for my call was your interest in old master copies." Carmine paused for a moment then turned. "Come with me."

I followed him into a back office. From a bottom desk drawer, he pulled out four photographs and handed them to me. They were of Renoir's still life, *Peaches*. The original, I knew, was on the Island hanging in Amy Stutesbury's house.

"I bought it from a pawnbroker in Lake Worth. He's more or less straight and comes across some worthwhile antiques. Of course it had to be a copy but it was so convincing. I mean it was perfect. I knew the original was owned by the Stutesburys, so I called her. You know Amy Stutesbury. She can be fickle. If you're not on the A-list, then you're a nonentity. Anyway, I never reached her but her secretary told me the painting was hanging where it always had, safe and sound. Matter of fact, she got a bit agitated so I let it drop. Then in March, the gallery was broken into and the Renoir copy was stolen along with a couple of prints. For some reason, I was sure what they were really after was the Renoir—the prints were a cover. But I didn't want to cloud the situation so I let the insurance pay and forgot about it. Until Maria mentioned you called."

"After the robbery I called the pawnbroker and he told me he learned through a third party that the guy who sold it to him had taken it out of the back seat of a Mercedes. Said he'd take it back and seemed relieved when I said it'd been stolen from my gallery."

"Did you have it examined?"

"No, I thought about it but never got around to doing anything except taking these pictures. There have been a lot of rumors running around about forgeries and worse. Do you know anything?"

"Not much, except that there's a forger out there. He's good, and he's done a lot of different paintings. I'd like to track him down,"

"Did you talk to Christina Hagan?"

"Sure did. She says she doesn't know anyone."

"Well she's been working overtime I hear."

"Do you think she could have done this copy?" I asked eyeing the photographs.

"Christine can paint anything. She's one of the best."

"Are you sure the painting was a copy and not the real thing?"

"What are you saying? That it was a real Renoir? I wish." He thought for a moment. "It was good, I'll tell you that."

"It's just a theory of mine. Nothing concrete," I said. "Could I have photocopies of these pictures?"

"Of course. But you can't tell much by these photos but the painting was good. It could have fooled anybody."

After Carmine made the copies I left the gallery back to the alley.

Carmine's information and the photographs strengthened my suspicions about a master forger. What if the painting Carmine bought was the original and not a copy? What if, like the Manley paintings, a copy was hanging in the Stutesbury house? Whoever stole the painting from the Mercedes had no idea what he had, so he pawned it. Perhaps the Mercedes was the forger's car. Maybe that was the reason he had to break into Carmine's gallery and steal it back.

I was wondering where all this fit in with the Manley murder when I noticed my path down the alley was blocked by the undertaker types I'd seen at Dahlia Kapofsky's apartment building.

"Who are you?" the one on the right growled in heavily accented English.

I started to look behind me when the growler, the larger of the two, grabbed me by the collar, lifted me off my feet and shoved me against a brick wall.

"You deaf? I asked, 'Who the fuck are you?'"

"I'm Maxie Roberts, an art dealer," I quickly said. I was fidgeting for a business card when he slammed my arm back.

They talked to each other in thick tongue-tied gibberish like the Lake Worth apartment concierge.

"What you want with Dahlia Kapofsky?"

"She worked for a client of mine and I—,"

He slammed his fist into my stomach. I bent over and grabbed my gut.

"You look like troublemaker."

"Not me," I said, gasping for breath. "I don't want any—,"

The other guy straightened me up and the first kneed me in the groin. I doubled over from the pain.

"You stay away from Dahlia Kapofsky. Forget about her," he shouted. "Or next time—," He waved a snub-nosed Smith and Wesson .38 revolver in my face.

I shook my head up and down like a puppy dog in the back window of a Yugo.

More gibberish, a few grunts, then they disappeared down the alley.

From Cold War days, I recognized the word, "*Nyet.*"

The undertakers were Russians.

For a good ten minutes I leaned against the brick wall waiting for the pain in my lower stomach to subside. By the time I could straighten up, Bernie's words echoed in my head. He was right. This was crazy. When did Maxie Roberts become a punching bag for all the lowlifes in Palm Beach County? And where did the Russians fit in? They've always been excellent forgers. Was the Russian Art Mafia catering to their *nouveau-riche* compatriots? Those tawdry tourists dressed in loud clothes with bad manners and billfolds bulging with dollars and Euros made after the Soviet Union collapsed? Not on The Island, of course. They'd stand out like fish and chips at Café L'Europe. You'll find them trolling the fine arts establishments of Fort Lauderdale and Miami, places where they feel more at home. They were definitely here—they bought and bought big. Were they forging the paintings or just buying stolen artwork and taking it back to Russia? This forger was sophisticated and wily. The Russian Mafia was not known for subtlety. I heard they prefer AK-47s to .22s.

I had to admit; the Russian connection was intriguing, if painful. After all, the Count was actually Russian, not Bulgarian. His parents had emigrated to the Balkan workers' paradise -- pre-Soviet takeover, of course.

Russians are not new to Palm Beach. Oddly it has one of the highest percentages of Russians émigrés in the country. One of our most beloved mayors, Paul Romanovsky-Ilyinsky, was a Romanov. His father had killed the mad monk Rasputin. "I'm the only Romanov to be elected to public office." he liked to say. Ilyinsky's election reflected our island's love affair with the eclectic and the royal.

An even newer breed of Russian was moving in. A Saint Petersburg billionaire, who, if you believe rumors, had made his money in phosphate, purchased a Donald Trump mansion for a paltry one hundred million dollars. He said he planned to raze the structure and build a new mansion making it the most expensive teardown ever.

Wonder if he's in the market for a painting.

Still clutching my gut I turned towards the Jag. Right now, I just wanted to get back to the gallery as fast as possible. I *can* take a hint.

CHAPTER 36

"Why are you limping?" Margot asked as I hobbled into the gallery.

"Stubbed my toe getting out of the car."

Margot stifled a disbelieving grunt and a smile and said, "Mr. Samuel Hoffman, Picasso man, called. He wants to see the *Crying Dora.* And Adam Aldrich wants you to call him."

"If Sam calls again, tell him I'll call him. Let him know that another party is interested in the painting," I said. "Better still. Why don't you set up a showing at his house?"

"At the standard commission?"

"Of course. Just sell it. I have a little errand to run first," I said.

Margot lifted up the receiver and dialed. "Good afternoon, Mister Hoffman. It's Margot Miller from the Roberts Fine Art Gallery . . . Fine thank you . . . Why yes . . . Of course, of course . . . Okay, Sam . . ." She winked at me and I left appreciating that only in Palm Beach can a young woman drive alone around The Island in a four-year-old purple Plymouth PT Cruiser with a million dollar painting sitting in her back seat and feel safe.

Adam suggested we meet at Ta-boo at five. Police telephone calls are routinely recorded and the sensitive information I had culled about the Palm Beach Ladies' Gigolo Club was for Adam's ears only.

I walked the eight blocks to Worth Avenue then took a right and up the half block to Ta-boo. Inside the restaurant was dark and I paused for my eyes to adjust. First I checked out the front dining area then walked back along the long bar past the monkey motifs on the wall to the main dining room in the back—The Island's cat walk. Taboo, especially at night, is where you can strut your stuff by the barflies. I asked the hostess for a corner table away from the fireplace. The few patrons were mostly late lunchers, probably locals. Later, in the evening, the crowd would drastically change. At night, Ta-boo was one of The Island's best pickup bars.

Adam ambled in five minutes later.

The pressure on Adam was telling, as the off-colored semicircles under his eyes testified. The Island denizens were demanding instant results. Their precious enclave had been deconsecrated and despoiled. A sacrifice was needed and the Count, available and suddenly redundant, fit the bill nicely. But pressure, political or otherwise, was not going to rush Lieutenant Adam Aldrick. He knew how to build a case, a case that the Palm Beach County state attorney could prosecute with half his brain tied behind his back.

Adam took the chair to my right swinging his leg to one side.

"It's the weather," he said.

"How do you chase down the bad guys with that leg?"

"That's what my automatic is for." he said and patted his left side. "But you know something funny, when I start to run it doesn't bother me. It's just when I still stand or sit."

We ordered two glasses of red wine and a plate of warm bruschetta.

"How is your case going?"

"To tell the truth, it's no longer my case," Adam glanced at the diners then ran his fingers slowly through his hair. "Well what do you have?"

I gave Adam the titillating but abbreviated version of the PBLG Club. To my chagrin he did not seem to be giving it the attention I felt it deserved. After taking a few notes he laid down his pen. I was offended and gave him my best pout. Was my Dashiel Hammell-level sleuthing being relegated to the status of idle island gossip?

"I wish I could thank you for this information," he said. "But you've just thrown me one heck of a curve ball and I don't want to get beamed with it.

"Okay, say there's some kind of sexual connection between Baldwin and Martha Manley. That doesn't change anything. We've got Baldwin at the Manley house without any innuendoes regarding our leading ladies. Draw your own conclusions. I couldn't even breathe a word of this, this little sex club, if I wanted to keep my job."

"Melanie Moore told me Sergio had a girlfriend."

"We know about your client's girlfriend," Adam said. "Visited the young lady like clockwork, every Tuesday and Thursday."

"Come on, Adam, are you suggesting he killed his wife so he could be with some bimbo? Isn't that reaching for a motive?"

"It happens. But that's not all. Martha Manley had a prenuptial with Ordenoff."

"Everybody has a prenup," I said "I heard that except for the artwork, the children get everything and most of that money is already in trusts."

"Not everything. If Sergio Ordenoff and Martha remained married for five years, he got five hundred and fifty thousand dollars. After ten years, a solid million. A nice escalation clause."

"So?"

"The five years just finished. Maybe he couldn't take another five years of marital bliss with Ms. Manley."

"Jesus, Adam. Five hundred and fifty thousand is the Manley bar tab for six months."

"We don't know that. But we've heard the Count has some expensive habits. He makes 900 calls to a phone sex service." Adam said with a chuckle. "Spent thousands of dollars."

"Everybody likes sex, Adam," I said.

"So you've told me," he said, tapping his notebook with his pen.

I ignored the dig and reached for a piece of bread when a shot of pain hit my side and lower stomach where the Russian contingent had done their best work. I winced and rubbed my side.

"You okay?" Adam asked.

I shook my head yes. "A little stomach pain that's all." Before he could ask more I said, "Somehow the forgeries, Martha's murder and the fire are connected. And the Manleys weren't the only people with forgery problems. It could be much wider spread than anyone can imagine. Dickie Durdle had a client that—,"

"Dickie Durdle. Isn't he the chap who got his foreskin caught in his fly while taking a midnight pee on Cocoanut Row?" Adam said.

I said nothing. As a matter of personal integrity, I refuse to defend the undefendable. "Have a little sympathy for the guy. Someone shot at him," I said.

"Are you sure?" Adam turned in his chair.

"That's what he said."

"Oh. Well, have him call me."

I was getting nowhere with the Palm Beach Ladies Gigolo club so I told him of my alleyway run-in with the darkly dressed gentlemen with heavy hands and bad manners.

"That's your little stomach pain? For all you know, they could be jealous boyfriends or Ms. Kapofsky's pimps. Do you want to file a complaint?"

"I can't afford to."

My eye caught a lovely lady strutting down the cat walk by the long bar with so glorious a blond mane she could have supplanted Blaine Trump as "Her Blondness." Following dutifully three steps behind her was one of Worth Avenues top jewelers whose shop was four doors down. We both turned as they passed by.

"You can look at some mug books if you want," Adam said, getting back to business.

"It'd be a waste of time. They all look the same."

"Suit yourself then, but it sounds like someone is trying to give you a warning."

"I'm just trying to help," I said.

"Help? I'm trying to solve a case. All you've done is muck up the waters."

"That's not fair."

"For the moment your new information will remain between us. Okay? But I'm telling you, Maxie, you're walking a thin line. Give me something that I can give to the sharks. I sure as hell can't give Putzer Melanie Cabot Moore, or suggest Martha Manley was part of a sex club. We need something concrete or else Putzer's going to throw your sorry ass in jail for interfering with an ongoing police investigation and I won't be able to help you."

He stared into the dark liquid in his glass as if somewhere at the bottom of the glass was an answer.

"Maxie, we've worked well together in the past and I trust your instincts. But you have to understand that this case has become political."

"And what about justice? Does politics trump justice?"

"Justice is relative. You learn early in this business the appearance of justice is more important than actual justice."

"Even if it means an innocent man is condemned?"

"If he looks guilty and there is a public clamor for punishment then innocent people are sacrificed in the name of justice. As I said, the appearance is more important to the system than guilt. It gives the public's faith in the system. Without public support the justice system would collapse."

"You don't buy into that do you?"

"I want solve the Manley case as much as anyone, but it makes no difference what I believe." Adam swirled his wine nervously. "I don't want to think about it right now." He stopped swirling and took a sip. "There is a Mostly Mozart concert at the Kravis in a couple of weeks. They're going to play a two of his piano concertos and the overtures from *Don Giovanni* and *The Magic Flute*. Are you going?"

"I'd love to but the kids are coming down that week. I'm worried about them being here with the guys who set the fire out there somewhere. I can't expose them to that."

"I'll assign someone to watch your place."

"That's all I need."

Adam finished his wine and stood up and grunted. "I got to run." As he turned he stopped short and made a face. He put his leg out in front of him and stretched it before disappearing through the bar.

190 Palm Beach Confidential

CHAPTER 38

It was dusk and two wines later by the time I left Ta-boo. The evening air was cool and winter refreshing. Walking back to the gallery I wondered if I was persevering or just being obsessive in my search for the forger. Obsession, I was told, killed my marriage. No, I insisted, it was perseverance, but I was overruled by Nancy. When does one become the other? For years I searched through flea markets and back-street galleries in a never-ending quest for lost masterpieces. Our weekends, between bouts of lovemaking, were spent in musty antique shops flipping through stacks of paintings, prints, and etchings. I found my share, including *The Lady of The Lake*. I blindly assumed Nancy shared my passion. What she shared was love.

Nancy often called me her Don Quixote, her Knight of the Sorrowful Countenance, charging windmills on my trusty Rosinante with erotic dreams of the seraphic Dulcinea driving me onward. During our infatuation stage she thought it was cute, a character flaw she was sure she could cure. Like a young woman nursing an alcoholic, there was no future in it. Dependence and desire do not love make. For Nancy, reality set in, exposing obsession for what it was. Love and liking were forced to take a back seat to practicality and position. By the time I realized that, she was gone.

Maybe I was more like Billy Balls than I'd ever want to admit: we both were in a perpetual quest for the big one. I'd found mine. And like a narcotic boost, the adrenalin-driven opiate apotheosis careening through my veins satisfied me for a while, until it became worn out and old hat. Bernie was right when he quoted Friedrich Nietzsche: *The secret of reaping the greatest fruitfulness and the greatest enjoyment from life is to live dangerously.* But at what cost? They tell me I am always sailing the thin line between hubris and hearth. Whatever that means.

These mind-boggling thoughts were not helping my mental state. I was feeling like the Florida coastline, low and vulnerable, a state exacerbated by forced bachelorhood. I longed for the feminine touch – a hug, a caress, even a cuddle. Indeed, *The Lady of the Lake* could offer scant solace to my desperate doldrums. My inner voice cried: *A woman, a woman, my art collection for a woman!*

Well, that shocking thought brought me crashing back to reality and its conjunctive clichés, supplemented by a call from Dickie Durdle. After the alleged shooting, Dickie Durdle was laying low. Exactly where he never volunteered.

"We have to talk," Dickie said to me in a disguised voice that sounded like Auntie May on testosterone. "Can you meet me at the Chesterfield Leopard Lounge in an hour?"

I said yes but this time I'd drive.

The Chesterfield Hotel off Cocoanut Row, three short blocks north of Worth Avenue, was a Palm Beach icon. Entering through the front patio garden, the intimate lobby and sitting rooms give one a feel of a home rather than a hotel. That intimacy abruptly ends through the doors to the right that lead to the Leopard Lounge. The core color is bordello red, a theme accentuated by the line of ladies with drinks in front of them sitting at the bar. In any other South Florida bar they would be working girls, except the mean age of these Leopard Lounge lizardettes was sixty-three. Hey, it's Palm Beach.

The band played dance music and three couples spun around on the light-encrusted dance floor. Dickie was seated in the corner at the far end of the bar with his back to the wall. Obviously he'd seen *The Godfather*. He was talking with two wide-eyed, slightly wrinkled dowagers at least twice his age. They were enthralled with Dickie, not that he was so entertaining or a financial catch, but he was male, and a breathing one at that, a commodity much in demand by the late-night ladies. As I walked up behind Dickie, eight pair of eyes locked on me for a good thirty seconds. I ordered a Cape Codder with no lime.

"Dickie, I think if you wanted to blend in with the locals you could have picked a less obvious place."

"This is perfect. It's the gay nineties. All the men are gay and all the women are over ninety. Do you know any assassins over ninety or gay?"

As a matter of fact I did.

The lady on Dickie's right was leaning over him. She either ignored his disguise or hoped against hope that he was straight enough to get it up once more.

Her companion said to no one in particular, "Good god, did she really do that? That's so basically Boca."

"Let's get a table," I said.

Dickie grabbed his drink and we moved to a corner cocktail table. Behind us I heard one of the ladies, "They must be gay."

That was the second time I'd heard that in two days. Not good.

"I think my Pissaro is a fake."

"Aseneth told me. What about the O'Keeffe?"

"I sold it," Dickie said. He allowed a curt smile. "Melanie Moore was quite happy. Anyway, do you remember Jon Gustafson?"

"Jupiter Jon?"

Dickie nodded. "He traded me three Juan Gris prints for a Matisse cutout. I always thought I'd gotten the better deal. I sold the Matisse to Joyce Newman. A week later she called and said it wasn't an original work. Good god, you know Matisse's cutouts. How can anyone tell? Well, like a good boy I took it back. You remember Jon was killed in a boating accident two years ago off the Jupiter Inlet? I'm now sure he was murdered to keep him quiet about the fake Matisse."

Dickie never let jumped-to conclusions interfere with facts. "*Art is dangerous,*" Anthony Burgess once said, and in Palm Beach it had gotten a bit more so.

"What do you expect me to do?"

"I don't know but this has gotten out of hand. I'm seriously considering leaving for California."

"Have a safe trip," I said. "Have any of your people mentioned anything more about the Manley collection?"

"That was a closely held collection."

"How about the kids? Frederick or Mary Martha?"

He shook his head.

"Anything new on Christina Hagan?"

"Just what I told you the last time. But you might try Warren Wright, her old boyfriend. Remember him?"

"The guy in that DUI case last spring on the Flagler Bridge?"

"Yep. I heard he's mad at Christina for dumping him. Said that's why he was drinking."

"How about Nigel Jenkins?"

"He's very well-liked, by all sexes."

"So I understand." A round of boisterous laughter rolled from the end of the bar.

"It's been said that he and Marcus were an item."

"What! Are we talking about the same Marcus Oberlin, former NFL Miami Dolphin linebacker with shoulders you could drive a Greyhound bus over?"

"Yes. Don't they have tight ends?"

"I didn't hear that."

"Well, Maxie, you must know not everyone in the queer community is a screaming queen. Big boys are welcomed, even demanded."

"I'll let that one go, thank you."

"Suit yourself," Dickie said. "By the way. Melanie asked me to please stay away from her daughter. I didn't even know she had a daughter, Maxie. Do you know anything about it?"

"Can't say that I do."

CHAPTER 38

The next morning at my office desk, I felt rested and almost cheerful as I stared at the empty space where the Picasso once hung. After paying the owner and Margot her commission, I had not a huge, but a nice, balance left over. A sure mood-raiser. My dilemma was: should I pay my bills or purchase that Sargent sketch. I was imagining the print hanging where the Picasso once hung when the telephone rang.

"I found Kiki. He's here," Zelda said.

"He's where?" I asked. Suddenly I had vivid pictures of a Hell's Angel gang camped out on the loggia guzzling my wine collection.

"Somewhere in the Acreage. I've got his address from a girl I used to work with. He's staying at her boyfriend's sister's house. If you want to catch him, we'd better do it as soon as possible. No telling when he'll split."

"You think it's safe?"

She laughed. "He's alone. But don't worry, you'll be with me. The Pariahs have an unwritten rule. They don't kill friends of friends." She laughed again. "At least not right away."

"Okay, I get it," I said. I didn't mind a little levity at my expense. It was the first time I'd heard Zelda laugh.

I picked Zelda up at the house and traded the Jag for the Everglades buggy and headed west. Kiki Cohen was holed up in a house in a rural development called the Acreage. Aside from hanging a hammock between two palm trees in the Big Cypress National Preserve, the Acreage was about the best place for a fugitive to hide. It was one of the thousands of Florida real estate scams perpetuated by developers since the state was taken from Spain in 1821. If Wellington represented the new mega-development, the Acreage was solidly set as an old Florida land scheme. The Great Depression, World War II, and the post-War boom had thankfully bypassed the Acreage until now. Much of Palm Beach County was again in the grasp of developers. Formerly pristine lands were falling under bulldozer blades at an alarming rate. Development pressures and urban sprawl had found this corner of the Everglades. Large houses have sprung up on lots formerly fit only for coral snakes and rabid raccoons. Parts of the Acreage, though, have kept its quaint charm.

Kiki had found that part.

I was deftly maneuvering the buggy around a pothole with a flattened armadillo in the middle when Zelda leaned over and said, "I want you to promise me that nothing will happen to Kiki."

"If you recall, we are both in a pretty bad situation, Zelda. Billy's murderers are still out there and Kiki may have some answers." I didn't want to emphasize that one of those murderers was probably Billy.

"I don't want you to say anything to the police or the lawyers."

"Let's make a deal. I need to tell the lieutenant that we have a witness. He's a friend of mine and I won't tell him where Kiki is unless I think any of our lives are at stake. Okay?"

Zelda gave a slight nod.

I was driving slowly to keep the dust down. Many of the roads were unpaved, a state some of the residents regarded as a mark of individuality and pride, far from civilization but too close to the Everglades if you asked the alligators and water moccasins scurrying through the canals. Large sections of the area were still underwater during part of the rainy season, much to the distress and ceaseless complaints of the newer residents. The old-timers didn't complain. They waited the high water out. The original inhabitants, the Seminoles, never complained either. Probably because they had all left a hundred years ago and were now living in luxury at the Seminole Reservation Hard Rock Casino outside of Fort Lauderdale.

Bikers, for the most part, are naturally gregarious creatures, thus Kiki's self-enforced isolation was an anomaly probably fueled by fear. So what did Kiki know, and who or what was he hiding from?

From beyond the tree line I heard a deep, bellowing roar.

"Tigers," said Zelda. "The couple on the next block takes in tigers and lions that have gotten too big for their owners or that zoos no longer want. Really nice people."

"Wonder what their beef bill is, three homeless per day?"

"Down the street, a lady has a bird farm where she raises hundreds of exotic birds. There's a llama farm two blocks over. I'm telling you; out here it's a sanctuary. You know, live and let live. No one gets into your business. I kinda like it."

"A regular animal farm," I said. Four legs good, two legs better.

I stopped the buggy in front of a low-lying cinder brick house that had once been painted aquamarine and cut the engine. A midnight blue chopped Harley Davidson motorcycle with high handlebars and fake bullet hole decals was parked in a dirt driveway beside a partially repaired all-terrain vehicle. The yard, overgrown with ragweed and young cabbage palms, had never seen the working end of a lawn mower. All in all, an xeriscpist's dream that gave the house a certain white-trash charm.

That charm was quickly dispelled when two large pit bulls raced from around back, straight at us. Only a rusting chain-link fence stood between us and a pair of snapping jaws. They leaped toward the top of the fence, barking wildly. Their mouths foamed with slobber and had sets of long, white fangs with no visible cavities.

Unsure if the fence would hold, I jumped back into the buggy, repeating, "Nice doggie, nice doggie."

With no hesitation, Zelda walked up to the fence, reached over and scratched their heads. She opened the gate and squatted.

"Peter and Paul, come here, boys," she said, holding out her arms.

I lost sight of her as the two massive pit bulls jumped and circled her. They licked her face, their massive rumps in constant motion. Obviously they were excited by Zelda, a condition I could readily appreciate.

Zelda stood and started down the front walk, crunching crushed seashells under her feet.

"Kiki! It's Zelda," she yelled out. "Kiki!"

She was halfway up the walk when the screen door creaked opened a crack.

"Goddamned useless mutts. Supposta be fucking watchdogs."

The beat-up screen door swung open and out poked the working end of a Remington twelve gauge shotgun, full-choke. A small hairy gnome-like creature stared at Zelda with bloodshot eyes. He shot a glaring glance at me.

"Who the hell is that?"

"He's a friend, Kiki. He's trying to help me."

Kiki cased the yard before he lowered the barrel of the shotgun and waved us inside.

Kiki Cohen was a skinny Hell's Angels wannabe with a wild goatee and long stringy brown hair pulled back in an off-centered ponytail. For a biker he looked like a pushover. He was all of a hundred fifty pounds of skin and bone. Wispy facial hairs discolored his cheeks and he had the feral eyes of a creature that naps but never sleeps. His body was covered with self-inflicted tattoos. On his right arm he sported two faded skulls facing each other over a waving banner that read, in blue, "Death To All Those Who Whimper And Cry." Obviously Kiki Cohen was a Bob Dylan fan.

Inside smelled of stale cigarettes, wet dogs, and week-old beer. Clearly the cleaning lady had not made an appearance in many months, judging from the distinct aroma of aged cat piss wafting through the house. I counted five felines feeding on the kitchen table, which might explain the lack of rats.

"Come on sit down, " Kiki said. "You want a joint?"

Hospitable enough, but Zelda and I both passed.

Kiki plopped down in an overstuffed chair with well-worn arms. The house looked like it had been furnished by a dump picker. An impressive collection of empty beer cans carpeted the floor. Which explained the rotten beer odor.

"Yeah, man," Kiki said. "Watch out for the beer cans. I lay them around so I can hear if anyone is creeping around the house at night," Kiki said.

Logical.

"What happened to Mary?" Zelda asked.

"She left. The bitch took my stash of meth. Can you believe that!" He eyed me again and sat up. "You ain't a fucking cop, are you?"

"He's cool, Kiki. Like I told you, he's helping me. I'm staying at his place and he got me a lawyer. He can help both of us find Billy's killer."

"The only thing that can help me is a one-way ticket to Australia." He sank back into this chair.

"Is that what you want?" I asked.

"What I want is to stay the fuck alive. The brothers can't help me. Shit, they left me out to dry. I don't know how the hell I can help you."

"Why don't you start with you and Billy?"

"You sure you ain't a cop?"

"Kiki," Zelda said softly.

"We was buds. You know, good friends. Billy was smart, you know. Didn't do a lot of dope. Kept his head above water. He was gonna make us rich."

"How was he going to make you rich?"

"He didn't tell me much but he'd hooked up with some rich fuckers and was taking them for a ride."

"Did this involve Martha Manley?"

Kiki's expression changed. "This is all fucked up." He jumped out of his seat and grabbed the shotgun. "I don't have to tell you shit." He swung the shotgun around and snapped off the safety.

"Kiki, Kiki sit down," Zelda yelled. She stood up and placed herself between Kiki and me. "Now."

Kiki paused then sat back down, and put the shotgun on the coffee table. He looked at Zelda then and quietly placed both feet squarely on the floor.

"Look man, all I did was drive him over to Palm Beach and let him out on the main drag by some big mother houses. He said, 'Don't park the car but keep on moving', because the police would question me if I was stopped anywhere near the house after I dropped him off. Billy told me to come back in thirty-five minutes and pick him up a half block down the street. I had to dress up and shove my hair under a hat. You know, look straight. That Billy was smart. Good with details."

"Yeah, he's dead smart," I said.

"Are you sure he ain't a cop?" Kiki said to Zelda.

"It's okay. Just tell him what you know. For me, okay?" Zelda said.

"Listen man, I thought he was knocking off one of those mansions, you know maybe some cash or jewels. I had no idea he'd offed anyone until I read that the old bag got blown away. Later Billy said, 'Don't worry,' he was working on another angle. Said he had something these guys would pay a fortune for. Never told me who they were but he gave me an extra thousand dollars and promised me another five later for helping him. Then he gets hit and now I'm here hiding and out five grand. I'm telling you, life's all fucked-up."

"Did he tell you how he was going to get the extra money for you?"

"Billy always said, 'If it makes money, it makes sense.' Boy, was he smart," Kiki said. "You sure you don't want a drag, man? It's pure Jamaican."

"Do you know why he killed her?"

"Nah, he never said nothing." Kiki reached over to the coffee table, retrieved a half-burnt marijuana joint and lit it. After taking a long drag, he slowly exhaled.

"Do you know if Billy had any partners, or was he working for someone?" I asked.

"Shit, I was his partner, I guess. At least that's what he kept saying. He might have been working for someone cause he had a lot of money before that bitch got killed." Kiki took another puff and placed the roach on the table.

"Do you have any idea if these guys hired him to kill her?"

"Hey, man, I don't know," Kiki said, raising his voice. "I keep telling ya, I don't know."

"We've gotta find the people who killed Billy," Zelda said. "They might be after us."

"I know. Believe me I know." Kiki looked up at Zelda. He fidgeted in his chair, tapped his feet, and pulled at his beard. He grabbed a beer can beside the shotgun and emptied it in one gulp, then dropped it on the floor and kicked it under the table. His head bowed, he stared at his feet.

"Zelda, I gotta say this," he said, finally looking up. "But I've always loved you. I know you were Billy's girl and shit. I wanna take care of you so bad, but just look at me, I can't even take care of me. I'm sorry." He dropped his head and began to rock back and forth in the chair.

"Thank you. Kiki, thank you," she said, looking at me, then the door. "You keep safe now."

"Yeah. Old Kiki the survivor. That's me."

Gingerly stepping over beer cans, Zelda and I quietly left. Outside the two pit bulls were lying down in the shade. In the Jeep as we buckled up, I turned to Zelda. "That answered a lot of questions," I said. "He's a prime witness." Probably the first time Kiki Cohen had been called prime anything.

"Remember what you promised about Kiki."

"This has gotten way beyond trying to protect a friend. He admitted to being a possible an accomplice to a murder and that might be why Billy was killed."

"I know."

"I have to tell the police about it," I said. "He might want to make himself scarce."

Zelda said nothing. She just stared straight ahead then said, "Poor Billy."

Kiki's information put Billy Balls at the scene of the murder. Perhaps Martha Manley caught him stealing something and he killed her. But Jack said only a few cheap jewels were missing. Then what? Had Billy Balls been hired to kill Martha Manley?

Billy was obviously expecting some big money. He'd been paid, and with that money he bought the Vette. Did he, after getting the job of a lifetime, decide to capitalize on it? He was probably paid ten, maybe twenty thousand dollars to put a single bullet into the head of an old woman, a woman he was servicing sexually. A piece of cake. A big pay-day for a small-time thief. But he wanted more. Instead of disposing of the pistol, as a true criminal should, he kept it. Why? To blackmail the people who hired him? His employers would not have been amused. Billy had to go. With Billy dead the only evidence linking them to the killing was the revolver. Therefore, the visit to Zelda's house where the killer found a helping hand. Mine.

And who were my midnight intruders? Bikers? Hardly. If it's Florida, you have to first think narcotics. Art? These guys wouldn't know art if it jumped out at them on I-95 in a clown suit. What was the art connection? That I was determined to find out.

CHAPTER 39

"I'm sorry you have to go through all this."

"It's all right. Billy was always knocking on closed doors."

We headed back along a dirt road paralleling a secondary drainage canal. I drove slowly to keep the dust trail down as low as possible. Obviously the hit or miss thunderstorms had not blessed the Acreage. Dust clouds rolled behind passing vehicles like a super hero's cape. Dirt-smudged bushes lined the side of the road. With its multitude of crisscrossing roads that all looked the same, it's easy to get lost in the Acreage.

I had placed my driving gloves next to the stick shift. Zelda reached over and lifted the left-hand glove with her thumb and forefinger as if she were carrying a dead field mouse by the tail.

"I've been meaning to ask, what are these?"

"Gloves. One hundred percent kidskin."

She shook her head and shrugged her shoulders. "Oh. I had no idea they let you do that to children."

I nodded and we both smiled.

In the rearview mirror I saw a cloud of dust billowing from a speeding car. Not wanting to eat buckets of road dirt, I sped up. If I could make the intersection a mile up the road, I'd turn and let him go by. If not, I'd do the old slow-down-and-drive-in-the-middle of the road eat-my-dust maneuver that got people mad but saved one from unwanted afternoon dust baths.

Another glance in the rearview mirror and I spotted a black SUV in the front of the cloud of light brown dust. *This guy is a real jerk*, I thought. Probably a damned redneck. At the rate the SUV was traveling it would overtake us in a half mile. I was not going to outrun him without speeding; the buggy was not a formula one. I switched to plan B. I slowed and deliberately drove in the middle of the road. He'd have to slow down or drive into the canal.

I heard the guttural roar of a gunned engine thunder up behind us. I looked again in the mirror and saw the chromed grill of a black Escalade outlined in the dust. It was not slowing down.

I hit the accelerator, spewing more dirt into his face, hoping he would get the hint and slow down. Instead, the Escalade leaped out of the dust cloud and plowed into the back of the buggy with a jolt and an ugly crunch.

"What the hell!" Zelda screamed.

"Hang on!" I shouted.

The buggy swerved sideways, its right wheels lifted up. I was thrown against the door as I fought to keep the buggy from tipping over. I swung the wheel around and the buggy straightened out, landing with a thud. Then we were struck again.

"Oh shit!" I yelled.

My head slammed back into the headrest. The rear end of the buggy jumped. We swerved wildly to the right, and the left side of the buggy rose up on end then skidded out of control to the right. The buggy lurched over the edge of the road then careened down the canal bank. With a sickening smack we plunged sideways into the water and flipped over. My head bounced violently into the steering wheel. The air bag exploded in my face and I was slapped back against the seat. Before I could react I was under water.

Black, mucky, swamp water burned my eyes and filled my nostrils. My lungs were on fire and I fought the urge to gag. I was drowning and I wanted to scream. Like a madman, I fought the air bag and shoved it aside, reached down and undid the seatbelt. In the black water I didn't know which way was up. I fought back panic. My arms flayed in the darkness and I hit my head on a roll bar. I was blacking out. I needed air. My hand found the edge of the outside window. I grabbed it and pulled myself out and free from the buggy, kicked off the roof and shot straight up. I broke the surface and gasping for air. My lungs and throat burned, and I coughed up black-acid water. Trying to catch my breath, I looked around for Zelda, then I saw the Escalade stopped on top of the bank about fifteen yards away. Its passenger window was down. I sucked in a bucket of air, dove deep, and swam as far underwater until my lungs screamed for air. When I surfaced the second time, the Escalade was gone. Treading water I spat out more gritty muck. My lungs and eyes burned. I was alive and I was alone.

Where was Zelda?

Frantically I looked around then, like a porpoise, Zelda bobbed to the surface ten yards from where I was treading water.

"You okay?" she asked.

"Of course," I yelled back.

Slowly, I side-stroked to the edge. Like an injured crab, I crawled up the canal bank and collapsed. With four smooth overhead strokes, Zelda crossed the canal.

"You sure you're okay?"

I just waved, still trying to catch my breath.

Zelda walked up the bank and sat down beside me. Below us, the rear bumper of the buggy protruded out of the murky water.

"What happened? Why didn't he stop?"

"Someone was trying to kill us," I said.

"Kill us? Are you sure? Who would want to kill us?"

"I don't know." I took a deep breath, "I'm glad to see you're okay. Jesus, what did you do?"

Zelda looked down at the canal. "When we got hit the first time, I undid my seatbelt and braced. When the car hit the water I waited until we stopped then swam through the window. I was on the varsity swim team in high school."

"I'm impressed," I puffed still catching my breath. "That's fast thinking."

"You ride with the Pariahs you learn to think fast," Zelda said. She was dripping wet and her wet clothes clung to her body, accenting a fine Sophia Loren figure.

Catching my eyes admiring her, she said, "It's my job to keep fit."

Sprawled on the bank and soaking wet, we looked like a pair of Mexican wetbacks emerging from the Rio Grande. I glanced up and down the road. Not a car in sight.

"Did you see the driver?" I asked.

"Nope, it happened too fast. And all the dust," Zelda said. "You're shaking."

"I'm cold," I lied.

"What are we going to do now?" Zelda asked.

"Walk."

CHAPTER 40

The 7-11 was farther then it looked, but the walk was cut mercifully short by a friendly, passing motorist in a blue Ford 150 pickup who gave us a lift. I kept looking back expecting at anytime to see the Escalade. My paranoia was not helped by the black plumes of smoke from sugarcane fires soaring into the air on the horizon like simmering volcanoes.

"Lots of people drive into the canals out here," he informed us. "They run over alligators and armadillos too."

Finally we reached the store. Pickup trucks and SUVs dominated the parking lot. Zelda and I looked like a pair of warthogs encrusted by baked-on road dust.

She said, "You think it might have been the guys who trashed my place?"

"I wouldn't doubt it. They must have followed us to Kiki's place or were there waiting."

"I'd better call Kiki."

For a moment I considered that Kiki might have set us up and was involved deeper than he admitted, but then decided he wouldn't do anything to hurt Zelda. Either way he was in danger, if not already dead. Two outside pay telephones hung on the walls at the far end of the store. Zelda dialed, waited, then hung up.

"He didn't answer." Zelda stared at the pay phone. "Do you think something might have happened to him?"

I wasn't sure if he had done the smart thing and left, or if the Escalade contingent had gotten to him.

"This is getting all screwed up," Zelda swore. "What are we going to do?"

"I have to call the police."

"I had hoped I wouldn't be hearing from you for a while," Adam said.

In as few words as possible, I described to Adam what had happened.

"Are you telling me that you talked to an accomplice in a homicide and didn't immediately call me?"

"I had no idea what he knew. We just left his place."

"We?"

"Zelda and me."

"You went with the suspect's girlfriend! What in God's name are you thinking? Damn it, Maxie, where the hell is this Kiki guy?"

I gave him the address. "He might need protection but I don't think he'll talk to you guys. You know, outlaw code and all."

"I'll throw his sorry ass in jail then I'll tell him I've told his friends that he's cooperating with us."

"Does that old shtick still work?"

"You'd be surprised what still works," Adam said. "I'll call you when I hear something."

The reluctant store clerk gave us the bathroom keys only after I slipped him a twenty from my soggy wallet.

"Been swimming?" he asked in a thick Bangalore accent after we'd freshened up.

"We'll take two hot coffees, too," I said.

"That'll be another four fifty."

CHAPTER 41

Fifteen minutes later, the tow truck arrived and took us to the crash site. Only the rear bumper and a tire stuck out of the water. The driver had no problem hooking up and pulling the buggy out of the canal. He assured us that cars driving into canals were a common occurrence.

"Happens all the time."

Zelda and I rode in the tow truck to Mike Minsky's auto garage. Thankfully, Mike was not there. I wasn't in the mood for any of Mike's pithy comments. I refused a loaner but asked the receptionist to call us a taxi and if I could use her phone. First, I called the gallery.

"Roberts Fine Arts."

"Margot, it's me," I said lamely. "Can you buy me a new cell phone at the Verizon store? I want the same number and plan."

"What happened to your phone or should I not ask?" she asked.

"It got wet."

Then I dialed Adam.

"A patrol car went out to the address you gave but found no one there," he said. "Your phantom witness has flown the coop."

"Was there a motorcycle in the front yard?"

"Nope. No working vehicles reported on the premises. I think if anyone had gotten to this Kiki guy they wouldn't have taken the bike. Chances are he left town."

"I hope so, for his sake."

"You hope so? Maxie, he was a key witness, maybe even an accomplice. Now he's gone. When were you going to tell me about this Kiki guy?"

"I was on my way over to see you when these guys ran us off the road."

"Yeah, right."

"Like I said, I was just going to talk to the guy."

"Maxie, don't you get it? That's our job."

It was close to dusk by the time we got home. My shoulder ached and I could add another large leg bruise to the list of abuses that had been heaped on my body over the last week. I bathed and changed, and resisted taking a nap. Instead I went to the kitchen where Margarita was, strangely, nowhere to be found. I fixed two vodka and tonics with plenty of ice, and took them out to the loggia to wait for Zelda.

She came out with her hair still wet, dressed in tight fitting jeans and a white blouse. Be careful, Jock, I warned.

"Thanks." She took the drink and sat down beside me.

I raised my glass in a salute. "As the old Confucian curse goes, 'May you live in interesting times.'"

"I thought riding with the Pariahs was exciting but this week has topped that," she said, drawing down her drink by half.

"Life with Maxie Roberts is always exciting," I said.

"Do you think we're safe here?"

"Of course, we are. The Palm Beach police station is a mile down the street. They could be here in three minutes. This island is like a fortress. If you want, I'll call the mayor and have the drawbridges raised."

"It's just that I don't know what to do anymore," she said. "This is not like me."

"It's been an exceptionally odd week for me, too."

Zelda cradled her glass in both her hands and surveyed the Intracoastal. The lights from the opposite shore shimmered on the water like nervous glowworms. I heard crickets chirping in the bushes and the echo of a motorboat slowly disappeared up the channel.

"Since Billy was killed, my entire world has gone topsy-turvy. I forget which way is up," she said.

"You're safe here." I gave her a reassuring smile and a pat on her leg, which I let linger longer than necessary. A warm flush ran up my arm. My mouth was dry. I jerked my hand back.

Zelda peered at me with her deep gypsy eyes. I thought I heard her sigh. She quickly finished the rest of her drink, stood up, and said, "Excuse me," and disappeared into the house.

Jesus, did I blow it? Did I come on too strong? Maximilian, you can be such an ass. I bemoaned my clumsiness and was about to give Jock one of my pointless lectures on inappropriate behavior when I heard my name gently called.

I turned and saw Zelda standing just inside the doorway. I gasped and spilled my drink on my pants. She was naked. Soft backlights from the kitchen outlined her figure in a sensual glow. The Lady of the Lake had stepped out of the painting and had come to me alive and well in all her glory. Jock was very happy.

I stood and went to her. *This is insane.* I was almost into overdrive, long past reason. I thought about Billy and the XL t-shirt she gave me to wear. She was used to big men. Usually when I fantasize while making love, I think of other women, not other men.

What are we doing? I know we're both adults but I feel so childish.

CLICK!

The doors of reason slammed shut and the portals of perception swung wide open. Choice shot like a stinger missile out the window. I had only one alternative. I slid my arms around Zelda, gave her one last up-and-down look, not believing my luck, and then I pulled her to me. With a mind of their own, my hands frolicked from her neck to her inner thighs.

I lifted her up in my arms and carried her into the spare bedroom. I laid her crossways on the bed without taking my eyes off her. As if by magic, my clothes fell to the floor. All of us, Zelda, Jock, and I were in a heightened state of excitement. Yet, I am a gentleman, brought up in the Southern style, and firmly believe the dictum *ladies first.* There was no rush. Absolutely none.

An hour later I was laying on my back with my heart still pounding in my chest. Zelda rolled over to give me a kiss. Her hand slipped under the covers and when it came out she had Oshian dangling from her fingers.

"What's this?" she asked fingering the grinning phallic.

"Um. Oh that? Well ahh . . . um . . . " I was trying to figure how to explain it was one of Magarita's mojos when we both looked down. Jock had gotten his second wind.

After another couple of romps and rolls, my senses slowly returned. It was late. Zelda was on her back asleep. The window was open, and the sound of water lapping against the dock and the smell of the sea stimulated my galloping synesthesia. I looked down at Jock in his semi-flaccid state. See what you got me into. Again!

I can talk to him like that in this condition.

The Arabs are right. Men have to wonder at and fear a woman's sexuality, their power over us. We have to marvel in jealous awe at their obvious deeper and longer, full-bodied orgasms.

I must have dozed off to asleep. It was eight-thirty in the morning and light outside, and the phone was ringing. I fumbled for the receiver and placed it against my ear.

"Hello, Maxie. Are you there?"

"Oh. Oh, hi, Nancy." I glanced over my shoulders at Zelda's sleeping form.

A pause.

"Maxie. What are you doing?"

"Ahh, um, nothing."

"Maxie. Are you being a good boy?"

Will you tell me how they know?

After promising to call Nancy back, I waddled into the kitchen, put on a pot of coffee, and headed for the bathroom to throw some cold water on my face. While I was not having morning-after remorse, I did have to rethink where I was going with this. I didn't need a Delphi oracle, Adam Aldrick, or Bernie Crown to tell me it was all wrong, sleeping with a woman who was traded at a motorcycle gang rally for a half-ounce of cocaine. Yet Zelda excited me beyond legal limits. As I brushed my teeth, her image danced in front of me. A cold shower was scant help. As freezing pellets of water took my breath away, there she was, hands against the tiles, standing on her toes with her hair wet and goose bumps doing the cha-cha down her back and me behind her. Jock, stop it! For God's sake, stop it!

CHAPTER 42

What do you have when you mix a dead socialite, a murdered motorcycle gang member reinvented as a gigolo, a half dozen art forgeries, a drowned Jupiter gallery owner, and an oversexed Count? Not even a bad, ribald joke. But I was sure it all made sense. Somehow. Adam, Bernie, and Aseneth all insisted I should let the police handle it. It wasn't my problem. They were right. My quandary was that I could never follow instructions; they were too confining. And that attitude kept getting me into a beehive of trouble.

Could I believe the Count? The story about Papa Manley and the Caravaggio and his motives for not turning it over to the children with the other paintings? After all he still believed it was an original painting. Was it all an elaborate story concocted for my benefit? I wanted to talk to the Count's girlfriend. She might have an angle on the paintings, on Sergio, maybe even on a motive. Adam was not about to tell me who the girlfriend was or where she lived and I wasn't going to ask the Count. That left Raymundo.

Wanting to avoid any possibly tapped phone lines, I drove over to the Manley manse. I pulled the Jag into the driveway and before I had turned off the motor, Raymundo had stepped out of the door to his over-the-garage apartment. The dour grimace on his face meant he was as happy to see me as I was him.

Without any formalities, I said as I closed the Jag's door, "I don't have to tell you that your patron is in serious trouble. He might be going to jail and I'm trying to help. I know he had a girlfriend and I need to talk with her. She might help save him."

He stared at me for a full thirty seconds. Then without saying a word, he waved me towards the house. I followed him through the side servants' entrance and the kitchen to the island counter. He opened a drawer and pulled out a notebook. He wrote a name and address on a piece of paper then handed it to me.

"Thanks," I said, folding the note in half.

Raymundo nodded.

Lisette Morgan lived in a third-floor mausoleum-like condominium two blocks west of South Ocean Blvd. Many of our leading men keep their spare ladies in apartments on The Island.

The uniformed doorman announced me then said, "Five oh eight. Elevators to your left." and tipped his hat. At the fifth floor I knocked and the door immediately swung open. Lisette was a shapely, thirty-something, well-tanned, well-endowed blond, though short for my taste. Not too short: just short.

I introduced myself and handed her my card.

"Miss Morgan, I'm here because I'm trying to help Sergio Ordenoff."

She stared at the card. "Sergio told me about you. Come on in, sir."

Sir? I hate that. Makes me feel ancient.

I sat down on a floral couch. The apartment was Spartan, with just enough furniture to make it comfortable. I tried not to notice the bare walls, an affront to an art dealer. Copies of *Cosmopolitan* and the *Star* were laid out on the round coffee table.

"Coffee?" she asked on cue.

I never refuse a cup of black brew. "Thanks."

She brought in two hot cups of instant coffee, which I lightened with two spoons of Coffee Mate and sweetened with two packs of NutraSweet to kill the taste. She sat in a straight back chair directly in front from me and crossed her legs, her hair held up on top of her head by a single plastic clip as if I had interrupted her in the middle of housework. She had on white shorts and a Key West t-shirt probably bought in one of the tacky shirt shops that line Duval Street. Her skin was an anemic white that had not seen the sun in years. She had rows of thin worry wrinkles over her grey eyes and a forced smile that displayed more pain than pleasure.

"You know that Sergio is in big trouble and I'm here to try and find anything that might help him"

"Can you do anything for Sergio?" she asked.

"I don't know, but I'm trying. I need to know about you two."

She shrugged. "Sergio is a real gentleman," she said. "And so kind."

"Married though."

"Of course, he never hid it. He said we'd get married if and when his wife ever passed away. I don't mean that he was capable of killing her. It's that she was, well, old."

"But not decrepit. And you thought you could wait years for him?"

"Believe me, I wasn't waiting. I've heard too many men's promises to believe them. The truth is I liked him and we enjoyed each other's company. He kept me happy. It's as simple as that."

"Did he give you money or buy you things?"

She squirmed in her chair and recrossed her legs. "No. I told the police. Oh, he bought me a few gifts." She fingered a simple delicate gold necklace dangling around her neck. "But nothing extravagant."

"Did Sergio mention anything about their friends or if something unusual has happened recently?"

"Not that I remember."

"How about anything about their help, the maid or the driver or a handyman?"

"No."

"They had a lot of paintings in the house. Did he say anything about them, like if they were for sale, or if they might be copies?"

She hesitated and shook her head. "No. No. I'm not into those things. Sergio was very discrete. He rarely talked about his private life, and never about his wife or her house."

Glancing around the apartment I saw no evidence of the Count's largess. Maybe it was as she said, a mutual attraction. Or had silent promises been made? Lisette had hung around Sergio for some reason. I did not picture Comrade Count Sergio Ordenoff as one of the world's greatest lovers. Then again, who am I to question the endless possibilities of true love?

Lisette's leg was rocking back and forth. "I don't want any trouble. I just want to be left alone."

"Do you still talk to him?" I quickly interjected.

"He called me on the day after his wife was killed. Told me not to worry and don't believe everything I heard or read in the papers. Then he called Saturday and mentioned you, but we haven't talked since then. He said it would complicate things if he was seen with me, and he didn't want me to get involved. The cops came anyway." Lisette's foot nervously tapped the floor. "It was not like what you think. I got to like Sergio and he liked me. I'll show you." She reached over and grabbed a small cherry wood box off an end table and took out two photographs. "Sergio and I went places together. Here's a couple pictures of us at the Jupiter Lighthouse and in Key West."

She handed me the photographs. The first was of Lisette leaning against a railing at Mallory Square. The second had the impeccably dressed Count and Lisette, in a white halter-top and red shorts, standing in front of the stately, sun burnt Jupiter lighthouse.

"May I borrow this?" I asked, holding up the Jupiter Lighthouse picture. She looked like she was about to object. "I'll return it," I said and secured it in my pocket then left.

"It was Martha's suggestion," Sergio said.

We were sitting in his living room in the same chairs we had our last conversation.

"You see, Mr. Roberts, Martha wanted me to be happy. She was a good woman."

"What do you mean 'her idea'?"

"We were at a party given by Maureen Driscoll. I met Lisette through a friend at the bar and while we were talking together, Martha came up and was very pleasant to her. Later she told me, 'If you two wish to cavort, that's fine. Just don't ever do it in my house and don't embarrass me.' You know, I hadn't really thought of it at the time. Well, I am a man and I did think of it, but the actual mechanics were Martha's doing. A couple of weeks later the opportunity arose and we took it. Discreet, just as Martha wanted. I never took away from Martha's time and I was always there for her. Except at the end. Then again, I don't know what I would have done. I'm not a courageous person."

"Do you think that Martha might have set you up with Lisette? You know, the devil that you know is better than the one you don't?"

"I never thought of it that way. You know Palm Beach. Strange things are accepted here that would be taboo anywhere else. Leaving Martha was never an option for me. I'm not good at being poor. Lisette knew I could not support us. And she never asked."

"She said that you said you'd marry her when Martha died."

"Not when, if. We all die sometime don't we?" The Count lowered his head and stared at the floor.

"So your relationship was basically just sex?"

"Part of it." He stood up. "Mr. Roberts. This is all just too much. Too much. My wife is murdered and I am as much a victim as Martha. I am a prime suspect. I've lost all my friends and I'm about to be evicted from my house. I could be arrested at any moment and I don't have the money to pay for a lawyer. Does that seem like a well-planned crime?"

I had no answer.

Apparently, Sergio Ordenoff had resigned himself to a fate bordering on martyrdom. People like the Count may have their Torquemada, but rarely suffer an auto-de-fe in the public square. Rather like a Tasmanian tabby, from whatever height they are tossed they inevitably land on their feet. Martyrdom is never attractive and on Count Sergio Ordenoff, it was superfluous.

CHAPTER 43

I had come to the end of my tether. I was stumped. I had amassed a lot of information in a new Manley file, and had its contents spread out on the kitchen counter. In neat rows, I had arranged pictures of paintings, names of artists, newspaper clippings about Billy's demise, a photograph of Martha and one of the Count. I was going to put it all together and drop the entire file into Adam's lap and, like Pontius Pilate, wash my hands of the entire affair. Let Adam separate the chaff from the wheat.

Eric and Nicole were coming in a week. Zelda needed a place to stay. With a killer or killers on the loose, I was still not sure it was safe for the kids to stay with me. My stockbroker, Peter Long, who had a house in Siesta Key on Sarasota Bay suggested, "Stay at my place. We'll be spending the holidays skiing in Vail. Bring your boat over." It was an attractive offer.

As if reading my thoughts, Margarita said, "Stop worrying. Here's some coffee for you two." Ironically, as Margarita knew, coffee calms me, like Ritalin and hyperactive kids. She sat down two steaming mugs. "Come now, drink." She waved Zelda to the counter.

As Zelda sipped her coffee, she fingered through the pictures. She pulled one out of the pile.

"Isn't that the guy that was on the TV?" Zelda asked. She held the photograph of the Count and Lisette at the Jupiter Lighthouse.

"That's the dear old Count."

"What's he doing with Lisette Morgan?"

My head shot up. "What?"

"Lisette Morgan. Petite blond with a skinny butt and gray eyes? The trannies loved her. She used to work in one of the big Tampa clubs. Had a class act, decked out in jewels and furs."

"Little Lisette Morgan was a stripper?"

"Pretty good one too, though she'd tell you she was an actress. She got in trouble with some club manager for doing tricks on the side. That's a big no-no."

Suddenly our little Palm Beach Island was crowded with strippers. Perhaps it wasn't all of a sudden. The real question was, *how did a small time Tampa stripper get invited to an exclusive Maureen Driscoll party?*

I dialed Lisette's apartment. No answer

Throwing caution and driving record points to the wind I raced over to her apartment building.

"Miss Morgan has left," the doorman told me. "She took a cab to the train station."

"When?"

"About an hour ago."

Again, ignoring everything I'd learned at my last driving school class, I sped over the bridge, took a sharp right by the Kravis Center to Tamarind Street train station. The Jag screeched into a parking space. I jumped out and ran to the loading platform.

A northbound train was chugging into the station.

"Where's this train going to?" I asked at the ticket window.

"Tampa."

I looked up at a hissing and grunting steel ten-car wall suddenly blocking my view of the loading platform and the crowd boarding. "All aboard!"

"Hey buddy, you gotta buy a ticket."

I paid and raced across the platform and leaped up the train steps as it lurched forward. I steadied myself and caught my breath before walking through the first car and upstairs to the upper deck and back down. The train was crowded with students, families, couples, and suitcases. But no Lisette.

I worked my way down the aisle of the next two cars and was about to pass into the next car when I heard, "Good afternoon, Mr. Roberts." My eyes caught Deacon Cleveland Cook smiling up from a window seat opposite two ladies dressed in their Sunday-best flowery dresses, wide-brim pastel hats, and wider smiles. They all had bibles opened to the Book of Job on their laps.

"You've been a very busy man."

"I know, Cleveland. It's been quite a hectic week."

"Hope you're not too busy to return an old friend's calls. You should slow down, go to church. Me and these two lovely Christian ladies are headed to Lakeland for a Baptist convention. And you?"

"Right now I'm not sure. I think I have a client for your paintings."

"That's not what I called about. Sit down. We have to talk. I have some information on a certain gentleman you mentioned."

"I can't right now, Reverend. I'm looking for someone on this train. Let me find her then we'll talk okay?"

"A young lady, I assume, alone, blond and rather nicely proportioned?" he asked.

His two companions looked at each other and shook their heads, suppressing giggles.

"Yeah."

"Next car, upper deck."

"Thanks, Cleveland. I'll be back. Ladies, if you'll excuse me," I said with a slight head bow.

The last car was half full. Lisette was in the second floor sky room staring out the window with her suitcase between her legs. I plopped down in the seat beside her.

"Why don't we have a serious talk, Miss Morgan?"

She pulled her purse to her chest. "I have nothing to say."

"Talk with me or with the police," I said. I took out my cellular and flipped it open. She raised her fingers to her mouth and again stared out the window.

"I don't want to cause you any problems. I want to know about you and Sergio," I said.

"Will you just leave me alone? Please, go away."

"I know all about your work in the Tampa clubs. All I want to know is how you met Sergio. It wasn't by accident, was it?"

Her legs held her suitcase firmly and her hands were folded together on top. Her grey eyes were scared and sad.

"I just need a little help here and some information. Then I promise you I'll leave."

I waited a full minute before she began, "I was just trying to make a few dollars. I never wanted to hurt Sergio. He was really so sweet. Treated me like a lady."

"Let's start from the beginning. Tell me how did you meet Sergio?"

"I was working in Tampa and this guy came into the club and offered me two month's salary at double what I was making. And I was making good money. He tells me I'll have a nice apartment and all expenses paid. All I had to do was meet this guy and be friendly with him."

"You mean have sex with him?"

"I told him right off that I was not going to do tricks. He swore it was an escort job. He said most of all I was to be real friendly with him. Make him feel at ease," she said. "Men feel comfortable around me."

"What was this guy's name?"

"He said it was Frank," she said softly.

"Frank?"

"Never told me his last name. He was a big guy, dark hair, well dressed with good manners."

"Was he Russian?"

"No. I don't think so. He didn't have any accent."

"Did he tell you who you were supposed to meet and be friendly with?"

She shook her head. "I didn't know until the party. It was more natural that way, he said."

"Tell me about the party. What happened there and who else did you meet?"

"It was a lovely house. Real big. Like right out of a magazine. Frank was there, of course, I met a nice guy named Manny Monterey, said he owned restaurants, and a tall good looking man named Jenkins."

"Nigel Jenkins?"

"I think so. Mr. Jenkins was with Sergio when I met him. They were talking when Frank and I walked over to them. I remember him well. He was not a shy one. I'm used to guys staring but he had that look. He said, 'Beauty like yours should be painted.'"

"And Sergio was with him?"

"That's right. Frank introduced me to Mr. Jenkins and Mr. Jenkins introduced me to Sergio."

"How soon after did you and Sergio start dating?"

She looked up at the ceiling as if counting the days. "I'd say about couple of weeks later Sergio called me, and then . . . well, you know."

"What did this Frank guy tell you he wanted?"

"I never really knew. After Sergio left, I would call him and he'd come over and ask what we had talked about. He was real interested in anything about Mrs. Manley. Asked a lot of questions about her."

"Like what?"

"Everything, you know. I began to get a bad feeling about the whole setup. At first I thought it was a con. And Sergio was so nice to me. I was going to split. I didn't want to hurt Sergio. Then Sergio's wife was killed. I'm scared. I just want to go home."

"Did Frank ever threaten you?"

"Not directly. He didn't have to."

"Do you know Dahlia Kapofsky?"

She shook her head.

"Billy Balls?"

"No."

"How about Zelda Zeitgeist?"

"Zelda. I know Zelda. She used to . . . "

"That's okay," I stopped her.

At the Fort Pierce stop, I got off the train and was standing on the platform trying to get my bearings when I heard a tapping sound. I looked up and there was Deacon Cleveland Cook at the train window mouthing the words 'We have to talk.' He put his hand like a telephone to his ear. I nodded, then flipped open my cell-phone and called a cab for the long ride home.

Was I to believe that Lisette Morgan was a plant placed to keep an eye on Sergio and, perhaps, Martha Manley? Again, Nigel Jenkins' name kept surfacing like a plastic bobber on a windswept lake. It didn't make sense that Jenkins was involved with Lisette. What would he gain? Unless Nigel Jenkins was The Island's personal pimp? Then I thought of Melanie Cabot Moore's description of Jenkins, "the tall, dark man about town." It seems he was much more about town then anyone realized.

I admit all my information was hearsay and circumstantial. But like an artist's under painting, stroke-by-stroke, a picture was forming. With each brush stroke, the flesh took on form and the colors took on life. But far from an idyllic Claude Monet garden setting, the emerging picture was an anxiety haunted Edvard Munch. I wasn't sure I wanted to see the finished product.

I picked up the Jag at the Tamarind train station and headed home. I was about to pass the Bethesda-by-the-Sea Episcopal Church when my head imploded and a bolt of lightning ricocheted around in my skull. I hit the brakes without looking, jerked the wheel to the curb and stopped.

Zelda. Was she a plant too? A female spy for every home? A motorcycle goddess with a Gina Lollobrigida body drops into my life like heavenly manna and I'm to blithely accept it as a godsend? I could be accused of naïveté, but completely guilelessness was not, I hoped, one of my personality flaws.

Unfortunately lack of common sense was.

CHAPTER 44

Exhausted, I collapsed on the family room couch. The television flickered some mindless reality program. The volume was off.

"You look tired. Would you like me to prepare something?" Zelda asked. "Margarita said she'd be back after nine. A friend picked her up for a Bingo game in West Palm."

"I'm not a helpless male. I can cook, you know. But if you insist, a soup will do just fine."

I watched Zelda maneuver around the kitchen island, sink, and stove. She opened the refrigerator door and I could hear drawers opening and closing.

"Let's see. You have mushrooms and shallots and some veggies. They'll make a nice soup."

"That sounds delicious." I laid my head back on the armrest and was about to change to the news when the telephone rang

"Do you want me to get that?" Zelda asked.

"No, let the machine take it." After the sixth ring, I heard a deep voice echoing from my answering machine. "Maxie, I know you're there. Answer the phone." It was Adam.

I swung my legs off the couch and against all good sense I scurried across the kitchen and grabbed the receiver. "How did you know?"

"How did I know that you were home? Sergeant Miller drove by your place ten minutes ago and saw your Jaguar pulling into the garage."

I took the cordless phone into my bedroom and closed the door. "Am I being watched or something?"

"Not yet, but you've been quite the subject of conversation around The Island," Adam said with a trace of sarcasm.

"You're not still mad about the lost evidence thing?"

"You bet I am. And you can throw in the lost phantom witness. Some very important people are calling about you and most are suspicious about your involvement in the Manley case."

"Am I a suspect?" I asked jokingly.

"You and everyone else on or off this island."

"You're kidding."

"Unfortunately, I'm not."

"Are my phones bugged?"

"If they were we wouldn't be having this conversation. But I wouldn't be so sure in the near future. A simple word to the wise."

"I appreciate it."

After Adam's phone call I milled over the intriguing possible connection between Lisette Morgan, this Frank guy, and Nigel Jenkins. What was Jenkins' involvement with a number of on-and off-island ladies and possibly Billy Balls? Was he pimping men and women to the upper crust? Was he the mastermind behind the PBLG Club? We all get our kicks differently. Maybe procurement was Jenkins. I know he doesn't need the money. Were Martha Manley and Melanie Cabot Moore part of a gang of over-sexed septuagenarians? I remembered inside the Bentley and Martha's hand lingering on my knee.

With her money, Martha Manley did basically whatever she wanted; like her quest for a hurricane. Perhaps she knew that a monster hurricane came ashore right over Palm Beach in 1928. I went to the bookcase, took down *Killer 'Cane: The Deadly Hurricane of 1928* and thumbed through the pictures. Gruesome. Three thousand dead in Palm Beach County alone.

For all its beauty, wealth, and power, Palm Beach is a frail, temporary refuge. Perched perilously on an elongated sand spit, the slug-shaped island offers scant protection from the watery forces which surround her slender neck like a pearl necklace. The water was the reason we were all here. Yet that same water, that necklace of liquid beauty, was ready at anytime to garrote the upstart islet. For most of its history, Florida was underwater. Our precarious peninsula has been submerged twenty-seven times in the last two million years. Living in Florida during hurricane season is akin to playing Russian roulette with God. Palm Beach is living on borrowed time. Maybe that's why so many believe the rules don't apply.

Enjoy it while you can.

At heart we're all narcissists. It's Darwinism at its purist, a survival technique. If I was to believe Adam, my very survival, or at least my freedom, was at risk.

CHAPTER 45

Even after dropping an Ambien, I slept fitfully, finally waking up at eight. After a long, slow shower, I dressed and trudged into the kitchen. Margarita was preparing breakfast. Zelda, nowhere to be seen, I assumed, was asleep.

"You looka terrible. You not sleep last night?" Margarita asked.

"I've got a lot on my mind."

"I know. Nicole and Eric are coming soon. You should get your problems fixed before they get here."

"I'm trying, Margarita, believe me, I'm trying."

"I have to grocery shop. Get sometings the children like."

I handed her a fifty for the taxi and my credit card for the groceries. Once a week, Margarita would take a cab to The Island Publix and stock up on groceries. When she first worked for us I tried to teach her to drive, but after two harrowing weeks' worth of near-accidents we both gave up.

I downed Margarita's breakfast. While worry never interfered with my appetite, I didn't have the stomach to read the *Palm Beach Post*. Over the last week, I'd been bombarded with too much information. The world and the walls were closing in. I needed to get out.

Once in the Jag, I lowered the top and headed south past Mar-A-Largo and Bernie's house. I don't know why, but I was feeling all wrong about my relationship with Zelda. Was it a relationship? And what about Kathy Krammer? It wasn't fair to compare them, but I couldn't help it. I don't think any woman could compare to Ms Krammer. Kathy and I weren't even dating, yet I felt guilty, like I'd betrayed her. I chided myself, *you're being silly*. Then again, perhaps a dozen roses might be appropriate after all. They say a man sends roses either for love or when he's done something wrong. In this case, even in my confused state, I think it was both.

I pulled over to the side of the road and called my florist on my new cell phone. "Deliver them to her office just before lunch." I told the florist. I wanted the roses paraded in front of the entire staff. Then I said, "Make that two dozen."

I dictated the card. "I'm sorry about the misunderstanding. I hope you'll let me explain over dinner at Café L'Europe."

Immediately after hanging up, I took a deep breath of the salt air. Round, foamy waves were breaking on the beach and a quartet of terns glided in the air with their heads down searching for fish. My eyes were carried out to the thin blue line where the sea meets the sky, the point along the much-maligned horizon, infinite with possibilities, where there's purity of space found only in dreams.

With the sun bright overhead and the wind straight off the ocean dripping with saltwater smells, Palm Beach was all mine. Factor in the culture, the interesting people, and the natural wonder, why would I want to live any place else? I pulled up to a light beside a Mercedes 500 SL convertible driven by a Carmen Miranda look-a-like. We caught each other's eyes. The light changed and, as I passed her, I tipped my cap and she smiled a large full smile. Possibilities. Endless possibilities.

Then I heard the annoying ring of my cell phone. If there had been a body of water within throwing distance I'd have chucked it. How quickly neo-necessities became irritants.

"You have a visitor," Margot said in a voice so low that I had to slow down to hear.

"Anyone I know?"

"*You are needed.*"

A line that is never a harbinger of good news.

The two official-looking gentlemen waiting for me at the gallery showed me their Palm Beach County Investigator's badges. I showed them the back office. It wasn't exactly a Mutt and Jeff team but the one dressed in blue was a good head-plus taller than the one dressed in gray.

"Mr. Roberts. We're looking into the murder of Martha Manley," said Mr. Grey. "Your name has been mentioned in relation to the victim and in a number of incidents afterwards. We understand you might have information that would help the investigation. We'd like to ask you a few questions."

"It's all on record. I've shared everything I know with the Palm Beach police," I lied.

"May I call you Max?" Mr. Blue asked.

"Maximilian will do."

"Okay. Maximilian. We understand you are living with a suspected killer's girlfriend. A Zelda Zeitgeist."

"Her home was vandalized, so she's staying at my house for a short time."

"What is your relationship with this woman?" Mr. Gray asked.

I didn't like where the conversation was headed. "Excuse me a minute. I do not mind cooperating with the authorities, but do I need a lawyer here?"

"Do you think you need a lawyer?" asked Mr. Gray.

That was a yes.

"Gentlemen, unless you wish to charge me with something, I suggest it's time we depart on goods terms."

"That's no way to make friends and influence people, Maximilian," said Mr. Blue. "If I were you, I wouldn't count on your friend Adam Aldrick's help. He knows which side his toast is buttered on."

"Butter or not, we all walk a slippery path. Remember, like Humpty Dumpty the high and mighty fall far and hard, with no one to put them together again."

They both thought on that one for a few seconds.

"You have an impressive collection. How did you afford all this?" Gray man asked, looking around at the paintings.

"Do you think the IRS would be interested?" Blue said to Gray.

"The green door, gentlemen," I said, pointing the way out.

I recognized the visit by Blue and Gray as a heavy-handed intimidation attempt by Peter Putzer. He was the paradigm of official opprobrium that I had spent an entire career avoiding. And now I was in the cross hairs of his myopic sights.

And to think I had voted for him.

CHAPTER 46

With jumbled thoughts tossing around in my gray matter like vermouth in a martini shaker, I pulled the Jag into the driveway and stopped short. My gloom immediately lifted. My eyes were met by a God-sent miracle. Parked by the front door was Kathy Krammer's blue Porsche Boxster.

I steadied myself. I took a deep breath, walked up the steps, brushed my hair with my fingers, opened the door, and then sauntered into the kitchen. Disappointingly empty. Then I glanced out to the loggia and froze in abject panic. *"The horror, the horror,"* I heard Marlon Brando's mutter echoing from *Apocalypse Now*.

Seated around the white wrought iron table, cooing like Raphael's *Three Graces*, were Zelda, Margarita and Kathy Krammer. I had a sinking sensation that I knew the principal topic of conversation and it wasn't idle island gossip. I looked for a graceful way to exit so I could retreat to my room to sulk but before I turned, "Hi, Maxie," Kathy called out.

I waved meekly. With retreat blocked, I steeled myself. My guardian angel prodded me with her sword and I involuntarily stepped forward. I believe she whispered *reap what ye sow*.

Kathy was smiling. It pained me that she was enjoying my suffering so.

"Good afternoon, ladies," I said in a near falsetto.

"I ran into Margarita at Publix and gave her a ride home," Kathy said.

"She a berry nice girl. I invite her for coffee." Margarita smiled, barely hiding her glee at my discomfort.

"Sit down," Kathy said, moving her purse from a chair.

"I wouldn't think of intruding."

"Sit," rang out the trio in unison.

I sat.

They were drinking tea or coffee or one of Margarita's toddies, which might explain their expansive humor. Zelda had her leg up on a chair, drying her freshly painted toenails. Kathy's hair, backlit by the afternoon sun, glowed halo-like. Not unlike the Lady of the Lake, I noticed.

"You want I fix you a drink?" Margarita said. "It's good."

"Maybe later," I said.

"I am impressed," Kathy said.

Trying not to cringe, I waited for the punch line.

"You live a dangerous life for an art dealer and are quite the hero, I hear, rescuing damsels in distress, fighting off marauders."

Nothing could be more dangerous than this, I thought.

"He's my knight in shining armor," Zelda said.

"Slightly rusting armor, I fear," I said, warming up.

"Oh, false modesty doesn't become you," Kathy said. "You must tell us everything."

"My guess is enough has been said at this table to fill a year's worth of Shiny Sheet gossip columns."

Giggles, chuckles and ha-has.

"Do I have to take this abuse without legal representation?"

"You have the right to take the fifth if you want," Kathy said.

"I thought I had."

"Let's have mercy, girls," Zelda said.

"I agree. We'll let him exercise his escape clause," Kathy said.

A round of agreement. I got up. "I would truly love to share a few moments with you ladies, but I have some pressing engagements."

"I'll walk out with you," Kathy said, grabbing her purse and my arm. "Margarita, that drink was delicious. You have to give me the recipe. Ladies, we'll have to do this again."

"Not on my watch," I grumbled.

Kathy and I walked inside.

"That was quite a harrowing adventure you two had. Did it have anything to do with the Manley case?"

"I believe so."

"Then you should tell the police."

"I have, and if you want my opinion, they're after the wrong man."

"I won't argue there. What does Beebee Alabama say? I know he likes to be kept informed."

"The cops get the information first."

"So you're helping Sergio Ordenoff?"

"Nothing against your clients, but no one says no to Beebee. Anyway, I'm more interested in finding the forger and the missing painting. I think I've made some progress. That is, if I don't wind up in jail."

"Care to share them?"

"I promise I'll let you know when I have something concrete."

"Obviously you are a man of many talents."

"I hope that's good."

"It could be," Kathy said. She gave my arm a squeeze.

"Thought you were peeved at me."

"I don't think anyone can stay mad at you for long."

"You haven't talked with my ex."

"Are you sure?" she asked.

My expression must have said it all.

"Just kidding." She squeezed my arm again. "By the way, thanks for the roses." She rose up on her toes and gave me a kiss.

CHAPTER 47

The keystone of the American justice system is based on two Olympian fallacies: innocent until proven guilty and ignorance is no defense. As to the first, arrest triggers an automatic and reflexive assumption of guilt and if the latter were true, then why the need for lawyers. As Beebee Alabama said, once set in motion, the legal system transmutes into a surreal exercise. For the Count, events had moved to the far side of surreal. The next morning, the early news shows went gaga over the Manley murder. Sergio Ordenoff was indicted for first-degree murder, conspiracy and another half dozen tacked-on charges. Overnight, our dour Bulgarian diplomat had mutated into a Kafka-like character moving in slow motion across a Hieronymus Bosch landscape with imps and daemons probing his dilated orifices.

Hoping to avoid a media circus, Beebee Alabama had advised Sergio to quietly surrender. He told the press that he had a verbal deal with Peter Putzer to bring Sergio in. But our crime-fighting superhero had other plans. In a morning raid, with the media in tow, the county sheriff and the state attorney arrested Sergio at his home. The television news shows were filled with shots of Count Sergio Ordenoff being lead out of his Palm Beach mansion in handcuffs, Sergio being helped into the police cruiser, Sergio arriving at the courthouse, Sergio disappearing into a barred hallway.

By noon, the continuing soap opera was playing out on the local media with a showcase news conference orchestrated by Putzer. He wanted Sergio seen in cuffs and in public like a hunting trophy, bread and circus, or justice as entertainment. Most islanders tsk-tsked, and whispered "can you believe" the news of Sergio's arrest. But as Sergio was led away, there were no degrading hands in front of his face, nor a jacket draped over his head to vainly protect his identity. To the end, Count Sergio Ordenoff walked straight, head high, leading with his chin. Elegant, detached, and decorous, he nodded politely to the reporters, the mark of a true gentleman. Sergio made us proud that one of ours never lost his sense of haut-caste even in the face of the electric chair. Melanie Cabot Moore was right. Class always tells.

All this theater belies the question—was he the killer? As I had seen first hand, the Big Lie and the spirit of Joseph Goebbels was alive and well in Palm Beach County. Aside from the fact that I thought the Count was being railroaded, there was little I could do except find the forger or the original paintings. I was sure either would lead to the real murderer.

"Poor man," Zelda said. "And with all that money."

We were in the family room watching the local news. After half an hour I had had enough and I handed Zelda the remote control.

"Mind if I change the channel?"

""Please do us all a favor."

Zelda was channel surfing when Margarita waddled in.

"They still talking about that nice man?" She opened the refrigerator and took out a plastic bag and placed it on the counter. "I got some limes to make you favorite, a key lima pie," she said, organizing the bag's contents over the counter. "By the way, Mr. Roberts, I think I saw someone sitting in a car watching the house."

Bad news, like good, comes in threes.

From the second floor bath I could make out a single male in an institutional gray sedan parked two doors down the street. It had to be County. I'd give him fifteen minutes before he got a visit from The Island's finest. A single man sitting in a car on a residential street did not go unnoticed for long in Palm Beach. They were wasting a lot of manpower and time on me. Or were they? For all I knew there might be a list of unindicted co-conspirators, topped by yours truly. I needed an attorney.

Grabbing the cordless telephone I was heading to the den to call Carl Chambers, Esquire, when I heard a familiar sound from my European days. It was Italian. Zelda was watching a National Geographic special about a holy festival in Italy.

"I always wanted to go to Italy," she said.

"I used to live there," I said, staring at the screen. A procession of locals from a small village in the Apennine Mountains carried a life-sized statue of Saint Dominic, the patron saint of snakes, on their shoulders as they wove their way through crowded medieval streets. The good saint was covered with a dozen large, well-fed specimens. Like a living shroud, the writhing reptiles slid on the statue from his shoulders to his toes. They dripped and drooped off the saint as an acolyte carrying a snake stick gently placed any errant adders back onto his shoulders. Saint Dominic had enough snakes coiled around his outstretched hands to make Saint Patrick slither in his grave.

Maybe a trip to Italy would be in my best interest. I could visit friends in Sicily who had rented the mansion where Aleister Crowley, "the world's most evil man," once lived and practiced black magic.

As I turned to leave the room, I caught sight of one four-foot snake dangling from the saint's arm, almost vertical like the snake in the paintings.

POW! A head flash. Eureka! "Jesus, that's it!" I shouted. Margarita and Zelda both looked up from the television.

Instead of a phalanx of overfed reptiles slithering over a plaster saint, I saw a microscopic hologram standing on its tail twinkling out from the dark depths of a forbidden Caravaggio. All those years of stern nuns, ruler-red knuckles, and Sunday school catechism classes came rushing into view. I knew who the forger was. Dominic. Not Saint Dominic but Dominic Carranza. It all fit. He was European, he had the skills and experience, he was an excellent, meticulous copyist, and he had disappeared around the time of the Manley killing. The reclusive copyist had to be the forger.

"Let me borrow your cell-phone." I said to Zelda. "I can't call out from here."

I walked out to the loggia and dialed Bernie Crown.

From his Viet Nam days, Bernie had gathered an impressive intelligence-gathering guild sharing, for a fee, information with various organizations, governments and NGOs. At one time a former President considered him for the CIA as Director of the National Clandestine Service until a FBI background investigation uncovered his alleged involvement in a few domestic and foreign black jobs.

"What the hell do they think the CIA is anyway?" he harped to me. "What do the damned Liberals want? Choirboys running the agency?"

He quietly withdrew his name.

"I need to find a painter named Dominic Carranza. You might remember him."

"You mean the Dominic Carranza who did that reproduction of Van Dyke for Mona Steinhouer?"

"One and the same. Christina Hagan told me that he dropped out of sight about two, maybe three months ago. Someone said his mother was dying."

"So, could this be our forger?" Bernie asked.

"Could be. Like you said about coincidence, there are too many of them to ignore."

"You on a secure line?"

"A cell phone not registered to me."

"It'll have to do."

Bernie's telephone was secure. He had his entire house swept for bugs every three days.

"Okay. Let me see here," Bernie said. I heard him say, "Computer. Find Dominic Carranza, C-A-R-R-A-N-Z-A." The keyboard clicked. "You sure he's still alive?"

"I hadn't thought about that," I said. He could be dead by now.

"We're delving into very foggy terrain here," he said. The less said on the phone the better. I'm going to try some of my Pundit people. Hang up and I'll get right back to you."

With all his sophisticated information gathering sources, his best local intelligence-gathering group was the Pundits, a cabal of The Island's most important males, who meet once a month for lunch and high-level gossip.

While I waited for Bernie's call, I checked my files on Dominic Carranza. I came up with a list of a dozen reproductions he had done for clients, including the copy of Jan Van Dyke's *Man in a Red Turban*. A studied, exacting work. And the most obvious, the *Eve and the Serpent* fresco he painted. Why hadn't I seen it before? Perhaps because I thought the forger was the killer and the gentle if touchy-tempered Dominic Carranza did not fit neatly into my preconceived ideal of a murdering monster.

Half an hour later the telephone rang.

"Maxie." I heard Bernie's rather distant voice. "What time do you have?" I told him.

"Well I have 2:64," he said. "Say in ten minutes." And then the telephone went dead.

CHAPTER 48

I had ten minutes. I made it in six and parked in a charming but secluded tropical cul-du-sac two blocks from the gallery named for John Phipps. The 264 Grill was quartered on the corner of South Country in the old Carriage House designed by Addison Mizner. Inside was soothingly dark, with an elegant homey air. I crossed the dining area to the bar, took a stool and ordered a coke, forgoing the succulent Maryland crabcakes.. Two minutes later the telephone ring at the end of the bar. "Mr. Roberts," the bartender said and handed me the telephone.

"Sorry about all this James Bond stuff, but your phones are bugged," Bernie said. "This is straight from the Pundits' mouth: this afternoon at twelve hundred, you'll receive a call at one of the pay phones at the Amoco gas station on the southeast corner of Federal and Belvedere. Someone will be calling you from Canada. Take it seriously."

"Canada?"

"Great country, a bit too cold. You know temperature extremes do strange things to people. People come down here and it's hot, different and exotic, so they think the rules don't apply anymore. The same with the cold. Take it seriously."

"I'm taking everything seriously. Who'll be calling?"

"Someone you'll want to talk to."

"It had better be the Pope. I need some miracles."

"Someone better, I assure you."

"What am I suppose to do?"

"Like Oedipus, count yourself a child of chance."

Oedipus? I felt more like a caged gerbil doomed to run in place forever.

"Be subtle," Bernie said, "but try to lose your keepers. If they see you calling from a pay phone they can always get the records."

I looked at my watch: it was ten forty.

I got back into the Jag and drove west to Haverhill Road, turned right, then right again onto Okeechobee. The gray car dutifully followed. I crossed the I-95 bridge and made another right onto Dixie Highway before pulling in front of Mike Minsky's auto shop. The gray car stopped across the street. I killed the engine and scurried inside.

"Not again," Mike whined as I entered the office.

"No, the Jag's fine. It's my bodyguards I want to lose."

He glanced out the window. "Close contact of the official kind, I see. Are we being a bad boy?" he snorted.

"Do you have a way out of here unobserved?"

Mike shook his head and smiled. "I love it. You didn't kill someone did you?" I glared at Mike. "Okay, go out the back through the left side by the restrooms and you can hop over the wall into the parking lot on Olive."

"Thanks."

"By the way, your buggy is almost finished."

I walked through the garage to the left of the work bays. The buggy was up on a lift. Out back I jogged across to a five-foot cinder brick wall, climbed over and sauntered through a parking lot until I came out onto Olive Street. It was a two-block walk south to Belvedere Road and the gas station.

At twelve, the pay phone rang on schedule.

"Mr. Roberts?"

"Speaking."

"If you remember we met years back at a showing. You might say we're in the same business."

"Dominic."

"Listen. I am on a pay phone so I can't stay on the line for long. I'll get to the point. I have information about Martha Manley and Billy Balls."

My heart skipped a beat. I heard a slight lisp as if he might have had a few drinks. "I'm listening."

"Her husband didn't have anything to do with her death, or with the reproductions. But we have to talk in person. Check into the Royal Oak Hotel in Toronto. There's an Air Canada flight that arrives at seven. I'll contact you at the hotel tonight."

"You want me to fly to Canada?"

"If you want the information, you'll come. Goodbye."

The phone went dead.

Toronto! It was winter. What was wrong with these guys? Didn't they know it was cold up there? They were supposed to flee to some warm, exotic place like Mexico or Rio. Years back before I fled to Europe, I dated Patricia Sullivan, a beautiful little redhead artist from Toronto. I liked Canada. I even liked Canadians. But the smart ones migrate here in winter. Most end up in Ft. Lauderdale along car-clogged Sunrise Boulevard, crammed in motel efficiencies and small apartment complexes with oversized, red maple leaf flags flying out front. They have my sincere condolences.

I was thinking I had just enough time to pack and make the flight when the pay phone rang again.

"Well?" I heard Bernie's voice.

"I don't know how you did it but he called. I'm leaving for Toronto on the next flight out."

"Like I said you can thank the Pundits. But forget the flight. The Gulfstream is ready for you at the Palm Beach Airport. Take care."

I trotted back to Mike's past the gray Chevrolet, gave them a wave then hopped into the Jag and headed home. Two hours later, after quickly packing and saying goodbye to Margarita and Zelda, I was winging my way north in Bernie's private jet.

It was dark when the cab dropped me off at the Toronto Royal Oak Hotel.

"Hope you enjoy your stay with us, Mr. Roberts," the waxen-looking desk clerk said. In winter all Canadians look pale—except those recently arrived from Florida, Cuba, or Somalia.

"My first time in the dead of winter."

"Oh, it's not so bad. It seems we have a message for you." He handed me a double-folded envelope.

I opened the message. Inside was a note in French. 'I'll call at nine.'

My eyes rolled to the top of my forehead. This is getting too weird, but I'd come too far to turn back. I had my luggage sent up to my room, then headed to the bar. After my second vodka and cranberry juice Cape Cod, I began to chide myself for making spur-of-the-moment decisions without thinking them out. Artist or not, Dominic Carranza might be a murderer and here I was in a foreign country, at night, ready to meet with him. I could blame Bernie, I suppose. My life insurance premium was paid, wasn't it?

I downed the last of my drink, thought about ordering another but decided against it and went to my room. Tired, I laid my head on the pillow. I was nearly asleep when the phone rang.

"Go out to Bay Street and walk two blocks east. Take a right, walk fifteen yards and a cab will be there. Give the driver this note."

"You do know it's twenty below out there?"

The line went dead.

From my suitcase I retrieved the only overcoat I possessed that could pass muster as winter attire. It was woefully inadequate, especially against Toronto's arctic lakeshore winds. I'm a native-born Floridian. It's a matter of regional pride not to have a winter jacket in your wardrobe.

In the lobby I wrapped my scarf around my neck and head, and feeling like King Tut's mummy, I stepped outside. It was dark. No, it was black and cold, but not as cold as I had imagined. But then Florida is not as hot in the summer as most people think. When I turned the corner, all thoughts of "it's not so cold" disappeared. A hard wind blowing off Lake Ontario sliced through me like airborne razor blades. I lowered my head into the wind and, per the instructions, walked two blocks, took a right, scurried up fifteen yards and stopped. I shot a glance up and down the street. Nothing. I backed into the protection of a recessed doorway and stomped my feet. My ears burned, the first stage of frostbite according to the National Geographic special I had seen earlier in the week. If I stayed out there much longer, I'd end up like the little match girl frozen on the sidewalk. Luckily, I did not have to wait long. A cab pulled up and I got into the back seat. It was empty except for the driver.

I handed him the envelope. He opened it and then, without reading the contents, placed the envelope on the passenger seat and headed out of the city. The night was clear. A near full moon shone on an eerily beautiful arctic landscape. Not a palm tree in sight. I shuddered. We drove in silence for forty minutes before I saw a sign to Guelph and the cab turned off the highway. Just before reaching the center of the town, we pulled into a faceless subdivision that could have been planned by any American developer. After a few looping turns, we stopped in front of a small house, the driver cautiously maneuvering the cab up a short driveway with piles of recently dug snow high on each side. The garage door rose and we drove inside. The door closed.

The driver turned to me. "Mr. Roberts," he said. "Please, follow me."

He got out of the cab, lifted the cab's hood, pulled an extension cord from the wall, and plugged in an electric dipstick heater. Without a word he opened a side door and stepped into the house. I followed.

The driver took off his hat and jacket and without turning around said, "I'm Dominic Carranza."

Standing before me was a phantasmagoric image of a man, changed beyond recognition. Dominic Carranza had aged. He had lost weight and had grown a beard. His hair was gray. A pair of bent granny-glasses and bushy eyebrows framed his brown eyes. His skin was ashen with small white flakes around his nose from the super-dry air. Smudges of paint spotted the sleeves of his brown-checkered shirt and his pants hung from his waist like slept-in laundry.

In the living room, a slim elderly woman with her hair pulled up in a tight bun sat in an overstuffed chair wrapped in a shawl watching television.

"Mama, this is Mr. Roberts," Dominic said.

She nodded and smiled and returned to her program.

"Come on in here," he signaled. "We can talk."

I followed him into the adjacent room. The well-lit room had a director's chair and a small stool set in front of a workbench. The dry air was filled with the smell of fresh oil and old turpentine. A heavy floor-to-ceiling curtain divided the room in half. In one corner was an oven probably to bake the paintings and age them with the fine *craquelure* cracks, a technique perfected by the master Dutch forger Han van Meegeren.

Dominic closed the door then sat down hard in the director's chair. I took the stool. On the workbench, I recognized two small twin postwar Oskar Kokoschkas self-portraits propped up side by side against the back. Silently, we both stared at the two paintings. The light over the bench was daylight bright amplifying the color and life of the paintings. The bold lines of the paintings as well as the subject's blue eyes and expressionistic face drew me in to the intense center. Both were masterpieces, but one I knew was a fake. With a simple glance Dominic had told me he was the forger and showed me his genius.

Here was a true artist. Dominic not only lived art, he looked the part. He painted in the classic style and composition. Shove Dominic into another century and he would have been Giotto di Bondone or Andrea Mantegna. He held art to uncompromisingly high standards.

Unfortunately, Dominic loved art almost as much as he disliked people. He turned potential buyers off with his painful shyness, which, over the years, was accompanied by a barely concealed belligerence. He could not get past the clients. He hated them. He hated their pretensions, their crassness. No one wanted a painting by an irascible artist who could not or would not explain his work to paying customers. Not the type of artist you want to show off at your island parties.

Thus, he made copies to survive. Each year hundreds of copyists, good artists in their own right, painted copies of the great and not so great masterpieces. Only, Dominic's copies were not just good, they were superb, the best. Too good. Such talent was a dangerous endowment, a Promethean gift. Like a mighty weapon it must be kept out of the hands of children. And Dominic Carranza was childlike in every respect.

CHAPTER 49

A sigh escaped his lips.

"How did you know it was me?" He asked.

"Your patron saint, Dominic. You signed your copies."

"Ah, *il serpentini*. Pride goes before the fall." A laconic smile crossed his face and he glanced away. Dominic leaned back, rocking in his chair before facing me and said. "Actually I'm surprised it took this long."

I nodded and waited out his response.

Finally he took a deep breath. "Things have gotten so far out of hand. Too crazy for me. You know, at first it was a challenge. If you can copy a master, you become a master. The greats painted from their souls, but if they made a mistake they could leave it. I could not afford to make a mistake. Every minute detail had to be copied, even their mistakes. The canvas had to be the right age and meticulously treated. The paints mixed just so. It was hard and I'm proud of my work. My clients were willing to pay the price of perfection."

"But they were forgeries."

"They weren't forgeries. They were reproductions. I do copies of the best works for clients who don't want to expose their paintings to theft or fire. I think there are some insurance benefits," he said. He twisted in his chair; his eyes darted nervously from the ceiling to the wall and back to me. "Starting about ten years ago I did a couple of reproductions for Nigel Jenkins. He said his clients wanted perfect copies so none of their art friends would know they were copies. I met the first client. Her name was Victoria Halsman. I remember her because she spoke with a slight lisp. I had a lisp once. Anyway, she sat down with me in Jenkins' office and told me she wanted exact copies of her original paintings down to the last detail. 'Good enough to fool Christie's,' she said."

He paused. A snicker cut across his face.

"You know how hard it is to get old canvas, especially in Florida. Almost impossible. Then once I had it, I had to clean it. I've got a new technique that eliminates all traces of chemicals. I thought of patenting the process."

Again he paused.

"Do you have any idea what it feels like when your work is comparable to the masters? My clients could hang their copies in their foyers without fear that any of their friends and associates would know the difference. Do you know how that feels? No, of course not. How could you? You're not a artist."

"Didn't you think that signing your paintings would come back to haunt you? Did you want to get caught?"

"You don't get it, do you? I was contracted to do *reproductions* for clients. What they did with them was their business. I did not do anything wrong. The *serpentini* were my insurance policy. I'm just an artist."

"Everyone tells me I don't get it. I don't care if I don't get it. We're far beyond art, Dominic. It's not just forgeries. We are talking about murder."

Dominic took out a handkerchief and wiped his nose, then folded it before stuffing it back into his pants pocket. The room went silent. I could hear a humidifier humming in the background and the muffled gargle of the television in the next room.

"So you made a reproduction for Victoria Halsman, then what?" I asked.

"Then I got flooded with work. Jenkins contracted me on an exclusive basis."

"Did you meet other clients?"

"No, only Victoria Halsman," Dominic said, fidgeting with a # 4 paintbrush. "She was killed a year later. I read it in the paper and didn't pay it much attention until the Manley murder. Then I met this Billy Balls guy. When I read he was murdered, I left the country."

"Hold on. You knew Billy Balls?"

"Not really knew him. I saw him once. It was in the reception room of Jenkins' business. I was delivering a painting. It was actually my last one. This guy, Billy Balls, came out of Jenkins' back office with Marcus. What caught my eye was not only the way he was dressed, but the tattoo on his left arm. A shark. Not a very good one but a scary copy of the sharks in Winslow Homer's *The Gulf Stream,* the ones circling the castaway. Or at least that's how I remembered it. Then I saw his picture in the paper. I'm no genius but I can put two and two together. That's when I left."

"So you saw Billy Balls and Nigel Jenkins together."

"Yes. And Marcus," he said. "I have no idea what they were talking about but I thought it strange when this guy Billy Balls walked out right past me sitting in the waiting groom as if I wasn't even there. And that was it. Never saw him again until his photo was in the paper."

"You know Dominic, I'm curious, tell me how did you paint the snakes so small? I mean they were as close to invisible as anything I've ever seen."

"I used a vicuña-hair brush." He reached over and took a single hair strand brush and passed it to me. I held it up to the light. It was so thin it was nearly invisible.

"Not bad," I said and handed the brush back. "When did you start signing the reproductions with the snakes?"

Dominic leaned back into the chair and looked up at the ceiling and said, "I had just finished the second reproduction for Jenkins and had laid it beside the original on the table, ready to send it to Jenkins. Like these two." He gestured to the two paintings on the counter. "I had gone out for a few drinks with some friends and when I returned I could not tell which was which. So I decided to leave a telltale mark to tell them apart then as a safeguard. Most of the paintings were copies of well known masters a few modern, expressionists, a couple Reynolds, a Zurbarán. I am an artist, right? So I have the right and obligation to sign them."

He folded his arms across his chest with the paintbrush still in his hand.

"Dominic, there's no denying you are an artist," I said. "I'll even say a genius. But tell me, didn't you ever ask anything about the clients? Didn't you want to know what happened to your paintings?"

"I'm not a curious person and definitely not that naive."

"But you are scared."

His face reddened and he yelled, "Don't you understand? They're going to kill me! They're killing the people I made reproductions for. Maybe they keep the originals and sell them on the black market. I'm the only person who can connect them and the paintings." He took a couple of deep breaths.

"Then where are the originals?" I asked.

"Could be anywhere." He waved his hand in the air. "Europe, Japan, Hong Kong. You know how the black market is."

"Even if they were offered on the black market, a buyer would want them authenticated," I said. "Any buyer dealing with thieves isn't about to buy a stolen painting without knowing it is real. There are only a few people who could analyze and authenticate a major painting. But I've asked around and came up blank. Any ideas?"

He shook his head.

"When we talked on the phone, you said that you had information that Sergio Ordenoff did not kill his wife. Can you tell me what you've got?"

"I told you. I saw this Balls guy at Jenkins' storage place."

"But that doesn't prove anything. It's just a hunch on your part," I said still fishing.

"Call it what you want. I know Jenkins or Marcus killed that woman, then killed the other guy."

"But you have no direct proof."

"No. But I have a list of the reproductions I did. And photographs of the originals side-by-side with the reproductions. I'm sure they are listed in catalogues and could be matched up with their owners after they were examined and tested."

"That's an idea and I'd like to help you," I said. "But you've got to help me. I'll need that list."

He sat up. "The only thing I see keeping me alive and out of jail is information. I would not have even agreed to talk to you except for Mr. Crown. He said I could trust you."

"You can trust me," I said staring Dominic directly in the eye. "But I have to inform the police. Look, an innocent man could be convicted for a murder he did not commit. You don't want that on your conscience."

"I told you. I just want to stay out of jail and get out this mess alive."

"That's two of us," I said. Then, to soften him up, "If what you're telling me is true, then you were conned like the rest of the victims. You should be okay. But I will need that list to show the police that you're cooperating. The investigation officer is a personal friend of mine. I'll explain everything to him just like you told me. I guarantee he'll be very grateful."

I watched as Dominic twitched in his chair and then put the brush on the table.

"Give me a few days," he said in a soft, low voice.

"Reality in this case is not pretty," I said. "I'm heading back to Palm

Beach." I paused. "What are you going to do now?"

"I'm not sure."

"The list is very important," I repeated.

"So you say."

"I can't force you to do anything, but the list would help your case, and Sergio Ordenoff. It might put Nigel Jenkins in jail."

"Under no condition will I return to the States." He pressed his lips together and looked me back in the eye.

"I'm not asking you to return to the States. But I'd advise you not to get lost. You don't want to be a fugitive running for the rest of your life." I pulled one of my business cards out of my pocket. "Here's my cell phone number."

He took it in a limp hand.

I turned to the two small Kokoschkas placed side by side on the counter.

"And these," I said, pointing to the paintings.

"A commission by a Montreal collector," he said. "I still have to work."

I examined the original and the copy. The copy was perfect. Dominic Carranza had captured the artist at his best, with the strength of his mature expression and style. I knew when I first saw a Carranza fake I had to meet the forger. I knew then that I'd find brilliance, and I had. But sadly, considering the circumstances, the joy I expected to feel was, instead, a cheerless, anxious void.

"I have to admit, Dominic, you are a master."

He allowed a smile to cross his lips. His shoulders dropped and he settled back in to his chair.

It was two in the morning. Dominic drove me back to Toronto. The ride back was quiet. I realized how tired I was and fought the urge to nod off. The lights of Toronto on a winter morning glowed before us as we zoomed over the highway.

Before we reached the hotel Dominic said, "My mother has a cottage near Kingston. I think I'm going to stay there."

"Give me a cell phone or something where I can reach you." When he hesitated, I added, "I can guarantee you that you don't want Bernie Crown looking for you." He stopped the cab a block from the Royal Oak and handed me dog-eared business card with two numbers at the bottom.

"I can be reached at the second number, but I'd be happy never to see you again.

"That might not be possible." I started to open the door then asked, "By the way, have you ever come across a Tintoretto landscape from Italy?"

I went straight to my room, grabbed my suitcase, checked out and took a taxi to the airport. The Gulfstream was fueled and fired up.

"I can't believe you guys are ready at this hour," I told the pilot as the fuselage door closed behind me. "Do you sleep on the plane?"

"Sometimes," the co-pilot said. "When you work for Mr. Crown, you're on call twenty-four seven."

"I hope he's paying you enough."

"We have no complaints, I assure you," he said. "Mr. Crown is on the phone."

He handed me the secure jet phone.

"Don't you ever sleep?" I asked.

"Can't afford to," Bernie said. "Hope you're enjoying yourself."

"It was a very informative meeting," I said

"I know," Bernie said. "I know. Call me when you get back." Click.

I handed the phone to the copilot.

"After takeoff, if you're tired, there're two beds in the back cabin," he said. "We'll have you back in West Palm by the time you awake." He touched the tip of his hat and disappeared into the cockpit.

As the jet taxied down the runway I thought to myself, *I'd found the forger but most likely not the killer.* Was Dominic the innocent tool of an elaborate art con, or was I being scammed? Nigel Jenkins was deeply involved. But was he the mastermind behind the deaths of Billy Balls and Martha? And if so, how was I to convince Adam?

Once in the air, I staggered into the back cabin. I undressed down to my shorts and crawled into one of the twin beds. Before the jet had reached cruising altitude I was deep asleep and did not wake until three hours later as we were approaching the West Palm airport.

CHAPTER 50

Once inside the terminal, I dialed Adam.

"I was just about to send the posse out."

"Are you confessing you miss me?"

"What do you have?"

"I'd like to ask you something first," I said. "Do you remember the Victoria Halsman murder?"

"Victoria Halsman. Now there's a cold case. What's your interest in it?"

"I was told she had a sizeable art collection."

"Yeah, I remember. The Massachusetts State Police asked me to interview her daughter who was staying at The Island house. The place was wall-to-wall paintings, reminded me of a museum. The last I heard, the case is still open and our Bay State brothers had nothing."

"No suspects?"

"Not yet," Adam said. "Now, do you care to tell me what the hell you were doing in Toronto?"

"Toronto?"

"Don't give me that crap. Your tails watched you take off and Mr. Crown's pilots filed a flight plan."

"I have a tail?"

"Yeah, right. You know, the ones you shook off your tail at Mike's garage."

"Well, Toronto was cold as hell, Adam. I would have gladly let you go in my place, but I was saving you from possible frostbite. You hate the cold."

"I hate you holding out on me."

"I'm a little punch-drunk. I haven't gotten much sleep lately. How about a bite at Green's? I could use some breakfast."

"See you in twenty."

Breakfast is a sure-shot at Green's Pharmacy. They serve it all day.

I dropped my bag in the Jag and headed west on Belvedere, then east onto Military. Not seeing any gray cars, I felt safe driving directly to The Island.

Breakfast smells assailed my nostrils as I stepped through the front North County Road door of Green's Pharmacy across from Saint Eddies. Green's was as close to a 1950s soda fountain drugstore as could be found anywhere. The drugstore and beach paraphernalia were stacked to the left and the diner operated on the south side. It was full. Adam had scored a stool at the far end of the counter. I ordered a coffee and a warmed banana nut muffin. Adam asked for coffee. In five minutes, the waitress deftly placed our orders on the counter and gave us a large smile, which Adam returned. He was in good humor. Odd, how I'd become attuned to Adam's mood swings.

"Here's the scoop," I said, and proceeded to tell Adam everything.

"This is all very interesting," Adam said.

"It's more than interesting," I said.

"Maxie, you've done a lot of work and I appreciate it, but Putzer is not buying the artist-as-killer story. He's got his man and he's sticking to it. I'll admit your story makes sense. I'll ask around, but we still have not gotten a formal complaint."

"And if Ordenoff is the wrong man?"

"He'll have his day in court," Adam said. "For Putzer to backtrack now after all the self-generated publicity, I'll need a hell of a lot more to sell him than what you've given me. There's no way he's going to change his mind over hearsay statements of a self-confessed fugitive forger hiding out in Canada." He took a sip of coffee. "You realize, of course, that if this forgery thing checks out, it could look even worse for your client."

"I keep telling you, he's not my client," I said. "If it's proven that Ordenoff had Martha killed, then I'll be the first to cheer that you got the right man. What I want to know is where are the original paintings and who tried to burn me out?"

"Unfortunately, we haven't got anything new on the fire," Adam said. "Meanwhile, do us both a favor, go home and rest. You look as bad as I feel."

"I just can't shake the thought of Martha dying like that."

"Dying is easy, it's the killing that's hard," Adam said as he got up to leave. "By the way, thanks again."

I tried to make a quiet entrance into the house but Margarita caught me sneaking into the den.

"You out all night," she said accusingly. "You a grown man. It's not good."

"It was business, Margarita. Honest."

"Business?"

"What if I told you I was in Canada and there was four feet of snow on the ground?"

"I never seen snow."

"You're not missing anything."

She huffed and retreated into the kitchen.

I sat down and turned on the computer.

Dominic told me he had done a reproduction for Victoria Halsman before she was murdered. She might have been the first victim in the current string of deaths. If so, there was a record. I Googled her name and got twenty-three hits. From an article in the Shiny Sheet, I found the headline: "Seasonal Resident Found Murdered In Hyannisport." Victoria Halsman, it said, had been killed in her summerhouse in Hyannisport, Massachusetts. Aside from the Cape Cod home, she'd had a house on Via Palmetto on The Island. Robbery was suspected as the motive. Her net-worth, according to the paper, was in the sixteen million range. A week later no suspects had been caught. The article was six years old and never mentioned a word about paintings.

CHAPTER 51

With the kids coming and the influx of northern clients, who I, the eternal optimist, was certain were waiting in line to buy paintings, I was running out of time. The Nigel Jenkins, Billy Balls, and Dominic Carranza connection was too pat to be coincidental. Yet in my mind, it couldn't be simpler. As Adam so poignantly pointed out, all I had was circumstantial hearsay, a few hunches, and the word of a fugitive forger. I needed concrete proof that the Manley paintings had been stored with Nigel Jenkins and that they were copied without her permission. Positive proof that even a legally myopic Peter Putzer could not deny. That proof, I felt, was back at the Manley place.

The Count had said that Martha kept meticulous records. Chances were that she had a file with a receipt or letter that would confirm her paintings had been stored with Jenkins. I called Raymundo and got a recording that the telephone had been disconnected. Perhaps, I thought, I'd catch him on the premises. I'd made so many trips there this week, the Jag almost knew the way by itself.

The driveway was empty and the house looked closed up tight, like a long gone snowbird's home. I rang the front door bell. No answer. I trudged around to the back. The five-car garage with Raymundo's apartment above was connected to the main house by an arched breezeway. I tried the door at the end of the garage. Nothing. I crossed the driveway to the kitchen door and knocked. Listening for life inside, I could hear nothing except for a mockingbird chirping away on top of a dormer eave. I knocked again. With a gentle push the door opened and I invited myself inside.

"Hello." My voice echoed through the kitchen. "Raymundo, are you here? It's Maxie Roberts."

Silence. The large empty home had a tomb-like stillness.

The kitchen was immaculate and had the sterile, chemical smell of a recent cleaning.

"Hello!"

The help was obviously gone, so I'd just have to do things myself. I crossed the kitchen, cut through the pantry and dining room past the bare walls in the living room to Martha's study. I scooted around her desk and pulled out the bottom drawer file the Count had shown to me when we were looking for Billy Balls' employment application. I fingered through the files reading every heading: Allentown apartment, Automobiles, Palm Beach house, Raymundo, Utilities. Nothing on paintings. I opened the next drawer. Sweat beaded on my forehead in the cool interior. I flipped through file after file. Nothing. No Nigel Jenkins, no Fine Art Custodians.

I was about to close the second drawer when I heard a rustle behind me and, before I completely turned, I was face to face with Raymundo standing in the doorway. In his right hand was a large .44 magnum revolver pointed at my chest. I raised my arms.

"What does the law say about shooting intruders?" he asked. "I heard they have to be armed. If you dig deeper in the top drawer to the right you'll find Mrs. Manley's .32 Smith & Wesson. Take it."

I raised my hands higher.

"I called and knocked . . . "

"That doesn't make it any less a B & E," he said and cocked the hammer. "Did you kill Miss Martha?"

"Of course not." Then, sounding braver then I felt, I said, "Did you?"

He took four paces closer. The revolver was still pointed at my chest. I could smell a trace of alcohol.

"The police were here asking questions about you," he said. "They think you're a prime suspect."

"You have to believe me, I'm trying to help Sergio."

"Help? You're like Shiva, the god of destruction. Since you showed up, Mrs. Manley was murdered, I've been treated as a murder suspect, the house has been raped, and now my boss is in jail. I think we can do without your help." He raised the revolver. "Why? Why would you want to help Mr. Ordenoff? Right now I don't think I'd believe anything you'd say to me. If you had been privy to the myriad of inane conversations I've heard over the last twenty years, you'd realize that words are vehicles of deceit, philosophically speaking that is."

Whoa! Was this Raymundo the mute?

Observing my visible surprise he started, "Strange isn't it? What you see before you is a common chauffeur. Actually, I was educated at Brown in Rhetoric, as a matter of fact, but I find driving relaxing, in a Zen-like way. You know, no pressure. That is until your employer is brutally murdered." He released the revolver hammer and holstered the gun. "Put your hands down. You look like one of the Three Stooges."

I hoped not Curley.

"Here." He pulled a handkerchief out of his pocket and threw it to me, "Wipe the sweat off your forehead."

"Thanks," I said, taking a deep breath.

"What did you hope to find?"

"A file or maybe a receipt that shows Martha or Frederick had stored their paintings somewhere."

"Why didn't you simply ask? Just before Miss Martha left for Europe after Mr. Manley died, she had her paintings crated and a van took them away. If I remember correctly, they were taken to some storage place in Palm Beach Gardens."

Raymundo came around the desk. He closed the bottom drawer with his leg, and then opened a closet door between the bookcases. Against the back wall was a built-in four-drawer mahogany file cabinet.

"Miss Martha kept the older files in here. Only the current files are in the desk."

Halfway through the second drawer he stopped.

"Maybe this is what you were looking for. It says Fine Art Custodians on the tab. It's empty." He opened the folder like a butterfly over the desk. "Why would anyone just take the contents and not the entire file?"

"Unless Martha had taken documents out to make copies or to show them to someone and didn't have time to return them or . . . "

"Someone might have killed her and taken them," Raymundo said.

"Might have," I said. "Wait, wait. Of course! Those were the papers in the trunk of Billy's Corvette."

"What Corvette?"

"Raymundo, you are quite an interesting person," I said. "But I gotta go. You've been a huge help, believe me. I think, with any luck, your patron will soon be free."

He looked incredulous and, for a moment, I thought he might try to stop me from leaving. Instead he shrugged his shoulders.

"One last item, Mr. Roberts," Raymundo said. "If you hear of anyone who needs an experienced and discreet chauffeur, do let me know."

By the time I made it back to the house, long afternoon shadows were creeping across the driveway. It wasn't until I had parked the Jag and glanced at the front door that I saw Zelda standing with her knapsack resting against the bottom step. I slowly got out of the Jag and walked up to her.

"I left you a note. It's inside. I've got a ride home." She smiled and said, "I'll be okay.

I didn't know what to say.

"I'll be okay," she said. "An old friend is coming to pick me up. He's a good guy. I trust him."

"Not the guy who traded you to Billy?"

"No." She looked up at me, her eyes moist. "At the risk of sounding corny, I'm going to miss you. You're a great guy but this ain't for me," she said, waving her hand in a circle.

"This is a new twist on love-them-and-leave-them."

"I like you too much to stay. Nothing good can come out of this. You know that."

With a smile she reached up, grabbed the back of my neck and kissed me. I wanted to hold her and tell he she didn't have to go, but before I could say a word I heard a deep un-Palm Beach-like rumble as a Harley Hog glided into the driveway topped by a muscular, crew cut Eurasian with an armful of tattoos. She said, "That Kathy girl, she's a keeper." Zelda swung her knapsack on her back and hopped on the back of the bike. She waved, and then in a blast of power, she was gone.

I went into the kitchen and plopped down on a stool. I was sorry she'd left but she was right.

A moment later Margarita came in. "You look sad. You okay?"

I nodded.

She retrieved one of her mystery mixtures from the refrigerator and placed it on the counter. "What happened to that nice Zelda girl?"

"I wish I knew, Margarita. Appears I'm condemned to a life alone."

"That's not what Oshim says," she said. "And he know everything."

Like Santa Claus, I reckoned.

Margarita's mix, followed by a double vodka and tonic, almost straightened me out. The you-have-calls light was flashing on the answering machine. I played the message back and heard Kathy Krammer's voice, "Like to bring you up to date on the Manley question. How about lunch on Friday?"

I stared at the machine. Did she know Zelda had left? I ran to the window, slowly parted the curtains and looked up and down the darken street. I half expected to see a blue Boxster parked outside in the evening shadows. But except for my new best friend in the grey car, the street was empty.

CHAPTER 52

With Margarita's concoction firmly ingested, I slept soundly, awaking at seven refreshed. Two caffeine-loaded coffees later and the cobwebs were swept from my mind. I made a quick assessment of what I knew. With Dominic and Kiki's statements, the much-bemoaned fog of war was lifting its nebulous veil and the bride it revealed was Nigel Jenkins. He had a perfect set up for a forgery ring. Wealthy art patrons stored their paintings in his vaults where he had all the time he needed to have them forged. He returned the copies to the owners and kept the originals. Before her trip to Europe, Martha had rented a vault at Fine Arts Custodians large enough to store her entire collection. Nigel Jenkins hired Dominic Carranza to make copies of the paintings. When the newly wedded Martha returned, Jenkins gave her the copies and kept the originals. At some point Martha began to question the authenticity of her paintings. Suddenly, instead of an enviable art collection, Martha had a fifteen million-dollar liability. She knew the Monet was a fake making the rest suspect. She wanted the paintings authenticated by someone who, unlike the major auction houses, would not be obliged to make that information public. Once the fakes were exposed, it would not have taken any investigator long to trace them back to Jenkins. Either Lisette or Billy Balls told him that Martha suspected the paintings were fake and it would not be long before she could trace them back to Jenkins.

The night before I was to examine the paintings, Martha had taken the Fine Arts Custodian papers out of the file. Billy Balls either, on his own or at the bequest of Nigel Jenkins, killed Martha and took the file. Billy kept the murder weapon and the file, and was blackmailing Jenkins. Jenkins had him killed, but did not know where Billy had hidden the pistol or the file. That is, until the night he found me at Zelda's house. With the pistol and the file gone, there was nothing to connect Jenkins with the forgeries or Martha's death.

Marcus probably did the more physical work, like murder and arson. Most likely it was Marcus who'd left his size fourteen shoe imprinted on my face in Zelda's garage. He must have been the dark figure fleeing the gallery the night of the fire, and I was sure he was Lisette's Frank.

I can still picture myself at Noreen Forester's Japanese party telling

Jenkins I was interested in the Manley paintings and hinting that they might be forgeries. He must have tried to burn me out to cover the missing Manley file or to scare me.

I had plenty of circumstantial information for Adam, but only the hearsay testimony of a forger and a missing biker. To seal the deal I still needed proof that Martha Manley had rented a vault at Jenkins' storage. That information was in the lion's den. Perhaps if I was to casually visit Jenkins he might say something that would incriminate him. Something concrete I could take to Adam. Jenkins had no idea that I had talked with either Lisette or Dominic. He did not know how much information I had, and I bet he wanted to pump me for as much information as I did him. It'd be an interesting chess match. It was a risk, but surely he would not do anything foolish with the receptionist present. I could be in and out of there in twenty minutes and on the phone to Adam with any new information.

I dialed the Fine Art Custodians; Jenkins answered on the second ring.

"Nigel, hi, Maxie here. I'm in Jupiter and was hoping to come by and talk about renting a vault."

"Come right on over. We're open twenty four-seven for our special customers," Jenkins said.

After a ten-minute drive, I pulled into the Fine Art Custodians' parking lot. It was empty except for Jenkins' Carrera and a black Lexus parked in front of the entrance in the shade. I shut off the engine and sat a minute taking deep breaths. This was either the bravest or stupidest stunt I'd pulled in my life. I thought of leaving. Instead, I dialed Adam and got his recorder.

"Adam. If you get this message give me a call in exactly a half an hour. It's eleven fifty, that'll be twelve twenty. I should have something important to tell you." If for any reason I was stuck inside, a well-timed call from a police lieutenant might help. I stared at my watch. I couldn't believe it was only ten to twelve. Except for the sun shining, it felt like midnight.

I checked myself in the rearview mirror. The bags under my eyes hung like sad sack prunes. I needed some serious sleep but I was on an adrenaline high.

No use waiting—I hopped out of the Jag and strode into the building. The atrium was lit up but the receptionist's desk was empty. I took the elevator up to the second floor and was greeted by Marcus Oberlin, who escorted me into the office.

"You're late," Jenkins said.

"Late?" I asked puzzled.

"Most people rent vaults during hurricane season."

"Oh. Well, I'm a confirmed contrarian," I said. "You know, since the fire, I'm thinking of keeping some of the more important pieces here for safekeeping. I was lucky once and don't want to press my luck."

Suddenly Cerberus bolted into the room, scurried up to me and sniffed my leg, his back end doing the samba.

"Nice boy." I reached and scratched between his ears. "I always forget how big he is."

Jenkins snapped his fingers and pointed to the backroom. "Come on Cerberus, inside." The Great Dane lowered his head and with his tail still wagging, obediently left the office.

"He does lack the killer instinct of a watchdog," Jenkins said. "But we still love him. Right Marcus?"

"Best damn dog in the county," Marcus said.

"We'll be pleased to have you as a client," Jenkins said. "Whatever you store here is as secure as Fort Knox. How big a vault did you have in mind?"

"A small walk-in will do. Something that could hold twenty paintings and not get crowded."

"You're in luck. We have two vaults that will fit your needs." He spread out a color-coded plan of the vaults. "These two," he said and pointed out two red squares. "Would you want to see them?"

"That's why I'm here," I said. "Insurance?"

"We're fully bonded but I'd advise getting a supplemental policy. You know how they are with artwork. They never want to pay out what it's really worth without concrete proof."

"I understand the Manleys have a vault here."

Jenkins paused. "Generally client information is confidential. But, yes, Mrs. Manley was one of our clients for a number of years, but she hasn't leased a vault from us for, I believe, going on five years now. "

"And Mr. Manley?"

"We've only been here seven years. I understand Mr. Manley passed away a while back, didn't he?"

"Did she have a vault large enough for all her paintings?"

Jenkins frowned. His eyes shrunk. "What do you want to know for?"

"Umm. I was thinking, you know, that I might need one as big."

Jenkins carefully folded up the plan on his desk. "The Manleys, the Manleys. It always comes down to the Manleys." He glanced at Marcus and then back at me. His jaw tightened and he drummed his fingers on his desk like one possessed.

"You are a little fucking, meddling ass shit," he barked.

I was trying to think of a clever retort when I was struck in the face by a size fifteen fist that threw me over the armrest to the floor. My next clear recollection was of Marcus yanking me to my feet. He thrust me back into the chair like a rag doll. Jenkins pulled a chrome-plated .9mm Glock from his desk.

"Why the fuck did you have to get in the middle of this? No one wanted you to interfere; yet you wouldn't stop. You kept coming like a yapping little rat dog."

"What are you talking about? Martha came to me."

"And she died for it. You didn't get the hint, you stupid fuck! They were happy with their copies. They loved what we gave them. They didn't know any better. They can't appreciate real art. Then you come around and have to upset the fucking cart." His temples were glowing a bright red.

"For Christ's sake, its just art, Nigel," I said. "It's not worth dying for."

"We'll see," he said. He raised the pistol at me.

I rolled off the chair and did a quick two step, ducking behind a blue and white Ming Chinese vase.

With two giant steps, Marcus was above me. He delivered a vicious kick to my lower back. I grabbed my backside and fell flat on the floor again, expecting once and for all to settle the age-old argument that you cannot hear the report of the bullet that kills you. Instead, Marcus grabbed me by the shoulders and jerked me to my feet. He took my wallet, cell phone, and car keys, then dragged me down the corridor.

"Nigel, what're you doing?"

Neither of them said anything. We stopped in front of a closet-sized vault.

"Lieutenant Aldrick knows I'm here. He's on his way over" I tried my gambit.

"Is he now?" Jenkins said, his voice hard and cold.

Jenkins tapped the keypad at the vault entrance. The door opened silently. Marcus gave me a vicious kidney punch that sent lightning up my spine and down my leg. I collapsed. He grabbed my arm, stood me up, then with one quick motion tossed me into a vault. I bounced hard off the back wall.

"Have a slow death," Jenkins said.

I was curled up in the corner trying to catch my breath, but I managed to ask, "Can you tell me one last thing? How many forgeries are there?"

"This isn't confession time, asshole," he spat. "But there are more than you can imagine."

I watched as the vault door closed. Then I heard the sickening metallic snap of the lock.

CHAPTER 53

Tomb-like darkness enveloped me and I froze, afraid that I might not wake up from this nightmare. My chest heaved and I started to hyperventilate. Stop, I told myself. Don't panic. Don't scream. Conserve air. I pulled my legs to my chest to relax and maintain my breathing. Slowly my eyes adjusted to the dark. I noticed, near the door, a tiny solitary red light glowing. Somewhere overhead I could hear the soft whirl of moving air. It was a ventilation system. Maybe I wouldn't die of suffocation, though prolonged starvation did not offer a more attractive alternative.

My ears attuned to the quiet and I could just make out noises from outside. I couldn't tell if it was voices or footsteps. Suddenly, the noises stopped. I strained, trying to hear anything. Then the red light went out and the ventilator's comforting hum ceased. They had turned off the electricity. Again I fought back panic.

I tried to remember the breathing exercises from the yoga classes Nancy had insisted I attend. I took long deep breaths and thought calming thoughts. My breathing slowed. I didn't kid myself; this was it.

I thought of the children. Eric would say of this situation, 'This sucks.' Nicole and Eric were going to miss me. In the darkness and silence with my eyes closed, I saw Nancy at our Lamaze classes. Eric's birth, and the first fish he caught and boated. He was three. I saw Nicole coming in first in the freestyle at the junior high school swim match. The family around the dinner table joking, reading passages from Homer and the Simpsons. We had been a family. What would happen to them? Probably do better with me gone. Bernie was executor to my estate. Nancy would take good care of the kids. She was always a good mother. And a great wife. Where did it go wrong? God, I've royally screwed up my life. Oh, Nancy, Nancy, I'm so sorry. So, so sorry.

My thoughts and my mind wandered. I was tired and lost track of time. I read that when drowning, your final memory is of sleep. Was this like drowning? I closed my eyes, a silent prayer on my lips. So much can be seen in absolute darkness.

I think I slept because I awoke wet. Beads of sweat dampened my forehead and I wiped them away with my sleeve. I was breathing deeply but, oddly, I had stopped feeling worried. The stale air tasted like steel wool on the back of my throat. I felt heavy, yet I was floating. It was night. If I tried, I could reach out and touch the stars. They were that close.

Suddenly I was playing by the canal behind my parents' house in West Palm Beach. I heard my mother calling from the back porch, then a sharp scraping sound, and a green frog, frightened, leaped from the bank into the murky water with a noiseless splash. Distant voices filtered through the heavy air. Angels, I thought. Then more scraping. No, muffled footsteps. I saw the little red light burst on like a laser beam and heard the vent hum in surreal fascination.

Had Jenkins and Marcus returned? Footsteps. Too many for two people. Fumbling in my pocket I retrieved a quarter and began to tap on the metal door. I couldn't scream. The chances of anyone hearing me were slim and I'd use up what little air I had. I kept on tapping. The metal-on-metal sound of the quarter against the vault door reverberated in the heavy air like a low C flat.

Muffled sounds outside the vault door. Then a pinging on the vault door. I tapped back. Thank God, someone was here. An eternity passed before the door opened and a wall of light blinded me. I closed my eyes and filled my lungs with air. Never knew that Florida air could taste so good.

I felt hands lift me and carry me out. They pried the quarter from my hand. When I opened my eyes, I was looking up at Adam.

"Seriously, Maxie. We gotta stop meeting like this."

I must have looked bad because Adam's forehead was wrinkled and worried. He helped me to my feet. One of the paramedics handed me a bottle of water. I downed half in one gulp.

"You can thank your police tail that you still have yours."

"Did they get Jenkins and Marcus?"

"No. They were watching you. When Jenkins and Oberlin left in a hurry they had no reason to suspect anything until an hour had passed and you didn't come out. We have an APB out for both of them. Probably skipped the state if not the country. Do you have any idea where they might have gone?"

I shook my head. "None."

"Looks like you were right. A lot of egg has been splashed on a lot of faces," Adam said. "It's not easy moving a lot of artwork around the country. We'll get them. Sooner or later we'll get them. Do you want to go to the hospital?"

"I'd rather go home."

"Your attorney is outside."

"My attorney?"

Adam helped me down the elevator and outside. Scores of cops and firemen milled around us. Then I saw Kathy Krammer's beaming face among the blue police. She waved then ran up to us.

"Do you need a good lawyer?" She asked.

"In more ways than one," I said. "Are you an ambulance chaser now?"

Tears welled in her eyes. She gave a little jump and hung her arms around my neck. "Damn you. I was so worried."

I hugged her back and felt her body, warm and soothing, press into mine.

"He's fine. But he'll need someone to drive him home," I heard Adam say behind me.

"I'll take him, lieutenant," Kathy volunteered.

"I don't need anyone to drive me," I started to protest. "I can drive."

"You don't have your driver's license. Unless you want a ride in a squad car to the station, I'd take the lady's offer." He winked at Kathy.

I knew when I was beaten. From under the back bumper of the Jag I retrieved a spare set of car keys. "You can have these," I threw Adam the keys. "Enjoy."

"I'll consider it a test drive. Never know when I'll be in the market for one."

CHAPTER 54

After I gave my statement, Kathy and I headed back to the house.

"You frightened the daylights out of me," she said as she made the turn off I-95 on to Okeechobee Boulevard. "I can't believe you went over there alone."

"I had it figured out, but Nigel Jenkins and Marcus did not follow the planned scenario," I said.

"Do they ever?"

No, I had to admit.

"And I don't think Margarita is going to be happy with you."

"That's all I need is a scolding."

Thinking back to the empty blackness in the vault, a stygian fear gripped my chest and I shivered. I almost died. I started to shake and tears welled up in my eyes.

"It's okay, Maxie," Kathy said softly and patted my leg.

While I claim to love a life of dissonance, I had to admit two near-death experiences filled my monthly quota. Then to Kathy, "You know something? I'm starved."

Margarita jumped up from her chair when Kathy and I walked into the kitchen.

"I was so worried. You scare me bad," Margarita said as she rushed around mumbling maledictions and supplications. "Take this and no complaints." She handed me one of her toddies, her eyes were wet. "I'm sorry, Margarita." I hugged her and drank her drink straight then fell onto the sofa exhausted.

"Lie back and relax, " Kathy said. "Margarita and I are going to cook something special."

My eyes had just shut when the phone rang and I foolishly answered it. Margot was on the line. "You've become quite popular lately."

"I know. I know. Just tell me the damage."

"I'll skip all the media people who want to talk to you. First, the Deacon Cleveland Cook called three times. Said it was urgent. About something you'd asked him to check out. And he mentioned Nigel Jenkins."

"Okay, I'll get back to him."

"And of course, Dickie Durdle, Twice. And Mr. Crown phoned. He said, he was out of town but would call when he got back. Three clients were wondering about their art, but I don't think you want to deal with them now. I said you'd call them back in a few days. When the press started in I took the phone off the hook."

"Good going. Keep it off the hook. Why don't you close up the gallery and take the rest of the day off."

"Do you want me to come by the house?"

"Thanks. But Margarita and Kathy Krammer have everything under control."

I hung up the phone. Hopefully, the media would not show up at my front door. I thought of the media group orgy in front of the Manley house when the Count was arrested. That was all I needed.

From across the family room I watched Kathy in the kitchen. She was dicing a couple of sweet peppers at the counter. Margarita was stirring a pan on the stove. A real domestic picture that I had not seen in three years. How I missed it.

With Margarita's libation swirling in my stomach, I felt relaxed enough to attempt a few calls.

I headed to the den. "I'll be right back."

"You need rest," Kathy said.

"I'm gonna disconnect the phone," Margarita said.

"A couple of calls, then you can cut the line if you want. Promise."

I dialed a Toronto number. Dominic answered.

"All hell has broken loose down here, Dominic. Jenkins tried to kill me. He and Marcus have taken off and there are hundreds of paintings locked up in the storage vaults. Any number of them could be forgeries."

"Actually I . . . I did very few copies," he stuttered. "I never made a copy without specific instructions from the owners."

"That might be a cute legal technicality, but this has gotten way beyond you and me, Dominic."

"I'm not coming back."

"I don't give a damn if you come back or not. But unless you want to see your face on CNN tonight, I want to know where to find Jenkins and Marcus."

"I don't know. Honest. Jenkins has a house in the Adirondacks and he told me once he had a farm somewhere near Lake Okeechobee, what he called his plantation."

"The man was a control freak. He planned everything, I'm sure he had a perfect escape plan to leave the country. I do remember he had a partner in South Africa. Once, after I delivered a reproduction to him, he said he'd had a long flight from Johannesburg. Told me he liked the country and was thinking of buying property there. Maybe he's there."

"You can't think of anything else?"

"I just worked for the man. We didn't socialize."

"And Marcus, what about him?"

"He was pretty a tight-lipped guy. I don't think we said ten words to each other. It was Jenkins who always did the talking."

After hanging up with Dominic, I dialed Dickie's cell phone.

"It's on all the news stations," Dickie said. "I was so worried and you know I don't do worry well. My fingernails are bit down to the quick. Aseneth phoned and said she was upset with you. You had promised her not to do anything stupid."

"You can go home now. It's safe," I told him.

"Maxie. They haven't been caught yet. I could still be in danger!"

"Dickie, believe me, they have much bigger problems to deal with. You are quite far down on their list."

"There's a list? You saw a list? Am I on the list?"

"Bye, Dickie."

I dialed what I hoped was to be my last call.

Cleveland Cook answered on the second ring.

"Mr. Roberts. You have been extremely remiss with your communication skills. I've left you messages."

"I know, Cleveland. I apologize. I owe you a dinner."

"Dinner would be much appreciated, thank you. I see the high and mighty are going though a restructuring of biblical proportions."

"Sermon fodder, Reverend?"

"Well sir, you remember our last telephone conversation? You asked me to let you know if I found out anything about the very same Nigel Jenkins that is gracing the local news. It just so happens I did. You know, Mr. Roberts, the sister-in-law of my first cousin's husband's brother is a housekeeper. A good, God-fearing woman. Lives in Pahokee. She cleans Nigel Jenkins' house or, rather, his farmhouse, twice a week. Said it was at the end of a gravel road half way between Royal Palm and Pahokee on a lake surrounded by orange groves and sugarcane fields. Says the house is a veritable museum. And it has an airplane landing field."

"Did she give you an address?"

"No, but she did say the turnoff was just beyond twenty-mile bend, right after one of those 'spanic cafes, you know, Hahblamous Spanish."

"I know the area."

"She was working there today and got a call this morning from Mr. Jenkins and was told to go home. He didn't say why or anything. Then she saw the news and remembered I was interested in him and she called me."

"Why didn't you say so before?"

"Mr. Roberts. Please. I left you many messages."

"I know, I know. It's my fault, Cleveland."

"Like I said, she's a good God-fearing woman and there was something she said about one of the paintings at the farm. It reminded her of the stain glass windows of the Forty-fifth Street Baptist Church. Christ on the Cross, but at a weird angle and it looked like he was floating. Surreal, I think."

"That sounds like a Dali, the one that was stolen from the Salvador Museum in Tampa."

"You know something, I think you're right."

"Thanks Cleveland. I mean it, thanks a lot."

"What about those fine paintings I gave you last week?"

Had it been only a week?

"Come by the gallery Monday and I'll have a check for you."

"I knew you wouldn't disappoint a man of God," he said. "By the way, you like sculptures of naked ladies?"

Jenkins had a farm near Pahokee? A few of the super rich, like Peter Pulitzer, had getaways in the Everglades—luxury fish and hunting camps where they went to escape The Island bustle.

I dialed Adam's cell phone. No answer. I left an urgent message to call me then I tried the station.

"He's out," the on-duty Sergeant said.

"It's important that I talk to him immediately."

"He's probably at a debriefing with the state attorney. I can't break into that meeting. If you want, I can give you the state attorney's assistant."

I would be damned before I gave that weasel Putzer this lead. If I saw him one more time on TV taking credit for others' work I'd puke.

With a sigh, I laid my head back down and closed my eyes. But before the sweet sirens of sleep carried me off into their world, visions of Dali, and Christ, and crosses to bear, danced like a pack of cards on my inner eyelids.

For two decades, I'd carried this cross of the lost Tintoretto, the Italian masterpiece stolen from the Murphy estate in Trivoli. If there was a chance, any chance, of saving another painting, I was going to do it. By now, Nigel Jenkins had probably left the country and the painting was hanging in his watery redoubt. Chances were there were others. I had to see them, rescue them, hold them in my hands. Was I atoning for losing the Tintoretto? I didn't know. I did know that I had to try.

I jumped off the bed and quickly calculated that the drive out to twenty-mile bend would take me twenty-five minutes. Taking a jacket out of the closet, I grabbed my Nikon camera from a drawer.

"What are you doing? I told you to rest," Kathy said, as I passed through the kitchen. "If you don't, I'll tell Margarita on you."

"I have one more errand to run."

"What, after all that's happened? You can't be serious."

"I know where some of the stolen paintings are."

CHAPTER 55

"You do?" Kathy said, putting down a stainless steel mixing bowl.

"That last call was from Deacon Cleveland Cook. He told me Jenkins has a farm outside of Pahokee where he kept some of the paintings. I can't get a hold of Adam so I want to check them out for myself and take pictures," I said.

"Hold on," Kathy said. "What are you going to do? Ride out there? What if Nigel Jenkins is there?"

"He's not stupid. He's long gone. These might be a couple of paintings he didn't have time to sell or ship out of the country." I raised my camera for her to see. "A few shots, then I'm home."

"Then I'm going with you."

"You can't."

"What do you mean, I can't. Aren't you forgetting one small detail?"

"What?"

"You don't have a car. That's my car parked out there and nobody drives my baby but me. Plus, if you want to get somewhere in a hurry, I'm your woman."

"Good point. You know, you'd make a good attorney."

"What about dinner?" Margarita cried as we headed for the door.

"We'll be back by six."

"No you won't," Margarita said. "Wait. Wait, I say."

I stopped. Margarita came around the kitchen island faster than I'd seen her move in years. She reached around her neck and took off a medallion she wore and slipped it over my head. "He'll protect you." Then she reached into her pocket, turned to Kathy and pressed another one into Kathy's hand.

"Go, if you have to. Go before I cry." She made the sign of the cross.

"I have a call into Adam Aldrick. If he calls here tell him to call my cell." I kissed Margarita on the forehead. "Thank you. We'll be back. I promise."

Kathy wasn't kidding about getting somewhere in a hurry. She drove like Mario Andretti on meta-amphetamines. We did ninety down Route 80, her fuzz buster on high. The reassuring hum of the Porsche engine generated two hundred eighty horse power a foot from our heads. I watched Kathy's skirt slowly inch up her thigh each time she lifted her leg to shift. Her legs could stop a freight train. Jock wanted me to ask her to pull over into a cane field for a quickie, but I knew the seats in the little two-seater did not go back. In fact, only two well-trained contortionists could make love in a Boxster. Come on, Porsche, get with the program!

Kathy caught my eye. "I know it's a little late to ask, but do we know what we're doing?"

"Good question, counselor. If I had known what I was doing I'd have never gotten out bed this morning."

"I mean, here we are speeding through the Everglades, trying to find a horde of art stolen by a serial murderer who, by the way, tried his best to kill you this morning and the cops don't even know where we are." She was right, but I noticed that she never let up on the accelerator. "Now tell me the real reason."

"I have a thing about stolen paintings that began with a Tintoretto." I stared ahead keeping an eye out for the bridge to the turn off. "I've been chasing these paintings for the last two weeks and I just want to see them. To hold them. To know that all the crap that's been thrown at me was worth it." I looked over at Kathy. "Am I crazy?"

"Sounds like a plan. Almost." She shot a hard look at me then smiled. "But do me a favor and try and get Adam on the phone again."

I dialed his cell phone but again got no answer. I left a message, then I tried the office. The same officer answered.

"They're still in meetings," the voice said

"Tell Adam that Maxie Roberts and Kathy Krammer are on their way to Pahokee near twenty-mile bend. It's important that he call me immediately."

"Could you repeat that please?"

I did.

"I'll see he gets the message."

I hung up. Again, I realized that in my rush I had not taken my nine-millimeter automatic from the night table. I was armed only with a Nikon 35 millimeter camera.

We raced by the flat fields of the Palm Beach Agricultural District. Acres of dark green, long-leaf fouteen-foot high sugarcane stretched flat and forever to a perfectly vertical horizon. As Kathy hit a hundred, the sugarcane flew by the window in a blurred mass of green. A half dozen columns of smoke from sugarcane fires rose straight and dark into the clear sky. The horizon looked like newsreel footage of Baghdad under siege.

We made a right onto Route 918. The pavement rose and fell like undulating ocean swells. Kathy slowed down to a respectable sixty miles per hour. Still, the bumps and rises sent us airborne more than once.

"There's the store on the right," I said.

Four dust-covered trucks and a 66 Buick were parked out front of a flat roofed one-story, concrete block store with a sign, *Hablamos Español,* hung in the window. "There's the road up ahead," I pointed.

Kathy made a right onto the dirt road. The low-slung Porsche scraped its axle every few hundred yards. Kathy slowed down and we crept due east. On either side of us were smoldering stalks of recently burned sugarcane fields. Large ash flakes glided down like weightless gray feathers and silently burst on the hood into pixie dust. Down a side dirt road, I spotted three farmers and a tractor with a blowtorch protruding behind that they ran along the field to set it on fire. The next large field was still green with unburned, ripe eight-foot-high sugar cane stalks.

Off in the distance, I noticed a clump of trees rising above the sugarcane. I thought it was an Everglades hammock, one of those island-like salients of land that dot the glades a foot or two higher than the surrounding terrain. It was actually a flat mound of fill about an acre square and ten feet high, dredged from a five-acre artificial lake that shone like a silvery mirror under the afternoon sun. At the lake's edge were a wide dock, a ski-boat, and a personal watercraft. Immediately behind the dock in the middle of the mound sat a two-story Mediterranean-style house with a wraparound loggia surrounded by mature sugarcane and orange groves. A large immaculate-looking barn rose majestically behind and above the house, but what caught my eye was a grass airstrip and hangar to the right of the barn. The hangar's doors were open and I could just make out a white twin Cessna 414 parked inside.

Kathy stopped the car a few feet from a gated archway and cut the engine. The gate was closed. A sign dangling from the arch announced we were about to enter Tara.

"Now what?" Kathy asked.

CHAPTER 56

I was pondering Kathy's question when my cell phone rang. "Maxie, what the hell is happening?" It was Adam. "What's this about Pahokee?"

"I'm with Kathy Krammer and we're at the entrance to Jenkins' farm. It's about six miles due north of twenty-mile bend. There's an airfield, and a twin-engine plane in the hangar."

"I don't believe I'm hearing this. How the heck did you get to Jenkins' ranch?"

"It's a long story but you'd better get here fast."

"Is Nigel Jenkins there?"

"I don't know."

"Don't go near the place. I'll have the Sheriff send over a couple of units and I'll see if I can get a helicopter in the air."

"You'd better hurry," I said.

"We're on our way. Stay put. Or better still get out of there."

I closed the cell phone.

"Adam says to sit tight," I told Kathy.

"Are we just going to sit here and wait?"

"I don't know. The thought of those paintings in there somewhere is bugging the hell out of me. I want to see them and I'm sure when the cops arrive they won't let me get near them. I'd love to go down there and get a peak at them first. What do you say?"

"I say we stay put like Adam said."

"Hate to admit it, but you're probably right."

"Look! There's someone there." Kathy pointed at the house. There was movement between the barn and the hangar. Two men stepped out of the shadows.

"Is it Nigel Jenkins?" I asked.

"I can't tell. They're too far away."

I took my camera and aimed down the 210 mm lens but could only make out vague figures working around the Cessna.

"It looks like they're going to take off," I said. "We've got to get some pictures of those guys before they do leave. If it's Jenkins, then it'll be more proof against him."

I snapped off a couple of shots from the car.

"We're too far away. I want to get closer," I said to Kathy without taking my eyes off the hangar. "Adam wouldn't object to a quick reconnoiter to check it out from a distance, would he? Are you game, counselor?"

"I'm right behind you."

I hefted my Nikon camera like an M-15 assault rifle and moved cautiously toward the fence. Resting the camera on a post I looked over the railing. The two men were gone.

"Do you see them anywhere?" I asked.

Kathy shook her head.

I shot a half roll of pictures of the farmhouse, the barn, and the hangar when I spotted them moving around the plane. They were loading boxes into it. The shutter clicked furiously.

"I'm sure it's Jenkins and he's getting ready to split with the paintings," I said to Kathy.

"I don't think we should get any closer," Kathy said.

"I think you're right." For once, common sense prevailed. "I've got that bastard in the pictures." I said, patting the camera. "No offence counselor, but no fast-talking lawyer is going to get this guy off."

"For once I'd like to be the prosecuting attorney."

"Thanks for backing me up," I said. "Let's get back to the main road and wait for the police."

I leaned over and gave her a kiss on the cheek. Like me, Kathy was breathing deeply, her eyes were wide and ready. The adrenaline rush was hitting her as much as me. But we both knew it was time to go.

With Kathy leading, we started back to the car. From behind, I watched her move. Her long legs striding, her hips swaying from one side then the other. My over stimulated senses were in overdrive and I never wanted a woman more than I wanted her at that moment.

I was about to say something I was sure was inappropriate when I heard the rumble of a motor. I turned and saw a dark-clad figure on an all-terrain vehicle careen out of the hangar, heading across the front lawn, right toward us. Halfway between us and the gate, the vehicle stopped. The driver was Marcus and he had a long rifle with a scope slung across the handlebars. He stopped abruptly, sat up, and raised the rifle.

"Get down," I yelled and grabbed Kathy.

We hit the ground in front of the car just as a bullet whistled over our heads. The windshield of the Porsche shattered, followed by a long report that echoed across the fields. Kathy glanced up at her car then back to me.

"We gotta run," I yelled.

"Where?"

"The cane field. Run for the cane field."

She jumped up and I followed her toward the sugarcane field. Our feet sank up to our ankles in the soft muck. Marcus had reached the gate and opened it just as we plunged into the cane. Large sharp leaves sliced at our faces and hands as we tried to run between the raised rows.

"Come on, jump from lump to lump," I said, grabbing Kathy's hand. She hiked up her skirt and took off down a cane row. She ran like she drove.

We scurried blindly through the high cane, running with our arms in front of our faces. I heard another report and the bullet whizzed through the cane stocks to my right, then another bullet ripped through the leaves like a scythe to my left. Marcus was close behind, but firing blindly. Our trail through the cane was easy to follow. With misplaced gallantry, I kept Kathy in front of me. Our only hope was the road about five miles away and the three farmers I saw burning the fields.

"Which way?" Kathy asked.

"I don't know," I said trying to catch my breath. "Straight."

Hunched over, we plowed through the thick heavy leaves. I ducked my head left and right. I glanced back to see if Marcus was gaining on us when I heard a racket above us and looked up. A flock of agitated cattle egrets flew overhead, then veered sharply to the west. Something had spooked them ahead of us. Then a familiar acrid smell filled the air. It was smoke. I heard a crackling sound. I shot a glance up to our left and saw yellow tongues of flames licking at the sky above the green sugar cane.

"Jesus, the field's on fire! To the right! Run to the right," I yelled.

Hot smoky air billowed above and before the flames. I could feel the heat and hear a sickening crackling like a thousand popping crackerjacks. The fire was moving fast, faster than we could run. Suddenly ahead, I saw light through the cane, then I saw water -- a wide irrigation canal laid a few yards away.

"I see a canal up ahead. Run for it," I yelled.

Like flying banshees, we broke out of the cane.

Without stopping, Kathy dove into the canal. I tripped and rolled headlong with a splash into the black water. I surfaced quickly. Kathy bobbed up two yards in front of me. Above us a raging wall of fiery fury leapt from the field, its fierce fingers groping the sky. A wave of sheering heat slapped at our faces.

"We got to get to the other side. Take a deep breath and stay under as long as possible," I said.

We both dove into the black underworld of the Everglades. Underwater, I could feel Kathy moving close by. I swam as far as I could before my lungs felt ready to burst, then I shot to the surface. Flames roared skyward above my head. I took a gulp of air and dove under again.

I tried to open my eyes but the stinging black water forced them shut. I swam blindly, hoping I was heading away from the fire. Each stroke was painfully slow. I gave a couple of hard kicks, then surfaced again.

The heat was intense. I could see the flames flickering. Without looking back, I surface dove down deep and toward the other bank. I had not seen Kathy and I could not sense any movement in the water. I swam as hard as I could and felt the rise of the bank before I saw it. I grabbed at waterweed growing on its side and pulled myself up and out. I heard crackling and smelled smoke, but the fire had died back as fast as it had burned. Light gray plumes streamed out from between the singed, green cane stalks.

I flipped around and looked up and down the canal. Kathy was ten feet away, holding onto roots jutting out of the bank. She didn't move. I took a couple of strokes towards her.

"Are you okay?" I yelled.

She nodded. "Are you?"

"Yeah."

We stared across the canal at the smoldering field. Like all sugarcane field fires, this one was a controlled flash fire; it burned fast and hot, then died out quickly. I imagined a couple of sugar farmers setting the fire a mile away having no idea the havoc they had caused. They might have saved our lives.

"What do we do now?" she asked.

"I'm not sure," I said, spitting out gritty, foul- tasting water. "But we have to get out of here."

.

CHAPTER 57

"Can you get up the bank?" I asked Kathy.

I think she nodded. She started to climb then fell back into the water. I swam up behind her and cupped my hands around her waist and lifted. After taking a couple of deep breaths, I followed her up the slippery embankment and fell onto the grass covering the top. Behind us was another field of unburned sugar cane. We were exposed where we were, but I was too exhausted to care. I looked back across the canal. The field was smoldering with scattered patches of fire.

"Can you see him?" Kathy asked.

"No. And I don't think anyone could survive that fire." Marcus had been right behind us and I was sure the flames got him. I glanced down at the black water. It was the second time in a week a canal had saved my life.

Kathy leaned back on the bank, her chest heaving. "Who set that fire? They almost killed us."

"Probably those farmers we spotted near the road. I've got my attorney with me. Maybe we can sue."

I scanned the landscape across the canal for Marcus in case he had survived the fire, like the bad guy in a Hollywood horror movie. As the smoke lifted, I could see through the standing charred stalks. Marcus was nowhere in sight.

Kathy and I were both dripping wet and covered with ash. Even soaked, Kathy looked great, her skirt split up the side and her blouse wet against her breasts. I took a few deep breaths and looked away.

I reached into my pants pocket and pulled out my soaking and quite dead cell phone. We were on our own and Jenkins was back at the farm with a plane.

"I have a cell phone in the car," Kathy said. "Do you think it's safe to go back?"

"I don't think we have a choice."

I looked up at the sky. "Where were the cops?"

We swam back across the canal and pushed our way through the smoking field toward the car. The ash was hot but our wet clothes gave us some protection. The going was easier with the leaves burned away and I could see a few yards ahead. I smelled the putrid stench of burnt flesh before I saw a smoldering blackened lump. Marcus was balled up in a fetal position. His charred skeletal face had no eyelids and it leered up in a lipless grimace. I almost retched. Kathy came up behind me.

"Don't look," I said.

"Jesus, I'm an attorney I've seen the worst," she said, pushing by me. "Oh my God."

I grabbed her hand.

"Poor guy, to die like that," she said.

"I believe he was trying to kill us."

"I know. I know."

Marcus's black hand still clutched the rifle. I pried his hand loose and hefted the rifle in my hand. The magazine was ripped open by ignited bullets discharging through the casing. I jerked the still hot magazine out of the butt and cocked the rifle. A bullet flew out. I pulled the trigger and the pin snapped on the empty chamber. It worked. I looked down the barrel, shook out the dirt inside, and blew into the chamber. I checked the scope. It was bent and useless. I reached down and retrieved the bullet. It was still good. I fed the lone round into the chamber. Snipers have a saying—one shot, one kill. Whatever, it was all I had.

"Are you going to use that?" Kathy asked.

"Only if I have to."

"I hate guns."

We stomped through the burnt cane stalks and came out onto the road. Kathy's car was a mess. The windshield was shattered and the hood had a bullet hole smack in the middle.

"Sorry about the car," I said.

"It's insured," she said, rubbing her legs with her hand. "God, that stuff's itchy."

"That's the damn muck. It's itchy as hell when it's dry."

Keeping low we moved around the side of the car. Kathy opened the driver's door. "Found it." She waved the cell phone over her head.

"I want you to call 911 and stay on the phone. I'm going to try and get to the plane and disable it."

"Maxie, don't be stupid. Wait for the police."

"I'm sure Jenkins is alone. If I don't do something, he'll be gone by the time the cops arrive," I said.

She started to say something, but I stopped her with a kiss on the mouth. "I'll be okay," I said. I brushed away a smudge on her cheek. Then I kissed her again. "Call the police," I said in a near whisper.

"Be careful. Please."

"I will."

I wanted to give her one more kiss. Instead I turned and, keeping as low as I could, I sneaked up to the gated entrance. I opened one side, stepped inside and closed the gate behind me and crept across the lawn towards the hangar. I had a clear view of the twin-engine plane and the crates around its base.

Nigel stepped out of the hangar. He saw me and abruptly stopped.

"Marcus?"

"Marcus is dead," I yelled. I stood up and raised the rifle so Jenkins could see it. "Stop right there, Nigel, there's no place for you to go."

Before I had finished, he dashed out of the hangar across the yard and disappeared into the house.

You're not going anywhere, I thought. I wanted him. I wanted him badly. He had tried to burn my gallery. My life's work. I could still see the contorted snarl on his face before he slammed the vault door shut. I was not going to let him escape. I ran to the house and up the front porch steps.

"Jenkins, give it up! The police are on the way," I yelled. Standing to one side of the door, I turned the knob. It was unlocked. I kicked the door. It swung open—just like in the movies. I took a deep breath and ran into the house and across the entrance hall, remembering from cowboy shows that moving targets are difficult to hit.

I scurried across the entrance hall. On the far side was a Victorian grandfather clock. I ducked beside it, pressing myself against the wall. Cautiously, I peaked around the clock into the other rooms and stopped short. Hanging on a large wall, soaring two stories above the living room, was a wall covered in a half dozen paintings. I immediately recognized half of them—a Pierre Bonnard nude, an Edouard Vuillard, and a Paul Signac.

Surrounded by so many paintings my thoughts ran wild and I had to look away. I backed up against the wall. Adam, you were so right. What am I doing here? I'm no cowboy. My chest heaved and I could feel my heart dancing the mambo in my throat.

"Fuck it," I said and ran through the first floor of the house.

Ahead was a flight of stairs. I hesitated, and then began climbing up slowly, step by step. I kept the rifle barrel pointed up. In the close confines of the house a long-barreled deer rifle with a broken high-powered scope was a definite disadvantage. It was hard to maneuver quickly without jamming it into a wall or furniture. What I needed was a short-barreled twelve-gage shotgun.

Did Jenkins have a shotgun?

Suddenly, instead of the hunter, I felt hunted. I froze, held my breath and listened. It was silent, stone silent except for the ticking grandfather clock. I thought I heard an eyelash blink. I glanced behind me and listened, then stepped up onto the second floor landing and looked down the hallway. There were four closed doors. I took a step toward them when a load-force blast exploded from below me, and a high whining bullet pissed by my jaw. I whirled around to see Jenkins at the bottom of the staircase, a nine-shot automatic pistol in his right hand. I fell to the floor and scrambled down the hall on all fours.

Below, I heard a door swing open and someone running. Glancing over the railing, I saw Jenkins disappear into the kitchen. I jumped up and scurried down the stairs and looked around the corner as Jenkins darted out the back door toward the barn. He was heading for the plane.

I set off after him. I had a single shot; he had eight bullets left. Not the type of odds I enjoy.

Reaching the barn, I peered around the door inside and gasped. Instead of holding horses and hay, the interior had been divided into two long gallery-like rows of well-lit hallways that ran along the length of the barn. Hanging on the walls were scores of masterpieces.

Focus! Don't look at the paintings.

I stepped into the barn beside a large Miró, then hopped over to the other side and pressed my back against the wall. A large portrait of Madame Matisse stared over my left shoulder. I didn't think Jenkins would shoot while I was leaning against a valuable painting.

A shot rang out and the Matisse frame splintered.

Wrong again.

I didn't see where the shot came from.

"Nigel! There's no place to go. You can't get away."

I heard a door slam shut at the end of the barn where it led into the hangar. I ran down the corridor to the door. Keeping to one side, I gripped the handle and threw it open. I peeked out. The large hangar doors were wide open and the Cessna looked primed and ready to go. A half dozen painting-sized crates were stacked by the cargo doors. Jenkins was nowhere to be seen.

He could be anywhere in the hangar and I couldn't stay where I was for very long, so I ducked back into the barn, leaving the connecting door open. I hefted the rifle and knelt down to an angle where I could see under the plane. I took aim down the rifle barrel at where I thought the wing fuel tank was. I closed my eyes and fired.

With the rifle recoil, I jumped back, expecting the plane to explode like in the movies. Instead, I heard a metallic clunk and the sound of fuel pouring out through a hole in the bottom of the wing onto the hangar floor. A large puddle formed at the base of the plane. The heavy smell of fuel filled the air. That bird was not going far. It was time to leave.

I threw the rifle down and dashed through the hanger doors. I was halfway across the lawn when an all-terrain vehicle roared out of the hangar straight at me. I sprinted toward the gate. I could hear the ATV gaining right behind me.

Before I reached the gate, I felt Jenkins right at my back. I jumped as hard as I could to the right. The ATV hit me in the thigh and I was thrown hard to the ground. Pain shot down my leg.

Jenkins roared past me and then made a sharp u-turn. I rolled over onto my side and tried to stand, but my leg would not support me and I fell back. Jenkins gunned the engine and headed straight for me. All I could do was wrap my arms around my head and roll away as fast as I could.

Then I heard a crash of splintering wood on metal. I looked up and saw the blue Boxster careening through the gate entrance and straight at Jenkins. Without stopping, the Boxster hit the ATV from behind. The ATV shot off at a radical angle throwing Jenkins out of his saddle through the air and over the Boxster hood. With a sickening thud he hit the ground. The ATV rolled over onto its side and died.

I stood up as straight as I could and limped over to Jenkins. He was on his side, his legs and arms doubled over like a broken doll. I turned him over. He groaned. A Munch red stain spread over his shirt. He was alive, but judging from the fresh blood oozing from his mouth and chest, he would not be for long. I took his pistol out of its belt holster.

Kathy backed up the Porsche and got out.

"Good God, Kathy, thanks."

She stood there, her hand to her mouth and started to shake. "I had to. I had to do it. He was going to kill you." Her lips were trembling and she had tears in her eyes.

I went to her and gave her a hug. " I know. It's all right."

"Oh, my God," Kathy cried as she looked down at Jenkins' broken body.

"You saved my life. Believe if you hadn't been here I'd be dead." I held her tightly and rubbed her back, then kissed her wet eyes.

"You've got blood all over you. Are you okay?"

I nodded and said softly, "It's his."

"You think you've won, asshole." I heard Jenkins mutter through a bloody grimace.

"It's not a game, Nigel. It never has been. I know you'll find this hard to believe but it was the art. Nothing but the art." I knelt down and lifted up his head. "Where are the rest of the paintings?"

He smiled with red teeth. "Try and find them yourself, fuckhead." His words were lost in a gurgle as he spit up a ball of bloody saliva. I doubt his comments will go down on any list of glorious last words. I let go and his head hit the ground with a thud. He coughed up more blood then turned his head towards the house. His eyes widened and a snarl crossed his lips. It was the same expression he had before he pulled his pistol on me that morning at the storage facility.

"We'd better call an ambulance," Kathy said.

I was about to say, let the bastard die but reluctantly I agreed.

I stood over Jenkins. There was an uneasy feeling in the air that I couldn't shake. Over the smell of burnt fields, pulverized muck and orange blossoms, I sensed a vague odor of paint solvent. It was unnatural and I didn't like it.

I sniffed. The smell got stronger, more pungent. I thought it must be the gasoline dripping from the plane on the hangar floor; then I realized it was coming from the house. A cold knife ran up my back and, before I could blink, a sheet of brilliance flashed in the second floor windows, then blew them out. I gasped as a wave of heat and debris nearly knocked me to the ground. Kathy shrieked. I jerked around as she fell backwards. I ran over and grabbed her by the shoulders and pulled her away from the house.

"You okay?" I yelled over the roar.

"I can't believe this."

Another explosion rocked the house, followed by another burst of flames.

Before I could stand up, the second floor was engulfed. Flames leaped through the roof.

"Oh, Christ! The paintings!"

I ripped off my jacket, threw it over my head, and ran to the burning house. I pushed my way inside, choking on grey smoke. A wall of red hell ripped through the entrance hall and up the stairs. I turned away and dropped to the floor to shield my face from the oven-hot shock waves. The intense heat bit at my eyes and face, and it hurt just to peek out from the protective cloth. Debris was falling from the ceiling. The house and the paintings were a total loss.

I backed out the door and drew a deep breath of air.

"Maxie!" Kathy yelled.

"I'm okay. I'm okay." I staggered toward her.

She pointed behind me. I spun around toward the barn. Part of it was on fire.

"No! No more," I screamed.

I ran to the front of the barn, flung open the double doors and stepped inside. The left end was an inferno of swirling flames and superheated air. Oil-based paintings hanging on the wall erupted like Roman candles. *God, no, this cannot be happening.* Like a demonic hand, fiery fingers of flames shot across the high arching ceiling overhead. The fire and heat rising to the rafters left a lower layer of cooler breathable air.

Without thinking, I pulled the first painting within grasp off the wall and dropped it on the floor. Then I raced to the next. I threw a Delacroix onto the pile, then a Withoos harbor scene and a Corot portrait. My eyes jerked back and forth trying to decide which ones to save.

Down the fiery corridor, I spotted the Caravaggio. I shot past a slew of masters and, in one motion, grabbed the Caravaggio by the frame and jerked it off the wall.

I twisted around when I heard a mournful howl over the flames. I stopped and listened. The sound came from around the corner. I shot a quick glance down a side hallway and saw Cerberus chained to a wall. Fiery tongues of flames licked at him from behind. He saw me and whined.

I dropped the Caravaggio and ran to him. I fumbled with the chain. With a hard yank it came loose. "Come on, boy," I said. He refused to move

"Come on, boy!" I yelled. "Don't do this. Not now. We gottta go!"

He still did not move. I grabbed his collar and dragged the hundred-twenty pound dog down the smoke-filled corridor and out the door to the lawn. "Stay," I yelled in his face, then, without thinking, ran back into the barn.

The fire had spread everywhere. The smoke felt like stiletto points slicing into my lungs. It was impossible to hear above the roar of the flames. My pile of paintings was burning. Along the walls, portraits stared out at me, fear shining in their eyes. The intense heat was like a slap of a hot iron at my face and I squinted into the flames. Caravaggio. I was going to get the Caravaggio or die trying.

The Caravaggio lay on the floor down the hall where I had dropped it. As I ran to it, a hissing flash shot up and stopped me short. I smelled burnt hair. Trying to catch my breath, I watched as the brilliant flare danced around the frame. I fought back the urge to jump into the mad flames and pull the painting out. The entire wall burst into a solid wall of crackling fire and roaring wind. The Caravaggio disappeared in a sheet of fire. Helplessly, I watched in horror as the world lost one of its great masterpieces. But I had no time to mourn. I was cut off from the front door, the entire ceiling lit up in a demonic inferno spitting twisted flames to the floor. There was fire all around. I was trapped.

Then I saw two eyes pleading with me across the fire. Tightening my jacket around my head, I dove through the wall of fire and landed on the floor in front of a Renoir. Gulping hot air, I grabbed the edge of the Renoir frame and jerked downward. The painting gave way and we both tumbled to the floor.

I rolled away from the wall. Bolts of fire and searing noxious smoke rolled downward. Like a blind man, I stumbled with the painting through the raging pyre looking for a way out. I could not bear the blistering heat on my face. My sleeves were smoldering.

My eyes burned and I squeezed them shut against the pain. Suddenly,

I thought, I'm not getting out of here. Panic rose in my gut. I jerked up, wanting to scream for help. I fell to my knees to get below the billowing smoke. I felt something at my neck and swiped at it with my free hand. Margarita's medallion flew onto the floor. I watched it roll to my right then looked up and, through the flames, saw a window and daylight. I crawled like a mad man on all fours toward the light. Using the picture frame as a hammer, I smashed through the window. The frame crumbled in my hand but I refused to let go. I crawled out over jagged glass and caught my leg. For a moment I dangled half in and half out. I dropped the Renoir out the window and jerked my leg. Shear white pain sliced through me as I fell to the ground and I fought to keep conscious.

Grabbing the smoldering Renoir, I crawled away from the barn dragging my leg. Once far enough from the fire, I got up, hopped on one foot until I could go no farther and collapsed. A piece of the painting was still in my hand. It was on fire. I rolled over and tucked the painting to my chest. I felt movement around me, water splashing over me. I was nauseated. The world flipped back and forth like a tide-whipped piece of driftwood. Then a white flash. Then darkness.

When I came to, Kathy was standing over me. Cerberus was licking my face. I took a deep breath and tried to sit up.

"Be careful," Kathy said. "Don't get up too quickly." She kneeled down and rested her hand on my shoulder. "You're such a fool."

I pulled my knees up to my chest and breathed deeply.

"What's that?" Kathy asked, looking at my hand. It was black. Still clutched in my charred fingers was a five-inch-square seared fragment of the Renoir. I looked at the house, and then the barn burning, and again felt nauseous. My scorched eyes watered.

"If you ever, ever do anything like this again, I'm going to kill you," Kathy said as she hugged me.

"Put it in writing and I'll sign."

She was crying. So was I.

I heard the helicopter before I saw it. I watched it land near the gate, away from the flames. Soon a dozen squad cars had the buildings encircled. Cerberus stood guard, refusing to leave his post by my side until the paramedics arrived. The fire, fueled by ten thousand collective years of genius burned, into the night.

CHAPTER 58

The next morning, South Florida exploded. Blazed across every front page, headlines screamed in bold print about the Crime of the Century, then, searching for ever more dramatic hyperboles, the Crime of the Millennium. Superlatives aside, it was the biggest art story since the Gardiner Museum theft in Boston

The *Palm Beach Post* ran a well-written four-page story capped with a ten-year-old archived picture of me at a gallery opening. Thankfully, no one published a shot of me with singed hair, crispy eyebrows, and blistered cheeks. There is, after all, restraint in the media.

I, fortunately, missed much of the media circus. For the first two days, the good doctors at Saint Mary's Hospital had me doped up beyond caring. The first night, I was vaguely aware of Kathy and Margarita by my bedside. I was told that Kathy gave me an occasional hug and kiss while Margarita prayed, which may explain the quirky dreams.

I remember a team of doctors hovering over me.

"You have second degree burns on your face, arms and legs," the first doctor told me. "Your hand suffered some damage but you should recover full use of it. You had a four-inch gashed in your thigh that required twenty stitches, but luckily, it was a clean cut. No tendons were severed and after a couple of weeks it should be as good as new."

When he pulled back the sheet to examine my leg, a six-inch Oshian rolled off the bed onto the floor.

"What's this?" He stooped to pick it up. He turned it over in his hand and glanced at Margarita.

I grabbed his hand. "It means a lot to me."

Both Margarita and the doctor smiled. "Alternative medicine, I see, comes in all shapes," he said shaking his head. He handed me the Oshian.

With my good hand I held onto it, nodded to Margarita, and mouthed the words "Thank you."

After the doctors left, Kathy said to me, "Remember, we have a date in

January. Are you going to be able to dance with that leg?"

"Dance? I'll be ready to do a sizzling Salsa. I promise you, Beebee Alabama will be impressed when we tango across the floor at the Children's Gala."

Dickie Durdle rose to the occasion. He spent much of the first two days with Kathy and Margarita by my bedside, and kept the reporters at bay by answering their questions while suggesting they visit his gallery.

Sometime during the second day, I was nodding in and out of consciousness watching a History Channel documentary, when I heard a deep voice echo from the ward hall. "Well. The miracle man is awake." With his hands buried deeply into his pockets, Adam Aldrick sauntered into the room.

"Adam." I raised my good hand over my head in mock surrender. "I was about to call you."

"Yeah." he laughed. "This time I have to admit you did. When my men got to Jenkins' farm, they couldn't believe anyone inside could have survived that fire."

"I admit, it was damn hot in there." I raised my bandaged hand to show Jack. "But most of the fire was burning above me in the rafters. It was worst than it looked."

"That I doubt. But I tell you, you were one lucky man. A damn fool, but very lucky. I've never seen anyone who attracted as much self-abuse as you. You're a confirmed masochist."

"To tell the truth, I don't know what got into me. Just thinking about the fire and what might have happened gives me the shakes."

"For your own good, I should have locked you up a week ago." Adam pulled up a metal chair beside the bed and sat. "All hell has broken loose. At the station, between the media, the Feds, and the victims, it's standing room only. The Chief doesn't know whether to thank you or curse you." He winked. "I'm trying to keep them away from bothering you here, but you might want to leave a.s.a.p. The gods must love you. You know, you don't look as bad as I thought you would. Anyway . . ." He slapped his hands on his knees. "I got to get back."

He stood up and snorted a laugh then headed for the door.

"Thanks for coming by. Next time we'll drink a Brunello."

"To celebrate something, I hope." He waved behind him and disappeared into the corridor.

When Nancy called, I told her that the reports in the media were exaggerated and I was all right. And yes, I could still take Nicole and Eric for Christmas.

I hoped I was convincing.

CHAPTER 59

I was discharged from Saint Mary's the next morning into Margarita's care. Kathy commandeered a Buick sedan to drive us home, where I slept for two days. Margarita said she would stay at the house while the kids were there. She usually spent Christmas with her daughter's family in Tampa.

"I promise you, I'll be up and running. Well maybe not running. But I'll be fit when they get here," I told Margarita.

"What about that dog? I gotta take care of you, I gotta take care of the house, and the kids. Now I gotta dog." As if on cue, Cerberus barked from the back yard.

A large floral display arrived with a card from Bernie and Aseneth. "We're off to Venice for Carnival. Join us when you can."

I hired a physical therapist who came to the house three times a week. By the fourth visit, I was limping without the cane.

The blisters healed up leaving only a couple of star-shaped scares. My right hand remained sore and cramped, and I was afraid of ever getting back it s full use, in spite of the therapist's assurances.

The day before the kids were to arrive, Kathy helped Margarita and I decorate an oversized tree we'd setup in a corner of the family room overlooking the Intracoastal Waterway. After carefully hanging a few white icicle lights outside, the house looked almost Christmassy.

But it wasn't until the day before Christmas, as I was seated on the deck watching Eric and Nicole playing in the backyard with Cerberus and the smell of Margarita's cooking wafting out of the kitchen, that I broke down and cried. All the stupid risks I had taken, putting my life on the line, and for what? I might have missed all this, the kids, my home, my friends. I had so much. I had, oh, so much. Thank you God, thank you.

Kathy came out of the house and hugged me. "It's all right. We're all here for you."

And through my sobs, I knew she was right.

During the week between Christmas and New Years, we visited Lion Country Safari and Butterfly World, checked out the Christmas lights on Florida Mango, and fished. Billie Osceola Tommie, dressed in full Seminole regalia, took us for an airboat ride to the tip of the Everglades, where he pointed out more wildlife than I thought existed.

On a breezy afternoon I took Eric and Nicole for a sail halfway to Bimini. While we were running with the wind on a starboard tack, Eric asked, "Dad, are you a hero or something?"

"I don't think so."

"They say you did something real brave."

"I did what I thought I had to do at the time. If I'd thought about it first, I wouldn't have done it. A true hero knows the consequences and does what he has to do regardless."

"But you almost got killed."

"Not really." I grabbed his head and pulled it to my chest and messed his hair. "Hold on to the line." I gave him the line to the main sail. "Keep it straight for that nun buoy on the horizon.

"Nicole. You want to help me set the spinnaker?"

We moved to the bow and I watched Nicole put all her weight into the line. She was a natural sailor and, like her father, loved the sea.

Eric and Nicole had grown so. Eric was a foot taller then last year and Nicole was filling out like a real woman. I thought I was doomed to see-ing them only on their occasional visits when Eric said, "You know, Dad, I'd like to go to the University of Florida."

My alma mater.

"I thought your mother wanted you to study in Massachusetts, or New York."

"I like Florida."

"Me too," I said. I don't think a father could have been any prouder of his son than I was at that moment.

Toward the end of the kids' stay, Nancy called.

"Are you okay?"

"Yeah, of course."

"I mean are you really okay, Maxie? You sound different."

"You know, Nancy, we had a good thing and I really appreciated it. I have this ongoing fantasy of us being together as a family, but I know that's impossible. And that's okay. Just look at Eric and Nicole. They're fantastic kids. You're doing a good job with them. You are a great mother and I can't ask for more."

Pause.

"Are you *sure* you're okay?"

"Except for the leg I couldn't be better," I said, then paused. "I'm leaving the country and the house will be empty. Margarita would love it if you and the kids would come down and stay here awhile."

"Maxie, what's going on?"

I reassured her my intentions were noble and reiterated my offer. When I hung up the phone I, for once, did not have a gut-grinding knot wrenching inside my stomach.

Immediately after the children left I paid a visit to the Fine Art Conservatory. Quietly, I hobbled into Lee Lohman's office and sat down. The smell of thinners and oils heavy in the air reminded me what a real artist's studio smells like.

"You look a lot better than at the hospital," Lee said.

"Thanks to Margarita's cooking."

"Boy, you've become quite the celebrity lately."

"Inadvertently, I assure you."

"The entire town is shook up. This is a serious mess." He crossed his arms on his chest.

"I know." I took out a manila envelope, placed it on his desk and pushed it toward him. Lee opened it and pulled out a plastic bag. Inside was the scorched patch of the Renoir that I had managed to save from the fire.

"Can you check it out for me? It's a Renoir. Late period."

"God, I can't believe it. This can't be one of the pieces lost in the fire?"

"Yes. As far as I know, it's all that's left."

"Wow." He pulled a white surgical glove out of his desk and slipped it on. He turned the piece over in his hand. "I'll get right on it."

"One other thing," I said. "Can you ask Gloria to come in? I'd like a word with her."

Gloria came in dressed in a knee-length white smock, her hair tied back in a ponytail. Her bright eyes widened when she saw me.

"You remember Maxie Roberts," Lee said.

"Hello, Mr. Roberts," she said softly.

"Have a seat, Gloria," Lee said.

She sat down and folded her hands on her lap. Her large eyes darted between Lee and myself.

"Gloria, how long have you been working for Lee?"

"About seven months."

"Lee has told me that you are one of the best restorers he's ever had."

"Thank you," she said.

"But we have a problem here." I laid down a manila folder with an old art report I'd picked up off of Lee's desk. Gloria sat up in her chair. "You've seen the news and I'm sure you know all that has happened and how serious things are. I want you to tell me about you and Nigel Jenkins."

Again, Gloria's eyes darted back and forth, then down to her hands.

"Don't worry, this has nothing to do with the police. I just want to know what your relationship was with him."

Her dark eyes watered up and she bowed her head as she started to cry. Lee came around his desk. "It's okay, Gloria," he said, gently rubbing her shoulder. He handed her a Kleenex. She dabbed at her eyes and blew her nose. "Just tell Mr. Roberts what you know."

She stared at her hands in her lap and started to shake her head. "I don't know," she said. "I met Nigel about three years ago at a gallery opening. He seemed like a nice man. He asked me to lunch, then we had a few dates. Nothing serious, believe me. We talked art, about restorations. He said he'd like to know who was having their paintings restored. He told me people who restore paintings often want to have a place to store them, or he could sell them a similar painting by the same artist or even a complementary painting. I didn't see any harm in it. It was never about money. I liked him. He seemed like a real nice guy. He was nice to me."

"You were at the Forester party last month with Jenkins, weren't you?"

"He asked if I would like to go. Not as a date or anything." Gloria dabbed at her eyes. "I'm so sorry, Lee. Please believe me."

"It's okay, Gloria. It's okay."

After Gloria left the office Lee asked, "What do you think I should do?"

"She's too good a restorer to lose. She's as much a victim of Jenkins as any of us."

It was the first week in January, a week before the Children's Gala, and I was staring at an airline ticket in my hand. This trip to Canada took longer than the direct flight in Bernie's Gulfstream. Kingston, the former capital of Canada before Ottawa, was an industrialized university town set snugly on the north shore of Lake Ontario. I drove my rental to a narrow country road on the outskirts and parked in front of a one-story steep-roofed cottage with two feet of snow piled on its roof. My shoes creaked on the hard-packed snow on the walkway up to the front door. I knocked and an elderly lady answered.

"Mrs. Carranza?"

"Yes?" she said, looking as fit as a teenager.

"I'm here to see Dominic."

"Comma in, comma in," she said. "Dominic, dere's a man to see you," she called out with a labored Northern Italian accent.

Dominic came in wiping his hands on an oily cloth.

"Hello, Dominic," I said.

He laid down the cloth on a chair by the door and brushed off his smock. "Well, I won't say I'm surprised." A slight smile crossed his lips. "You look like you got beat up or something."

"Burns. We had a bit of a fire recently."

"Come on into the studio." He led me into the back room. "I heard all about the demise of our Mr. Jenkins. Nice job."

"Did you think he deserved to die?"

"For killing Martha Manley and the others, yes."

"You might be right on that account," I said. "Dominic, how long have you been painting?"

"All my life."

"Has there been a day in your life you didn't paint?"

"As the ancients used to say, '*Nulle dies sine linea.*' No day without a line."

"I admire your discipline. In fact I admire you a lot."

He said nothing. I could smell freshly perked coffee.

"Have you ever seen this before?" I handed him the remains of the singed Renoir I saved from the fire.

"One of Jenkins' paintings?"

"Yes. This is all that remains of them."

He nodded. He took the burnt canvas in his hands, "Such a shame. But even in this fragment the beauty is still there."

"Yes, beautiful."

More nods.

"And guess what? Would it surprise you to know it's a fake?"

Dominic was silent.

"A fake, just like all the others that were burnt. Don't you find that interesting?"

Nothing.

"Well, Dominic, correct me if I'm wrong. Jenkins hired you to make reproductions of paintings his clients had stored in his vaults. You knew Jenkins was substituting the original paintings for your copies, so instead of one copy you painted two then gave them to Jenkins and kept the originals. Jenkins believing he had an original and a fake returned the copy to the owners and kept what he thought was the original," I said. "No one was the wiser."

Dominic remained silent.

"I have to say it was brilliant, except that so many people got hurt."

"I didn't hurt anyone."

"Still, people died," I said. "You don't want to spend the rest of your life in jail where you could never paint like this again. Do you?"

The color fled his face and I thought he was going to collapse onto the floor. He steadied himself and looked away. He bowed his head, moving it slightly side to side. Dominic seemed to age noticeably in front of my eyes. He hunched over a bit more and stared down at the floor as if looking for something, then I heard a long strained sigh rise from deep inside him.

"Jenkins never knew art from crap," he said. "One of those phonies who worshiped the false gods of their own ignorant, self-important egos. You know I did the first one a little over ten years ago. More as an experiment for myself. I figured I'd keep the second copy for myself. But then I decided to try an experiment and keep the original. No one noticed. Then it snowballed and got out of control. I could not stand to see the paintings in the hands of that asshole, Jenkins. All these people claiming to know real art. They don't know shit. And I proved it. My copies were as good as VerMeer or Goya or any of the old masters."

He looked at me. The color had come back to his face.

"You enjoyed fooling them, didn't you."

"No . . . no . . . no. Not fooling them. I hated their lies. They're all phonies. I sat for hours staring at a painting before beginning to work. Each second there is a new revelation, the emotion, the story locked in the painting that the artist was trying to tell us. And these people think their money can buy them knowledge and instant class. It makes them feel important."

"You're starting to sound like Jenkins. All artists sold their paintings. It was their job. They had to make a living. You're a great artist, Dominic," I said, making a direct appeal to his vanity, "but these paintings have families. They have to go home."

He stood up. "You came alone?"

"Yes," I said, staring him straight in the eye. "One way or the other, this ends here today."

He looked away. "You know there is only one way," he said. "Follow me."

I fell in step behind him to the hallway, then down a set of narrow steps into the basement. Fresh oil and turpentine stung my nostrils.

He turned on the lights, then opened his arms out wide, like a bishop blessing a crowd.

Along the walls in the basement of a modest ranch house hung more masterpieces than most of the world's great museums possessed. Rows of others leaned against the walls on the floor like tired long-distance runners. There had to be at least a hundred and fifty paintings on the walls and floor. So much beauty, so much genius concentrated in one small area.

I could see how Dominic might have gone mad. But it wasn't my station in life to police or judge Dominic Carranza. My eyes finally settled on the table cluttered with a rainbow of colorful paints and oils. On it was the Caravaggio. A tingle ran up my backbone and down my arms and legs. My heart raced and I'd stopped breathing. I steadied myself before I moved forward. I hefted the painting and held onto it as if it were a phantom, or an angel that might vanish at any moment. Carefully, I backed up and sat down, placing the painting on my lap. Slowly, my breathing returned to normal.

Here was proof there was a God who spoke to us mere mortals through his artists.

"These paintings are special," Dominic said. "Very, very special."

I saw in his eyes the pride a father has in his children.

"And me?" Dominic asked.

"Do what you've always done. Keep on painting."

CHAPTER 60

Returning the paintings without another hullabaloo of publicity was almost as difficult as finding them. While there were many grateful people, many resented that they had been duped. And others, the most irate, had to return overinflated insurance checks. A couple of owners refused to believe that the works hanging in their homes were fakes. Within a year nearly half of the paintings made the auction house catalogues and were sold or donated. The happiest people were the insurance companies who had paid out for the first round of fire-sale forgeries. They offered me two percent. I graciously accepted.

Dominic never returned to Florida. He remained in Canada suffering through the punishing winter. Did I believe Dominic Carranza was an innocent dupe? Hardly. But some high priest would have to offer him up as a sacrificial lamb on the altar of art, not I. Soon after, I heard he married an artist's model forty years his junior. Crime does pay.

A page-twelve, two-paragraph article stated that all charges against Sergio Ordenoff in relation to his wife's death were dropped due to lack of evidence. While Peter Putzer managed to spin the sudden shift in perpetrators from the Count to Nigel Jenkins and company, I was amused as our state attorney squirmed in front of the cameras when a reporter asked him if Sergio Ordenoff was going to sue for false arrest.

After a few "Missing Paintings Found." headlines, the forged paintings scandal quietly died. Few of our art patrons wanted to comment in public.

Even Adam seemed satisfied that with the death of Jenkins and Marcus, justice had been served. The Manley children, in their eagerness to get their hands on the estate free and clear, paid Ordenoff three times the specified amount in prenuptial agreement he had with Martha, and he returned to Europe, if not quite rich, at least free. After an exhaustive analysis, the Manley collection, per Papa's instructions, was donated to the Norton Museum and the Palm Beach house placed in the capable hands of Mary Gottya Real Estate.

I realized I had completely misread dear Frederick the IV when he had handed me back the original check for one hundred thousand dollars.

"You know, my sister wanted Ordenoff hanged. She never forgave Mother for marrying him, but I wanted the killers in jail or preferably dead. And thanks to you, they are." He grunted.

"Thanks, Freddie." Now I felt like a real hit man.

CHAPTER 61

It took a week for me to work up the courage to make another cold trip to Canada. This time, my destination was Montreal, one of my favorite, if understated, cities. It also gave me an excuse to practice my French.

I had two addresses. The first was a specialty packing company.

"I'll need a padded, wooden crate three-by-four-by—two feet, ready to be sent to Italy by noon," I told them.

"That's a little fast," the owner said.

"I'll pay you double," I said.

The second address, written on a piece of paper given to me by Dominic Carranza, was the stock brokerage firm of Carlson, Reynolds, and Jackson. The Jackson was Jonathan J. Jackson, partner in good standing. The third-floor office was respectable if modern, a curious mixture of mahogany paneling and large glass windows. Jackson's office was the second door to the left, a corner office.

"Hi. Is Jumping Johnny in?" I asked the receptionist.

"Jumping Johnny?"

She looked up with her mouth slightly opened. I'm sure no one had called Jonathan J. Jackson 'Jumping Johnny' in years. "I meant J. J. Jackson."

"He's in a meeting. Do you have an appointment, sir?"

"A standing twenty-year appointment," I said and, before she could protest, strolled past her and into his office.

Jonathan Jackson was a little older, but much as I remembered him. Blond hair combed back, sans ponytail, and blue eyes that glowed green when he was angry or confused. They were green. His wardrobe had changed since our hippie days in Italy where we smoked marijuana and hashish in Trivoli. He was talking with two oriental men in three-piece suits, yellow power ties, and pencil moustaches when he looked up at me.

"What the . . . Who are . . . " He started to rise, then stopped before falling back in his chair.

"Hello, Johnny."

Hanging behind his desk, in a place of honor, was the Tintoretto Johnny had stolen from the Italian villa twenty-five years ago. Before he could react, I marched around the desk, reached up and with a tug pulled the painting with its frame and the lamp from the wall. I snapped off the little lamp from the frame and let it fall to the floor.

I turned to Johnny. "Don't bother getting up."

The receptionist ran into the room. "Shall I call security?"

"That's all right, Miss. I was just leaving."

I turned my back and without another glance at Jumping Johnny, walked out of the building with a three-million-dollar painting under my arm.

That evening as I sat at the gallery office looking out over the courtyard garden I couldn't help but wonder if Dominic Carranza might have painted three copies of the paintings instead of two. He had said they were special. "Very, very special."

Wherever they were, I hoped they were resting comfortably. I'd done my part.

An email confirmed that the Tintoretto had arrived safely back home at the Murphy villa in Trivoli.

I had a decision to make and was preparing to leave the gallery when I heard the distinctive horn of a Rolls. It was Bernie's Corniche. He was driving; Aseneth was in the copilot's seat with Dickie huddled in the back. The maniacal menagerie had arrived.

"Your last message said you were in Bulgaria."

"We were. Come on, we're off to the Café L'Europe for caviar and vodka."

I hobbled into the back seat with Dickie.

"You owe me big time, Maxie."

"Dickie, that I do. How about a tin of Beluga?"

"Two tins. Of Triple O Molassol?"

"Done."

Along with good friends and good conversation, a generous portion of champagne and caviar always manages to put life in perspective.

A week later, I caught a glimpse of Aseneth in the Palm Beach Notables in a red dress accompanied by Mr. Bernard Crown in a dark gray silk tuxedo, attending a charity gala.

Aseneth returned to Bogotá and Bernie left town for Argentina, then flew to Europe with stopovers in Damascus and Beirut. Something about a large deal brewing in the Middle East. I suppose if anyone can bring peace to the Middle East, it was Bernie.

Back at the gallery I was feeling good about life. Last night Kathy and I had taken in an early movie at City Place then dinner at Bellagio's. This morning, Dickie Durdle phoned to tell me he had found a signed Salvador Dali print that I had coveted.

On my desk I had construction plans rolled out flat. It was a small project, an enclosed closet, about a foot deep and four feet wide and undetectable. Except for the finish to make it invisible from the outside, I was going to do most of the work myself. Until then, a heavy curtain would suffice. Behind it was the Caravaggio I had taken from Dominic. The Count had the "unseen" Caravaggio and I knew it would remain "unseen." As I glanced at the painting I would let others decide if therein laid a serpent. Right now I just didn't care.

I did see Zelda one last time, from the front door of the Landing Strip. I slipped the doorman a hundred-dollar bill in an envelope and watched as he crossed the floor and handed it to her. Before she looked up, I was gone. I didn't trust myself to be close to her. My hormonal threshold was extremely low.

Fortunately, I had scant time to feel remorse or wallow in the quagmire of nostalgia. The Children's Home Gala was in two days and Ms. Kathy Krammer, Esquire, would be firmly ensconced on my left arm. Margarita was teaching me a few new Salsa steps. At the gala, limp or no limp, I planned to spin the lady lawyer around and around and perhaps, if I get lucky, off her feet.

My eyebrows were growing back, the sun was shining and the fish were running.

I stared at the three-day pile of *Palm Beach Posts* on my desk, reached over, picked out the Friday edition and turned to the fishing report. The latest cold front had brought down the billfish. Sails were hitting hard in the Zoo. Out of my desk's bottom drawer, I pulled out a sign that my kids had given me when they were preteens and all mine. I walked past the gallery of staring eyes and knowing glances to reception and handed the sign to Margot.

"Hang it in the window. And you have the rest of the week off."

"With pay?"

"Why, of course with pay," I said and was out the door.

I slid into the Jag. It was nippy, in the low seventies, but I put down the top. The air smelled of saltwater and expectation. I gunned the Jag around the corner and glanced at the yellow and black sign in the gallery window.

Gone Fishing.

THE END

AUTHOR'S AFTERWORDS

Palm Beach Confidential is a work of fiction. *The Lady of the Lake* by Dante Gabriel Rossetti does not exist, though he did many paintings of his wife Elizabeth Siddal. There is no Monet *Water Lilies at Dawn*. Most of the other works of art mentioned, except for the Caravaggio, can be found in museums or private collections. Maxie Robert's house as well as the gallery are entirely invented. Maxie Roberts, Nancy, Eric and Nicole Roberts, Kathy Krammer, Adam Aldrick, Count Sergio Ordenoff, Beebee Alabama, Nigel Jenkins, Dickie Durdle, Maurice Oberlin, Mike Minsky, Martha Manley, and the rest of the Manley family are all products of my imagination.

Most of the places referred to in the novel are invented. However, many restaurants, galleries, hotels, clubs, churches, and museums do exist. The Café L'Europe, Ta-boo, Cucina dell'Art, Testa's, Nick and Johnnie's Grill, Renato's, and the 264 Grill are well known Palm Beach restaurants. A favorite Island breakfast haunt is Green's Pharmacy. The faithful will recognize Saint Edwards, Saint Ann, and Bethesda-by-the-Sea with its ancillary consignment shop, The Church Mouse. A few of the Island's fine art galleries, John H. Surovek, Philips Galleries, Irving Galleries, Select Fine Arts, Arcature Fine Art, and Fourth Dimension Studios are real. Also real are hotels such as The Colony, The Chesterfield and its fabled Leopard Lounge, The Breakers and its Circle Room. Some of my favorite places- the Norton Museum of Art and the Society of the Four Arts Museum, its sculpture gardens and art library are all part and parcel of the fabulous Island called Palm Beach.

No Palm Beach book would be complete without mentioning its famous private clubs: Palm Beach Country Club, Sailfish Club, Beach Club, Everglades Club, and Mar-A-Lago.

Certain places are no longer with us. The Landing Strip which burned down under mysterious circumstances, and the AU Bar was reborn as the Palm Beach Grill, a Houston's in disguise. Gone, too, is Amici's, long one of my favorite Island restaurants, and The Theater has left us longing for quality motion pictures.

I'd be remiss if I did not mention friends Jeff Jacobus of Classic Bookshop, Dr. Harold Bafitis of the Plastic Surgery Institute of the Palm Beaches, and Dale Longstreet of Indian River Coffee where they roast a special blend I designed called Killer 'Cane -- a cup of coffee that will blow you away.

— **Robert Mykle**
Palm Beach Gardens, Florida